Chinese Subculture and Criminality

Recent Titles in
Contributions in Criminology and Penology

Policy Administration and Progressive Reform: Theodore Roosevelt as Police Commissioner of New York
Jay Stuart Berman

Policing Multi-Ethnic Neighborhoods: The Miami Study and Findings for Law Enforcement in the United States
Geoffrey P. Alpert and Roger G. Dunham

Minorities and Criminality
Ronald Barri Flowers

Marijuana: Costs of Abuse, Costs of Control
Mark Kleiman

Doing Time in American Prisons: A Study of Modern Novels
Dennis Massey

Demographics and Criminality: The Characteristics of Crime in America
Ronald Barri Flowers

Taking Charge: Crisis Intervention in Criminal Justice
Anne T. Romano

Beyond Punishment: A New View on the Rehabilitation of Criminal Offenders
Edgardo Rotman

Police Pursuit Driving: Controlling Responses to Emergency Situations
Geoffrey P. Alpert and Roger G. Dunham

Vigilantism: Political History of Private Power in America
William C. Culberson

CHINESE SUBCULTURE AND CRIMINALITY

Non-traditional Crime Groups in America

Ko-lin Chin

Contributions in Criminology and Penology, Number 29

Marvin Wolfgang, Series Adviser

Greenwood Press
NEW YORK • WESTPORT, CONNECTICUT • LONDON

Library of Congress Cataloging-in-Publication Data

Chin, Ko-lin.
Chinese subculture and criminality : nontraditional crime groups in America / Ko-lin Chin.
p. cm.—(Contributions in criminology and penology, ISSN 0732–4464 ; no. 29)
Includes bibliographical references (p.).
ISBN 0–313–27262–X (lib. bdg. : alk. paper)
1. Chinese American criminals. I. Title. II. Series.
HV6791.C53 1990
364.3'089'951073—dc20 89–71441

British Library Cataloguing in Publication Data is available.

Library of Congress Catalog Card Number: 89–71441
ISBN: 0–313–27262–X
ISSN: 0732–4464

First published in 1990

Greenwood Press, 88 Post Road West, Westport, CT 06881
An imprint of Greenwood Publishing Group, Inc.

Printed in the United States of America

The paper used in this book complies with the Permanent Paper Standard issued by the National Information Standards Organization (Z39.48–1984).

10 9 8 7 6 5 4 3 2 1

To Catherine

CONTENTS

FIGURES

FOREWORD

When a young Chinese scholar came to me for advice on his living among his countrymen in Chinatown, New York, to become nearly a participant observer among Chinese gangs to study their deviant and criminal activities, I was very apprehensive. I feared for his life, for I had heard of a graduate student in San Francisco who lost his life trying to study the same phenomena there. But Ko-lin Chin was persistent and finally convinced me that he would be assured safety.

His prodigious labors have resulted in one of the most exciting studies that I have been privy to from the outset. This study is a marvelous combination of the best qualitative observations with careful historical analysis that I have seen in many years. We learn not only about the historical Tongs of generations and their geographic expansions, but also of their infiltration into current criminal gang activities across the United States and Canada.

The efforts of the President's Commission on Organized Crime in the United States only touched the surface of Chinese involvement compared to Ko-lin Chin's probing analysis. This study is empirically rich and theoretically sound both in historical and sociological terms.

Marvin E. Wolfgang

PREFACE

During the summer of 1984, a friend of mine, with two partners, opened a restaurant in Philadelphia. I spent the summer in the restaurant doing a field study on the subculture of Chinese waiters for a methodology course. Within a few months of the grand opening, however, the owners were forced to sell the restaurant because business was slow. A heated argument ensued, with the owners disagreeing about how the proceeds should be split after liquidation. The partner who was the chef immediately sought help from a Chinese gang; he never thought of going to court because of his illegal status. The second partner, who also had connections with Chinese crime figures, counteracted by asking his shady friends to represent him in the negotiations. My friend, who had no powerful figure to protect him, had to talk for himself.

I was at the restaurant while the negotiations was underway among the owners and the two groups of gang members. An accord was quickly reached between the chef and the second partner, largely because of a mutual understanding between the two gangs, who wanted to avoid a bloody confrontation over such an insignificant affair. After the second partner and his "friends" left the restaurant, the chef's gang, all teenagers, surrounded my friend and flashed out their guns. They asked my friend to pay them $3,000 in cash the next day and told him that he and his family could be hurt if he refused.

My friend quickly settled the matter by paying the gang the money they demanded. He felt he had no other choice. His strong animosity toward the American criminal justice system, resulting from unpleasant past experiences in dealing with the police and the courts, precluded his reporting the crime to law enforcement authorities. When the chef asked the gang members for his share of the $3,000, he got beaten up. The gang then left the city with all the money and never bothered themselves with the problem they were asked to solve.

A few weeks later, another friend of mine, who worked as a waitress in a Chinese restaurant, witnessed the killing of the owner's daughter by Chinese gang members. The daughter, an American-born Chinese who knew nothing about the Chinese underworld and its extortion schemes, was shot in the head when she tried to call the police after being puzzled by the gang kids' demand for *li shi* ("lucky money"). My friend, who had arrived in the United States only one month before the murder, was so traumatized by the event that she immediately quit her job and flew back to Taiwan. She never came back.

These two deeply disturbing incidents led me to switch my research interests to Asian criminality and its manifestations within ethnic communities in the United States. Since the liberalization of the U.S. immigration law in 1965, tens of thousands of Asian newcomers have come to settle here. Although most Asians are law-abiding and hard-working, a few are heavily involved in criminal activities. Street gangs and adult crime groups formed by Chinese, Japanese, Vietnamese, Filipinos, and Koreans have flourished in the ethnic enclaves.

As these groups became well established and as Asian immigrants became upwardly mobile and founded new ethnic communities in the suburbs, the crime groups gradually changed their patterns of illegal activities. Asian criminals who began their careers as extortionists and robbers have become providers of illegal services and goods through protection rackets, gambling operations, loansharking, alien smuggling, and heroin trafficking.

It took twenty years for American law enforcement officials to realize the seriousness of Asian crime groups. Federal authorities are especially concerned with the emergence of the Chinese in the heroin trade and the possible transfer of Hong Kong organized crime groups to the United States in 1997, when the British cede the colony to the People's Republic of China. These issues were highlighted when the President's Commission on Organized Crime held public hearings in 1984 and predicted that Asian crime groups would be the foremost organized crime problem in the United States in the 1990s.

Aside from the sensational media reports and the task-oriented official reports, there are few comprehensive studies of the nature of Asian crime groups and the scope of their criminal activities. As a result, many diverse Asian organizations are loosely labeled as Asian Organized Crime, and all shady Chinese organizations are called the Chinese Triads or the Chinese Mafia.

Such an imprecise understanding of the nature and structure of Asian crime groups could have grave consequences for the criminal justice system and policymakers. When law enforcement resources are allocated to hunt and destroy an illusive organization that is ill defined, the effort is bound to be ineffective and futile. When policies are made to target only certain highly publicized organizations, criminal elements that are not related to these organizations are escaping the scrutiny of the law. In short, if we are to use the limited law enforcement resources allocated for combating Asian organized crime effectively, we must know precisely the norms and values, structure, criminal patterns, and interrelationships of Asian crime groups.

Inspired by the work of Wolfgang and Ferracuti (1982) on the subculture of violence, this book is a sociological study of the culture of the Triads (originally, Chinese secret societies), tongs (self-help associations established by Chinese immigrants), and street gangs. It explores where, how, and why these groups were formed, developed, and transformed. What were their roles and functions in the political economy of Chinese societies in China, Hong Kong, Taiwan, and the United States? The book also discusses the relationships of the groups to each other, and the values and norms of the subculture in which these groups thrive.

Chapter 1 provides a description of the intensified concern of law enforcement officials about the Chinese crime groups in the United States. It outlines the various efforts initiated to cope with the problem and the reasons why social control agencies reacted to these groups the way they did. The chapter also presents the major theme of the book: the nature of the connection between Triad subculture and Chinese criminality, and the internalization of Triad norms and values as a crucial step in the process of becoming a Chinese gang member.

Chapter 2 describes and compares the history, values, recruiting practices, organization, and activities of the Hung and the Ching, two active groups of Chinese secret societies. It depicts the social and historical contexts in which secret societies emerged and flourished, the roles and functions of secret societies in the politics of China, and the current status of secret societies in Taiwan and China.

Chapter 3 analyzes how secret societies degenerated into the organized crime groups now in Hong Kong. It also explains the structure and activity of these criminal organizations. The possible transfer of Hong Kong organized crime to the United States is also explored.

Our focus then shifts to tongs and street gangs in the United States. Chapter 4 deals with the often symbiotic relationship between Chinese communities and tongs. A sociological analysis of the disorganization of the communities and a historical analysis of the development of the tongs are followed by a discussion of the tongs' organizational structures and activities.

Chapter 5 provides a detailed history of Chinese street gangs in the United States, concentrating on the gangs' development in San Francisco, Los Angeles, Monterey Park (California), and New York City. The issues covered include why and how Chinese street gangs formed and how they were transformed from street-corner groups to organized gangs.

Chapter 6 introduces the causative and intervening factors in the rise of Chinese gangs. The discussion focuses on the impact of family, school, opportunity structure, and community adult organizations on gang delinquency.

Chapter 7 explores the criminal patterns of Chinese gangs in New York and other cities. Chinese gangs' involvement in protection and extortion, robbery, prostitution, street violence, and drug trafficking are examined.

To explain why these street gangs persist, Chapter 8 identifies personal and group characteristics of the gangs, and compares Chinese with other ethnic gangs. In addition, law enforcement and community reactions to the Chinese gang problem are described.

In an attempt to predict the future direction of Chinese organized crime, the last chapter analyzes the world of "Jiang Hu," a shady yet powerful Chinese underground society in which the values and norms of the Triad subculture are transmitted and observed. In addition, the chapter discusses the issue of ethnic succession in organized crime and evaluates the role of Chinese criminals in the heroin trade.

This book is intended for a wide variety of readers. The information presented should be of value to students of sociology, criminology, criminal justice, anthropology, psychology, political science, education, urban studies, and ethnic studies. Policymakers and law enforcement authorities, too, should find the book helpful in understanding why and how tongs and gangs have a symbiotic relationship with Chinese communities and also in understanding the nature of the Triad subculture, in which many structurally unrelated crime groups are enmeshed. My hope is that this book will deepen our understanding of an often-misunderstood subculture and will lead to realistic, effective, and humane ways of reducing the kind of tragic events that I described in the beginning of this Preface.

ACKNOWLEDGMENTS

There are many people who have helped me with this study. First of all, I would like to take this opportunity to thank Marvin E. Wolfgang for the inspiration and learning on which my work in the field of criminology has been based. To him I owe my greatest debt.

Many scholars have read and commented on my work. Their criticisms are all well taken and appreciated. They are Robert Figlio of University of Pennsylvania, Robert Kelly of Brooklyn College, Jeffrey Fagan of Rutgers University, John Hagedorn of University of Wisconsin, Malcolm Klein of University of Southern California, Irvin Spergel of University of Chicago, Betty Lee Sung of City College of New York, Richard Stephens of Cleveland State University, and Francis Ianni and Steve Hilgartner of Columbia University. Of course, I bear full responsibility for all shortcomings in this book.

A study like this needs support from many people who are active in the Chinese communities. Among them, my special thanks go to Alex Peng of the *World Journal*, David Chen of the Chinese American Planning Council, Simon Chow of the Hamilton Madison House, Charles Lai of the Chinatown History Project, Man Bun Lee of the Lee's Family Association, and Henry Cheng of the Chinese American Voters Association of Queens. I also want to thank those who agreed to be interviewed but preferred to remain anonymous. They are the ones who should be credited for providing me with much rich information. Without their help, this study would not have been possible.

People in the criminal justice system have also went out their way to help me. I deeply appreciate for the support of John Galea, Joseph Sheldorfer, Neil Mauriello, Robert Lum, and Michael Wong of the New York City Police Department, John McKenna of the San Francisco Police

Department, Nancy Ryan of the Manhattan District Attorney's Office, James Harmon of the President's Commission on Organized Crime, James Goldman of the Immigration and Naturalization Service, Tom Rynne of the U.S. Customs Service, John Feehan and Richard LaMagna of the Drug Enforcement Administration, and Phil Baridon of the U.S. Department of Justice.

My colleagues also deserve special thanks for their interest and support. I would like to express my gratitude to Bruce Johnson, Mary Eckert, Steven Belenko, Paul Dynia, Iona Mara-Drita, Freda Solomon, Martin Rouse, Colleen Cosgrove, Rumoldo Arriolla, and Alexandra Gorelik.

I also much appreciate the support of Mildred Vasan, the Politics and Law editor of Greenwood Press, and Arthur Hamperian. Isabel Actub, Pamela Fisher, and Elizabeth Hovinen have edited the manuscript at various stages. Their expertise in editing has enormously improved the readability of this book.

Last, but not least, I reserve my most special thanks for my wife Catherine for her patience and support throughout this study. This book is dedicated to her.

1

INTRODUCTION

Before 1965, the crime rate within the Chinese communities in the United States was very low. Chinese immigrants were generally law-abiding, hard-working, and peaceful (Beach 1932; MacGill 1938). Official statistics show that the most common offenses were victimless crimes such as prostitution, opium smoking, drunkenness, and disorderly conduct (Tracy 1980). Offenders were primarily adults who indulged in these culturally sanctioned recreational activities as a respite from work.

Among Chinese adolescents, delinquency rates were also low despite difficult circumstances (Sung 1977). Most Chinese newcomers settled in crime-prone inner cities; most Chinese youths attended schools that had high delinquency rates; and most Chinese parents worked long hours in laundries, restaurants, and garment factories, and had little time to supervise their children. Although they had to learn a new language and adjust to a new school system, young Chinese immigrants worked hard to stay in school and keep themselves out of trouble. MacGill (1938) attributed the low delinquency rates among Chinese adolescents to their family bonds, religious beliefs, and ethnic pride. She predicted that as long as Chinese boys did not adopt American culture, they would not drift into delinquency. Delinquency among the Chinese would increase, she thought, only if the Chinese family broke down as a consequence of acculturation.

In considering these low delinquency rates, however, it is important to note that before 1965 there were very few Chinese teenagers in the United States, a result of the Chinese Exclusion Act passed in 1882 and the National Origins Act of 1924 (Sung 1979; Liu 1981; Fessler 1983). The Immigration and Naturalization Act of 1965 was a turning point in the history of Chinese immigration because it not only made China a "preferred" nation but also established priorities for admission based largely on family relationships; those already living in the United States could initiate the immigration process for their families overseas (Takagi and Platt 1978; Kwong 1987).

The increasing number of Chinese immigrating to the United States affected the stability of the Chinese communities in unprecedented ways. Traditional groups in these communities were ill prepared to cope with the influx. Because there were few social service agencies to help the newcomers, they were left mostly on their own to resolve housing, employment, education, and health problems (R. Chin 1971; Huang and Pilisuk 1977).

This breakdown in support, coupled with the growth of the Chinese population in isolated and fragmented communities, brought a corresponding increase in crime rates among the Chinese (Sung 1977). Young and adult Chinese criminals are alleged to be involved in homicide, gambling, prostitution, extortion, loansharking, money laundering, alien smuggling, financial fraud, and, most recently, heroin trafficking (Robertson 1977; Bresler 1981; President's Commission on Organized Crime 1984b; Posner 1988).

GROWING CONCERN ABOUT CHINESE CRIME GROUPS

Since the early 1980s, activities of Asian crime groups have been the subject of great scrutiny by officials in the United States. Many hearings were initiated to discuss the emergence of the so-called nontraditional organized crime groups. For example, the President's Commission on Organized Crime held public hearings in New York City in 1984 to uncover the structure and operation of the emerging Chinese, Japanese, and Vietnamese organizations (*New York Times*, October 24, 1984, A1). During the hearings, police officers from the United States and other parts of the world, Asian criminals, and victims of Asian gangsters testified before the commission. These hearings exposed to the public for the first time the initiation rites, organization, and activities of Asian crime groups; the biographies of alleged Asian crime bosses; and the threats of these criminal groups to American society. In 1986 the Senate Permanent Subcommittee on Investigations held hearings on Asian criminal groups in Washington, D.C. (United States Senate 1986). A year later, the Select Committee on Narcotics Abuse and Control of the U.S. House of Representatives conducted hearings on the involvement of nontraditional crime groups in heroin trafficking (U.S. House of Representatives 1987).

Law enforcement agencies across the country have also sponsored conferences to discuss the emergence of Asian organized crime. Since

1978, police officers in the United States and Canada have participated in annual meetings to exchange information on the activities of Chinese criminal organizations. In 1987, the Middle Atlantic-Great Lakes Organized Crime Law Enforcement Network (MAGLOCLEN), one of the six regional information-sharing systems (RISS Projects) funded by the U.S. Department of Justice, sponsored a conference on Asian organized crime. The Oakland (California) Police Department also held a national convention to discuss crime and violence in the Asian community.

To aid law enforcement authorities in understanding the Asian crime groups, the Federal Bureau of Investigation completed an investigative report on oriental organized crime (U.S. Department of Justice 1985). Three years later the Criminal Division of the U.S. Department of Justice wrote another report on the issue (U.S. Department of Justice 1988). A recent federal report, based upon interviews with ninety-three federal prosecutors nationwide, also indicated that Asian crime groups play important roles in heroin trafficking (U.S. Attorneys and the Attorney General of the United States 1989). Although all three reports used the terms "Asian" or "oriental" to denote the crime groups concerned, their major focus was on the Chinese secret societies and street gangs.

San Francisco, Los Angeles, Monterey Park (California), New York, Vancouver, and Toronto now have Asian or Chinese gang task forces to cope with Asian crime groups (President's Commission on Organized Crime 1984b). In New York City, besides the Chinese Gang Task Force, the Oriental Gang Unit, known as the Jade Squad, was established to investigate Chinese gangs (Leng 1984; U.S. Department of Justice 1989). The Drug Enforcement Administration in New York City has an Asian Heroin Group (also known as Group 41) that deals mainly with drug trafficking among the Chinese (*New York Times*, August 11, 1987, B1). Other cities such as Oakland, Chicago, Boston, Dallas, Houston, and Arlington (Virginia) also devote law enforcement resources to Chinese gangs. In reaction to the emergence of Chinese crime groups, the Immigration and Naturalization Service also established special task forces in Washington, New York, Boston, Houston, San Francisco, and Los Angeles to deal exclusively with Chinese criminal elements (*Organized Crime Digest*, August 9, 1989).

In order to fight the internationally active Chinese crime groups, federal agents in the United States have begun to work closely with social control agencies in Asian countries. For example, in a recent undercover operation, the Federal Bureau of Investigation (FBI), the New York City Police Department (NYPD), the Drug Enforcement Administration (DEA), the Royal Hong Kong Police, the Royal Canadian Mounted Police in Toronto,

Calgary, and Vancouver, and police in Singapore have cooperated in penetrating a major Chinese drug trafficking group (*New York Newsday*, February 22, 1989, 5).

The media and the movie industry have also become aware of the crime problems within Asian communities. Major newspapers in San Francisco, Los Angeles, Dallas, Washington, and New York have published special reports on Asian crime groups (*New York Times*, January 13, 1985, A1; *Washington Times*, January 28, 1986, A1; *Dallas Morning News*, September 14, 1986, A1; *San Francisco Chronicle*, March 26, 1988, A2). Television stations in New York have run special series on Chinese gangs in their prime-time news reports (*Centre Daily News*, May 27, 1987, 24). Hollywood produced *The Year of the Dragon*, *China Girl*, and *The Tongs* to depict how secret societies, tongs, and Chinese street gangs in New York's Chinatown were involved in drug trafficking, murder, and extortion. "The Chinese Mafia" has now become a popular term, and even *Penthouse* magazine published an article on this underworld (Surovell 1988).

Shortly after the hearings of the President's Commission on Organized Crime, a police chief predicted that "Asian organized crime will end up being the No. 1 organized crime problem in North America in the next five years" and "will make the Sicilian Mafia look like a bunch of Sunday school kids" (*New York Times*, January 13, 1985, A1). Another law enforcement officer suggested that the "Chinese have put together a criminal venture that is well-defined, highly sophisticated, and ruthless. It has the potential of making the Mafia in America look like a fraternity of wimps" (*Washington Times*, January 28, 1986, 1A).

REASONS FOR INTENSIFIED CONCERN

What has caused this increased interest in Chinese crime? After all, the Chinese and the tongs have been in the United States for more than 150 years. Ruthless clashes among tong members killed more than three hundred people during the tong war period (1894-1913) in California (Dillon 1962). The power struggle among the tongs later spread to the East Coast, and many more so-called "*boo how doy*" (hatchetmen who were salaried soldiers of the tongs) were gunned down in Boston, Chicago, and New York City (Gong and Grant 1930; Liu 1981). The tongs have been accused of running opium and gambling dens, prostitution houses, and extortion rackets since their establishment. Yet tongs were ignored by both law enforcement officials and the public. Why then, after so many years, did the tongs, along with Chinese street gangs and other criminal groups, emerge as the major target of law enforcement agencies in the 1980s?

A confluence of factors brought about the intensified interest in Chinese organized crime. First, as noted, the number of Chinese immigrants has increased dramatically since the mid-1960s. At the turn of the century, there were only 89,863 Chinese in the United States (Kwong 1987). By 1960 the Chinese population had increased to 237,292, and it doubled each decade thereafter (to 435,062 in 1970 and 812,178 in 1980) (U.S. Department of Justice 1988). Approximately 1,079,400 Chinese live in this country, excluding tens of thousands who are here illegally. As the Chinese population grew, Chinese communities around the nation expanded rapidly, and some of the communities became major tourist attractions (Light 1974). Thousands of new immigrants moved into the San Francisco and New York Chinatowns (Fessler 1983), and new Chinatowns were established in New York City; Monterey Park, California; Oakland; Miami; Houston; and San Diego (*New York Times*, September 14, 1986, 7; February 10, 1988, C1). Chinatowns thus became economically and politically significant to local governments. The media and public officials can no longer ignore what happens within them.

Second, criminal acts committed by Chinese are no longer confined to the traditional Chinese communities. Before the mid-1970s, such crimes occurred mainly within Chinatowns. Now, Chinese living in New Jersey, Connecticut, and Long Island are being threatened, murdered, or robbed by Chinese gang members (*Centre Daily News*, January 29, 1988, 24). When the more affluent and better educated Chinese are victimized, they are more likely than Chinatown residents to report the incident to the police, and these reported incidents gain publicity.

Third, Chinese gangs now victimize not only Chinese people but also other ethnic groups as well. For example, six New York Chinese gang members kidnapped, gang-raped, and killed a white woman (*World Journal*, October 22, 1982, 24). In several other incidents, non-Chinese were wounded by gunfire while they visited Chinese communities (*New York Daily News*, May 22, 1985, 3; *China Daily News*, July 18, 1989, 3). Sometimes Chinese gang members even wounded or killed people of other ethnic groups in areas outside Chinatowns (*World Journal*, April 7, 1988, 24). As people of other ethnic groups began to be victimized by Chinese gang members, media and law enforcement attention came to be more intensely focused on Chinese gangs than it had previously been.

Fourth, major Italian-American crime leaders were successfully prosecuted and imprisoned in the 1980s. Law enforcement officers believe that Chinese criminal elements are replacing imprisoned Mafia figures in organized crime (President's Commission on Organized Crime 1984b).

Fifth, the number of Chinese criminal organizations has increased tremendously. In New York City alone, there are at least seven street gangs and several adult groups, with chapters in various large cities on the East Coast and in the South (K. Chin 1986). In California, besides the Chinese street gangs and tongs, crime groups from Vietnam, Taiwan, and Hong Kong are believed to be on the rise (*New York Times*, July 9, 1987, A20). Power struggles among and within the groups have led to many murders and shootouts that shocked the communities and the nation (for example, *New York Times*, December 24, 1982, A1).

Sixth, Chinese criminal groups are now involved in drug trafficking and money laundering—areas of special concern to law enforcement officials (President's Commission on Organized Crime 1984a). These criminal groups are alleged to be responsible for a large part of the heroin smuggled into the United States. According to the Drug Enforcement Administration, the amount of heroin the Chinese are handling is simply "mind-boggling" (U.S. House of Representatives 1987). For instance, a group of Chinese drug traffickers was arrested for attempting to import a thousand pounds of heroin into the United States (*New York Times*, March 15, 1988, B5). The close connections between Chinese criminal elements and heroin producers in the Golden Triangle, an area near the borders of Myanmar (Burma), Thailand, and Laos, lead U.S. officials to believe that Chinese crime groups will continue to dominate the heroin trade in America.

Finally, Britain will cede Hong Kong to the People's Republic of China in 1997, and federal law enforcement agencies in North America assume that criminal elements there are going to seek new "havens" abroad because the Chinese government punishes criminal organizations harshly. The United States, Canada, and Australia are considered to be the prime targets because of their well-established Chinese communities and humanitarian legal systems. A few Hong Kong crime groups are believed to be already active in the United States and to be corroborating with local Chinese criminals (U.S. Department of Justice 1988).

IS THE CHINESE MAFIA A MYTH?

Researchers have concluded that there is a worldwide Chinese criminal organization, with headquarters in Hong Kong and Taiwan (Robertson 1977; Bresler 1981; Posner 1988). Bresler is firmly convinced that there is "an organized international conspiracy with a strict hierarchy, operating from a central base in the Far East, with a Mafia-type control over its members, and an almost limitless capacity for criminal evil stretching across the world" (1981, 246). Posner, after investigating the Chinese crime groups around the world for two years, suggested that "Chinese Triads are the most powerful criminal syndicates in existence and that they pose the most serious and growing threat confronting law enforcement" (1988, xviii).

While American law enforcement agencies, investigative journalists, and the media were focusing on the Chinese crime groups, Chinese Americans were shocked and angered by the well-publicized and sensationalized hearings, reports, and films on Asian crime groups (for example, *China Times*, October 24, 1984, 3). Chinese community leaders questioned the real motives of the President's Commission on Organized Crime and rejected the allegation that well-organized criminal groups are active in their communities. A social activist in San Francisco insisted that the issue is "all very exaggerated" and there is "nothing like the Mafia here" (*New York Times*, January 13, 1985, A1).

Few Chinese deny that gang members are active in their communities. The gangs are involved in extortion, robbery, and protection of gambling places. Community residents are also aware that certain tong members play an important role in the operation of gambling establishments. However, they do not believe that the tongs and gangs are routinely involved in nationwide or international criminal conspiracies. To them, the idea of a powerful, conglomerate criminal organization called the Chinese Mafia with worldwide connections and global ambitions is simply a racist concept backed by little evidence (*China Times*, October 29, 1984, 3).

In order to evaluate the reaction and viewpoint of the Chinese community, it is necessary to understand that this is a time of enormous opportunity for Chinese businesses and interest groups in the United States. For them, more Chinese immigrants mean more business, more money, and more power. Along with Chinese immigrants, investment money is pouring in from Hong Kong and Taiwan (*New York Times*, December 29, 1981, A1; *New York Post*, October 20, 1988, 58). The opportunity to do business with the People's Republic of China created no less excitement among Chinese than among American business people. The Chinese here can now shuttle between Beijing (Peking) and Taipei to strike lucrative business deals. The current Chinese crime problem has thus created enormous tension for Chinese businessmen and interest groups; they know that they have much to lose if the issue continues to be prominent.

In my attempt to ascertain the truth about Chinese criminal activity, data collection has proved to be the most difficult task. Not only are there no systematic and reliable statistics on crime rates within the Chinese communities, but comprehensive and scientific reports on Chinese crime groups are also rare. Because of the sensitive nature of the phenomenon, most Chinese immigrants are reluctant to discuss the crime groups active in their communities. As a result, this study relied on four types of sources: ethnographic interviews, field notes, official reports and documents, and newspapers and magazines.

People who were familiar with Chinese crime or who had been victimized were interviewed. Among them were members of secret societies, tongs, and street gangs; social service providers, leaders of community associations, reporters, police officers, prosecutors, federal law enforcement officials, and victims of Chinese crime groups.

In order to supplement interview data, I spent some time in the field. Most of these participant observations were carried out in gambling dens or bars where gang members hang out. I also reviewed and analyzed classified and unclassified official reports and documents, and I examined indictment materials and sentencing memorandums related to two notorious Chinese crime groups.

Finally, hundreds of English and Chinese newspaper and magazine articles on Asian crime groups were collected and categorized by type of criminal organization, geographical area, and type of crime. Newspapers and magazines offered enormous amounts of information on the issues discussed in this book.

TRIAD SUBCULTURE AND CRIMINALITY

The study of organized crime and street gangs has a long tradition in the fields of sociology and criminology. Since Thrasher's (1927) study of 1,313 youth gangs and Landesco's (1968) study of organized crime in Chicago, social scientists have been intrigued by the many criminal organizations flourishing in ethnic communities—organizations made up both of youths (Shaw and McKay 1942; Whyte 1943; Cohen 1955; Miller 1958; Cloward and Ohlin 1960; Short and Strodbeck 1965; Yablonsky 1970; Poston 1971; Klein 1971; Miller 1975; Moore et al. 1978; Horowitz 1983; Schwendinger and Schwendinger 1985; Hagedorn 1988) and of adults (Cressey 1967; Ianni 1972, 1974; Nelli 1976; Reuter 1983; Arlacchi 1987). Most of these studies have focused on Italian adult organizations and black or Hispanic youth gangs. Little is known about criminal organizations of ethnic groups from the Caribbean, Africa, and Asia.

In order to understand Asian crime groups, the research and law enforcement communities need to broaden their perspectives. Concepts that are adequate for explaining Italian, black, and Hispanic crime groups may not be adequate for examining criminal organizations of Asian origin.

Because Asian people have diverse cultural heritages, we also need to identify the unique features of each Asian ethnic group.

In the development of Chinese crime groups, the values and norms of the Triad subculture have been paramount. Triad (a triangle of heaven, earth, and man) societies were established by ousted Chinese officials and the alienated poor during the late seventeenth century to overthrow the Qing (Ch'ing) government, which had been established by the invading Manchu people (Ping 1935; Morgan 1960). Branches of the Triad societies in the United States were called tongs. When the Qing government finally collapsed and the Republic of China was established in 1912, local and overseas Triad organizations tried to incorporate themselves into the political machine of the new republic. For various reasons, the societies' attempt failed (Pung 1987).

After the Qing government was overthrown, politically motivated Triad leaders left the organizations to pursue political careers. But those who were not absorbed by the political machine returned to the well-established Triad organizations for power and status. However, without a patriotic cause to pursue, the secretive and anti-establishment nature of the organizations easily helped transform them into criminal groups. Because most members were uneducated and there was no central administrative body to represent and direct the fragmented societies, political as well as crime groups could penetrate and control them. Not only did the societies disintegrate structurally, but their values also became situational and flexible. As a result, various groups were able to superimpose their own ideologies on those of the secret societies (Y. Sun 1977).

The political unrest in China during the first half of the twentieth century facilitated the societies' degeneration as various powerful groups came to rely on the societies to enforce their rules among the masses. When there was resistance, members were urged to use intimidation and violence. In return for the societies' services, the powerful groups sanctioned the societies' involvement in operating prostitution, gambling, and opium houses (Seagrave 1985).

During this time, secret societies in the United States continued to flourish. However, without a patriotic cause and strong leadership, the purpose of some of the organizations soon deteriorated from revolution to crime, and tong members also became increasingly involved in operating prostitution, gambling, and opium houses (Gong and Grant 1930; Dillon 1962).

In 1949, the Kuomintang party under the leadership of Chiang Kai-shek was defeated by the Red Army headed by Mao Zedong (Mao Tse-tung). While millions of Chiang's followers fled to Taiwan, thousands of Triad members transferred their operations to Hong Kong and Taiwan. The tongs immediately proclaimed their support for the Kuomintang government in Taiwan, while the Chinese Communists uprooted the Triad organizations from China by executing hundreds of Triad members (Pung 1987).

Triad members who fled to Hong Kong formed several local Triad societies. Many peddlers and workers in the then chaotic British colony joined the groups for protection. Soon, Triad members infiltrated the Hong Kong police department and monopolized various racketeering activities. Triads in Hong Kong thus further degenerated into purely criminal groups with no political aspirations (Zhang 1984).

Triad members who followed Chiang to Taiwan were unable to expand their criminal activities because the Kuomintang tightly controlled every aspect of the Triad organizations. Triads, most of whose members were in the army, were forced by the Kuomintang to become a political tool in the war against communism (*China Times Weekly*, January 26, 1989).

Tong members in the United States identified closely with Triad members in Taiwan. Thus, tongs also became a political arm of the Kuomintang, ensuring that Chinese communities in the United States would not be permeated by the Chinese Communists. During the Cultural Revolution, a radical political movement in the People's Republic of China, the tongs played a crucial role in suppressing the spread of Communist ideology among Chinese American youths. The tongs mobilized and organized young people within the communities to fight against the left-wing radicals, many of whom later became gang members (*Mei Wah Report* June 14, 1988; June 28, 1988). When the United States established diplomatic relations with the Chinese Communists in 1979, the tongs rapidly lost their position in the vanguard of the Chinese communities. As their political motivation diminished, they also shifted from being protectors to being exploiters of those communities.

As this brief history shows, Triad values and norms have changed over the past two centuries. Initially, Triad subculture stressed patriotism and righteousness. Membership was offered only to a limited number of people with no criminal record. Once members were recruited, leaders closely scrutinized their activities. Later, loyalty to the Triad groups replaced patriotism and righteousness. The tongs, for example, protected Chinese immigrants from racial discrimination and provided important services during the tongs' developmental stage. Brotherhood was the core value. Although tong members' involvement in victimless crimes such as prostitution and gambling increased dramatically, they still cherished the values of loyalty and righteousness, and were reluctant to become involved in predatory crimes. However, when the manifest or latent functions of these self-help groups became less important, the groups gradually replaced their patriotic or benevolent causes with criminal activities. Membership was granted to almost anybody who wanted to join, and leaders lost track of and control over their followers. Members became interested in enhancing their individual gains. Nowadays, the Triad values of patriotism, brotherhood, righteousness, and loyalty remain only in proclamations. The next chapter examines the emergence, structure and recruiting practices, and subculture of Chinese secret societies.

2

TRADITIONAL SECRET SOCIETIES

In ancient Chinese society, the population was composed of predominantly poor and illiterate peasants and laborers. Very few people belonged to the two distinctive classes that dominated the fate of China. The "*Ru*," or the literati, were admired for their knowledge, good writing ability, and familiarity with Confucian teachings. They were conservative, refined, and family-oriented public administrators who were far removed from the underclass. In contrast to the literati, the "*Xia*," or knights, wandered from kingdom to kingdom and relied on their expertise in fighting to protect the poor and the vulnerable from corrupt government officials and greedy landlords. They were appraised for their loyalty, righteousness, and strong conscience for the society and the poor (Tang 1974).

Based upon the philosophy and tradition of the *Xia*, many secret societies developed in China since the period of the Han dynasty (206 B.C.-A.D. 220) (Chesneaux 1972). Since then, ambitious politicians or army generals recruited and mobilized people who belonged to the subculture of the *Xia* to fight against incumbent tyrannies in many political upheavals. The literati, who played prominent roles in the administration of public affairs during peacetime, have rarely risked their lives on the battlegrounds (Fairbank 1987).

Not only have the *Xia* proved that they are courageous and unselfish in time of crisis, but they have also showed that they are righteous and trustful in time of peace. Other than the family, there were no other social organizations that could provide the kind of camaraderie the secret societies offer to their "family members." As a result, notwithstanding the illegitimate status of the secret societies, many Chinese, especially those who were away from home, joined one of the societies to protect themselves.

Two prominent and active groups were the Hung and the Ching. Neither organization was a coordinated entity but rather was composed of many fragmented and conflicting chapters or branches (Ward and Stirling 1925;

Ping 1935; Shaw 1935; Chen 1946; Wei 1949; Shuai 1961; Shu n.d.; Morgan 1960; Peoples University and the First National Archive 1980; Teng 1981; Chi 1985). Most studies of Chinese secret societies are historical analyses of the organizations' roles in religious and political arenas.

The term "Triad societies" applies only to the major group of secret societies, known as the Hung. The Ching, another major group of secret societies, are not considered Triads. However, for analytical purposes, the term Triad subculture is used in this book to denote the subcultures of both Hung and Ching societies. Other less significant groups can be categorized into either one of them. The Hung societies are also known as the Hung Mun (Hung League), Tien Ti Wei (Heaven and Earth Society), and San Ho Wei (Three United Association). Ching societies are also called Ching Men (Ching Family), Liang Pang (Rice Gang), or Ching Pang (Ching Gang). Hung societies and Ching societies are generally known as Pi Mi Sher Wei (Secret Societies).

THE LEGEND OF SECRET SOCIETIES

The emergence and development of the Hung societies are not known, and there are few historical documents available about the groups. Most research on the organizations has had to rely on oral history and popular myth. Thus, the findings of this research should be viewed with caution.

In the mid-seventeenth century, Manchu warriors had dethroned the Ming emperor and established the Qing (Ch'ing) dynasty, which ruled China for more than three centuries. According to legend, the Hung societies were established during the tenure of the Qing emperor Kang Xi. In 1672, the Qing's territory was often invaded by the Xi Lu barbarians. Emperor Kang Xi sought help from local organizations to fight these barbarians. At that time, a monastery called Shaolin, in Fujian (Fukien) Province, had 108 Buddhist monks who were well trained in martial arts. These monks responded to the emperor's call and conquered the Xi Lu barbarians. When the monks returned from the battlefield, the emperor rewarded them with money and gifts. After the monks returned to Shaolin, two senior officials of the Qing dynasty wanted to overthrow Kang Xi but were afraid of the Shaolin monks. In order to neutralize a potential opposing power, the two officials persuaded the emperor to destroy the monastery before it developed into a revolutionary force. The emperor conceded and sent troops to raid the monastery. Shaolin was set on fire, and most of the monks were killed. Only five monks escaped, and they became the First Five Ancestors of the Hung societies (Morgan 1960).

The five monks escaping from the Manchu troops were helped by five patriotic fighters. These five men were later honored as the Second Five Ancestors. A scholar who had worked for the Qing government welcomed the First Five Ancestors and set the stage for a meeting of patriotic men who wanted to oust the Qing dynasty. On a certain day in 1674, these people gathered in a place called the Red Flower Temple. One of the Ming emperor's grandsons, Zhu Hung-tsu, also attended the meeting. While the ceremony was underway, a red light appeared in the sky. The participants interpreted it as a symbol of blessing from the heavens and decided to call the revolutionary organization the Hung, in honor of the Ming emperor's grandson and to commemorate the red (*hung*) light in the sky. Since then, Hung members fought the Qing army in many ill-fated wars (Shu n.d.).

Some Hung members emigrated to Southeast Asia and North America and started new branches of their societies there (Fung 1947; Mak 1977). Overseas Hung branches are generally called "tong," "kung sor," "kung kuan," or "hui." Hung members around the world supported Sun Yat-sen, the leader of the revolution that in 1912 finally overthrew the Qing dynasty and led to the establishment of the first democratic government in Asia (Shuai 1961; Chesneaux 1972) (see Chapter 4 for details). Between 1912 and 1949, some Hung members emigrated to Hong Kong and established many criminally oriented Hung branches (Morgan 1960; Zhang 1984). I will discuss this issue in detail in the next chapter.

The other major group, the Ching, is believed to have been founded by Hung leaders in the late seventeenth century. Initially, the organization was established to assist the Qing emperor in transporting rice from rural areas to cities. Members were predominantly sailors and laborers. When the Qing government later dissolved the organization, it was reorganized and transformed into political groups that also proclaimed to "overthrow the Qing and restore the Ming" (Chen 1946).

Ching societies reached their peak from 1920 through 1950, a period when China was divided by political parties, warlords, and foreign powers. Ching groups virtually controlled Shanghai and the French and British concessions there (Seagrave 1985; Fu 1987). Using their close connections with local leaders and the colonialists, they dominated the opium smuggling, gambling, and prostitution rackets in the city, and were also involved in murders and drug trafficking (McCoy 1973).

BROTHERHOOD, LOYALTY, AND RIGHTEOUSNESS

In addition to the spirits of the *Xia*, two popular novels had a profound impact on the structure and values of secret societies in China. The first,

San Guo Yan Yi (The Three Kingdoms), describes how three generals became "brothers" through an elaborate ceremony of taking oaths, burning yellow papers, and drinking each other's blood mixed with wine. After swearing to be "brothers"—to be loyal to each other and to die together—the three generals went on to conquer most of the country. The second novel, *Shui Hu Zhuan (Outlaws of the Marsh)*, recounts the adventures of vagabonds who establish an enclave in a remote mountain called Lian Shan. The vagabonds were loyal to one another and committed to fight against corrupted officials and other bad elements who were viewed as enemies by the poor (Li 1981).

Hung members emulated the initiation ceremony narrated in *The Three Kingdoms* and treasured the values and norms of the Lian Shan people. According to Shuai:

> What are the impacts of Shui Hu Zhuan on Tien Ti Wei? Tien Ti Wei's song denotes: "We worship heaven as father; we worship earth as mother; we worship sun as brother; we worship moon as sister." To worship heaven as father and earth as mother means to eliminate the attachment to one's own kinship and district so that people from various kinships can get together as members of a large family. This ideal of Tien Ti Wei's is exactly the replica of the Shui Hu Zhuan, which announced that "In the past, we scattered all over the country; now we belong to Zhong Yi Tong (Hall of Loyalty and Righteousness); the stars are our brothers; heaven is our father and earth our mother." . . . Members of Lian Shan belong to an organization in which there are no classes, no social distance, no favoritism, or hatred among members. Tien Ti Wei also demands egalitarianism, brotherhood, and equality among members. (1961, 38-39; my translation)

Thus, the societies were built on the idea of brotherhood. In order to secure the members' loyalty, Hung societies stressed that they were, in essence, one large family unit. Urban dwellers and immigrants who were cut off from their own families found the nature of the groups very appealing.

While the society's ideas about family and brotherhood brought and held tens of thousands of alienated poor together by offering them status, fellowship, excitement, and security, the revolutionary nature of the society caused it to develop secretive, anti-establishment, and predatory norms to protect and support themselves.

All Hung members take the thirty-six solemn oaths of loyalty (Appendix 1). These oaths guide members in their relationships with other members and with outsiders. Of the thirty-six oaths, only one (No. 36) relates to the societies' political ideology; another (No. 31) defines righteousness; and three (Nos. 5, 33, and 35) concern secrecy; most of the rest pertain to loyalty to Hung members and the organizations.

Although the oaths of loyalty are not designed for committing crime, the rigidity and absoluteness of these norms demand members to have little regard for the norms and values of the establishment. Subtly and vaguely, the oaths sanction members to rob and kill those who are at odds with the societies. Thus, social control agencies could be substituted easily for the initial targeted enemy—the Qing officials. Furthermore, the rights and benefits of the public could be seriously compromised under the Hung societies' principles of loyalty to brethren and rebellion against public officials. Bresler has pointed out the social implication of the Chinese people's overemphasis on loyalty to one's "family."

> As an ethnic group, the Chinese are extremely intelligent: not for nothing does Chinese civilization antedate the Western variety. Furthermore, like many other human beings, of whatever race, colour or religion, who live out their lives for the most part in almost intolerable circumstances of poverty and squalor, many of them possess a cold indifference to the sufferings of anyone not within their concept of "family." One's "family" is all. Loyalty is owed almost exclusively to the natural family and to the extended "family" of the original village or district of the town where one now lives. Amid the vast stretches of mainland China, loyalty and patriotism could not take in a feeling of brotherhood and love for those living 2,000 miles away across unknown deserts and mountains, even though they might be of the same skin colour and belong, according to anthropologists, to the same overall ethnic group. This attitude to outsiders can become a streak of utter ruthlessness when applied to criminal endeavor. (1981, 11)

Another crucial piece of information about Hung values is the "philosophy" of the Hung (Appendix 2), also known as the "Thirty-six Strategies." It teaches members how to commit murder, robbery, burglary, and other crimes. The strategies are opportunistic and violent, and they have been learned and internalized by Chinese criminals.

Besides having loyalty oaths, regulations, and strategies for confronting the enemy, Hung societies have secret oral and behavioral methods of communication. Their ruthless punishment by the Qing troops forced them to develop precautionary measures for communicating with strangers.

The ideology of the Ching societies is political and is explicitly stated in the manual for members. The principal goals are to eradicate communism in China, to neutralize Soviet influence in China, and to support the Kuomintang in its efforts to recover China. The opening statement in the *Jian Yi Jia Li Xu Zhi*, a manual for Ching members, says it all:

> At the moment, Soviet imperialists, under the idea of primitive society—communism—have instructed the Chinese bandits such as Mao Zedong and Zhou En-lai to occupy our land illegally, destroy our traditional culture, treat our people as slaves, and slaughter the loyalist and the innocent. The Chinese bandits are more ruthless than the Manchus, more destructive than the egalitarian. . . . By virtue of loyalty, we are going to destroy the Communists' conspiracy to transform China into a puppet of the Soviets; by virtue of righteousness, we are going to paralyze the Communists' shameless conspiracy. (my translation)

From this outline of the Hung and Ching ideologies, we can extract five core norms and values of the secret societies. The first is loyalty, cherished by members as the most important. However, loyalty extends only to their country, their organization, and other members. One does not have to be loyal to outsiders. To be loyal to the organization means a member will not exploit the organization, will not reveal the inner workings of the organization to outsiders, and will not work against the organization by establishing another secret society without the permission of the organization. Loyalty to the brothers means that a member has the responsibility to protect and support all other members in time of peace and crisis and not to take advantage of the brother who is wanted by law enforcement officials.

Righteousness is the second most observed virtue. Again, members are required to be righteous only to their peers. Members must protect one another from outsiders, trust each other, and be willing to aid a member in need of help. To kill or victimize outsiders for the sake of members and the organization is considered righteous behavior. The idea of neutralizing the powerful and helping the poor is also part of righteousness. Members view themselves as self-appointed agents for redistributing justice and wealth to the poor. They are antagonistic toward merchants, landlords, and public officials, and always grasp the opportunity to victimize them in order to avenge the underclass.

The third virtue is nationalism. Members are proud of their nationalistic and patriotic spirit. They look down upon the more refined and educated scholars and officials for their lack of courage and action for the country in time of crises.

The fourth norm is secrecy. Members must never reveal their membership or the inner workings of the organization to outsiders. They learn various secretive communicating techniques such as body language, poems, and slang.

The fifth is the concept of "brotherhood." One of the most repeated slogan of the secret societies is that "All men are brothers." As a member of the secret societies, a person must treat other members as "brothers" and offer his or her help without reservation.

None of these norms or values is intrinsically criminal. However, as noted above, the strong emphasis on loyalty and righteousness only to members of the organization and to a particular political party shows the societies' total commitment to their values regardless of the social ramifications of their actions.

BECOMING A SECRET SOCIETY MEMBER

Each Hung society is recognized as xx Mountain xx Tong (Hall). The Shan Chu (Head of the Mountain) is the highest leader of a society, and the Fu Shan Chu (Associate Head) is normally the person who runs the organization. The Hu Yin is equivalent to the administrator, while the Hu Jian is responsible for enforcement activities. Eight Internal Tongs are occupied by eight senior officers who function as the cabinet of the society. The Eight External Tongs consist of eight senior but peripheral officers (Shu n.d.) (see Figure 1).

The structure of the Ching is different from that of the Hung. According to a Ching member interviewed by the author, the foundation of the Ching societies is the relationship between a master and his students, which is analogous to that between father and son. All students of a master are considered "brothers" and are equal in rank and prestige. The Ching societies initially have twenty-four ranks. As the societies expand, another twenty-four ranks are added. A new apprentice's rank is always one lower than his master's, and a member's rank is permanent. After being in the society for more than ten years, a respectful member may recruit his own students, but only if his master has *shou shan* ("closed the mountain")—that is, has retired.

The application process for Ching societies is rather complicated and takes about two to five years to complete. The process has four stages. In the initial stage, a potential applicant has to know a Ching member who

Figure 1
Organizational Chart of a Traditional Hung Society

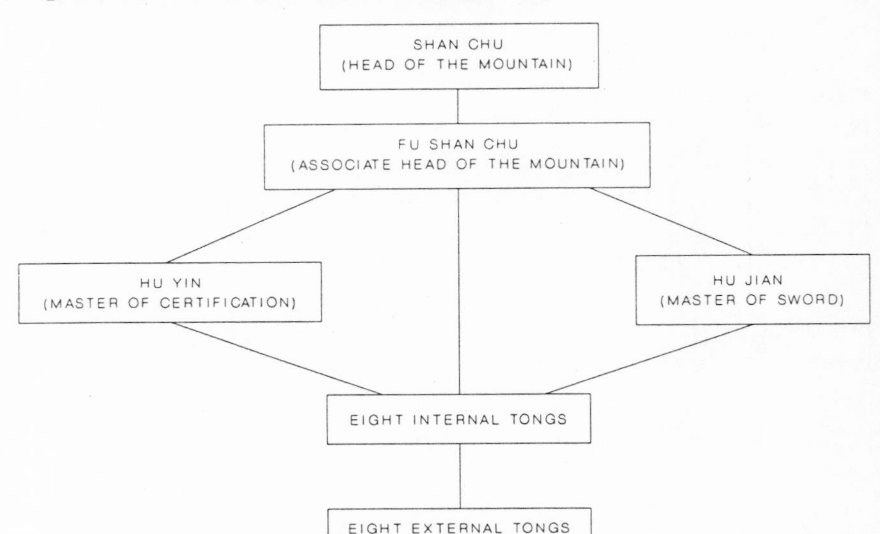

is willing to introduce him to a recruiting master. After the introduction, the applicant can submit a *qing tie* ("application") to the recruiting master.

In the investigation stage, the recruiting master investigates the applicant's background for about one to three years. The recruiting master finds out whether the applicant will be loyal and "righteous" to the organization and its members if recruited. The applicant's criminal record is ignored.

In the observation stage, the applicant meets the recruiting master's students and the rule master. The rule master is responsible for teaching the applicant the rules, principles, and regulations of the organization. The recruiting master and the rule master then closely observe the applicant for another one to two years. At this stage, the rule master explores the applicant's real motives for joining.

In the final stage, if both masters are satisfied with the applicant, the applicant will meet his principal master and be formally initiated. The new member receives a membership booklet that contains information about the member and the masters, as well as the societies' rules and regulations.

Membership in secret societies is fluid and mobile. Certain rules enable the transfer of members to other societies and the recruitment of members from them. For example, the Shan Chu, or the master, can *shou shan* ("close the mountain"), meaning that he is not involved in society activities anymore and his organization is dissolved. He can also *fu shan* ("reopen the mountain"), meaning that he has reinvolved himself in society affairs and his organization is recruiting members again. By *zhuan shan* ("change the mountain"), leaders and members can join other societies or maintain membership in two or more societies simultaneously.

Many people join the secret societies for two reasons. The first is curiosity. They want to know what it is like to be a member of a legendary secret organization. The other reason has to do with practicality. They believe that being a member enhances their ability to survive in a competitive environment. Members find that they have many "brothers" to turn to whenever and wherever they need help.

HUNG AND CHING: ONE BIG FAMILY

Hung and Ching societies are cordial to each other and view themselves as members of a large family. Both societies support each other. If Ching societies' brothers need help, Hung brothers will support them and vice versa. It is acceptable for a person to maintain dual membership, and such a person is highly regarded by both societies. However, there is one regulation about dual membership—that is, a Ching brother is allowed to join any of the Hung societies, but not the other way around. There is a saying, "If a Ching member joins the Hung, he is a dragon." (The dragon symbolizes a courageous fighter.) There is another saying, "If a Hung brother joins the Ching society, he should be severely punished." The reason is that the transformation of a Ching member to a Hung member is in harmony with nature, in which green (Chinese *ching*) leaf or fruit turns to red (Chinese *hung*) color when it is aged or ripened. To turn green (to become a Ching society member) from red (a Hung society member) is considered abnormal because it is antagonistic to natural law. One source indicated that Hung members are not allowed to join the Ching societies because Hung leaders view Ching societies as pro-Qing (Ch'ing) associations (Morgan 1960). A Ching brother who joins Hung societies is normally assigned an important position, which is at least a senior position in one of the eight external tongs.

There are three similar features between the Hung and Ching societies. Both groups are patriotic and nationalistic and support conservative right-wing political groups. They emerged almost simultaneously, with the Ching societies in the northern part of China and the Hung societies in the southern part. Both groups' major goal was to overthrow the Qing and restore the Ming dynasty.

Second, both societies' members are primarily workers of low socioeconomic class, soldiers, or peasants who dwell at the bottom rank of society and are alienated from conventional norms and values. Members of both societies have little faith in government officials and intellectuals because they view the latter as opportunistic people who lack the virtues of loyalty and righteousness. History has convinced the members that officials and intellectuals have often betrayed the incumbent government to support the newly emerged power. In regard to this issue, a Hung leader stated explicitly in the closing ceremony of the Overseas Hung League Meeting that:

> In the Hung societies, we have members who are scholars, politicians, farmers, workers, and businessmen. Some members have enormous amounts of knowledge, some have little, and some are illiterate. People have accused the Hung League of recruiting many members who are marginals and unconventional. That is true. However, if we look at the other side of the coin, we see that a lot of learned people and very knowledgeable people have often committed disloyal and unrighteous acts. I am a learned person myself, and I have to remind myself that learned persons are often inferior in comparison with unlearned persons. Although those uneducated people are at the bottom rank of our society, they are loyal and righteous, their personalities are great, and their contributions to their country are enormous. Look back at the initial stage of the Communists' takeover of mainland China; those who immediately supported and followed the Communists were not ordinary countrymen, but the educated and the scholars. Normally, these people appear to be very arrogant, and yet, in the midst of crisis, they are the ones who could not keep their principles, who lost their character, and who are easily bribed. From this fact, we can conclude that the greatness of a person's personality has no association with his educational level. (Shuai 1961, 151; my translation)

Third, both groups of societies were vulnerable to exploitation by political and military groups. Since members are mostly uneducated and there is no central administrative body to represent and direct the fragmented societies, the societies were easily penetrated and controlled by various political and criminal groups. The societies are not only structurally disintegrated but their ideology is also situational and flexible. Thus, various interest groups have been able to impose their own ideologies onto the spirit of the secret societies. For instance, Ching members were hired by the Manchu as dockworkers to unload rice from ships. Besides, the Manchu also infiltrated the overseas version of the Hung societies—the tongs—and established a coalition (the Pao Wong Tang—the Party for the Preservation of the Qing Emperor) in an attempt to neutralize Sun Yat-sen's efforts to provoke nationalism among Chinese immigrants (Y. Sun 1977).

In sum, Hung and Ching societies are similar in the following ways: (1) both were originally patriotic and nationalistic organizations; (2) both groups established their foundations on the loyalty of underclass people such as peasants, laborers, and soldiers; and (3) both societies were vulnerable to outsiders' exploitation.

The major dissimilarities between the Hung and Ching societies are their level of secrecy and their structures. First, although both are secret societies, the Hung societies' efforts to maintain secrecy are not as intense as the Ching societies'. The Hung societies were actively and openly involved in direct confrontation with the Manchus, whereas Ching societies maintained a low profile in such situations. Besides, the overseas Hung brethren have held their annual meetings openly in various parts of the world. If a person belongs to both groups, he normally would reveal only his membership in the Hung society (Shuai 1961). Thus, people know that there are semi-public Hung societies among Chinese immigrants, but few people are aware of the Ching societies.

Second, the Hung societies are vertically structured, whereas the Ching societies are horizontally structured. Although Hung members are all considered brothers, there is a rigid hierarchical system and each member occupies a well-defined position within it. In contrast, there are only masters and students in the Ching societies. Although there are forty-eight ranks altogether within the Ching societies, these ranks are significant only in recruiting and courtesy matters. A member's rank is not positively related to his power or prestige within the group.

THE REVIVAL OF SECRET SOCIETIES

When the political party that Sun Yat-sen founded, the Kuomintang, was defeated by the Chinese Communists in 1949, Hung members who served in the Kuomintang army followed the leader, Chiang Kai-shek, to Taiwan. From 1949 to 1980, the Hung organizations were active in neither political nor criminal activities. However, when Taiwan became more liberal and opposing political groups were formed in the 1980s, the Hung societies there revived. According to Chi (1985), since the early 1980s, the societies have been mobilized by the Kuomintang to support pro-Kuomintang political candidates during local elections or to neutralize the influence of many social movements. Occasionally, the societies are hired by local politicians to aid in political campaigns. In several instances, Hung members have used violence to intimidate political opponents.

Having remained behind the scenes for almost forty years, the Hung societies dramatically changed their policy in 1988 by conducting an initiation ceremony that was open to the public. The media were invited, and Hung leaders performed the whole process of initiation rites to the stunned reporters and television cameramen. Besides, the leaders announced the establishment of their own political party. During the meeting, some Hung leaders even suggested that they may soon register their organizations with the government as lawful civic associations, a move that they thought might help unite the fragmented groups into a well-integrated, powerful organization and that also might prevent them from being infiltrated by criminal elements. Nevertheless, other leaders oppose this plan, preferring that the societies remain secret (*World Journal*, November 13, 1988, 6).

There are many fragmented Hung societies active in Taiwan, with more than 100,000 active members. Most Hung leaders are former generals, and members include soldiers, intelligence personnel, and professionals. There is little evidence to suggest that Hung members are yet involved in criminal activities or being infiltrated by major Taiwanese criminal organizations such as the Bamboo United and the Four Seas.

Ching members fled to Hong Kong or Taiwan when the Communists took over China. In Hong Kong, after several years of successful drug smuggling, the societies prepared to launch a major recruiting ceremony to solidify their presence in the colony. However, their plan was ruined when a police order canceled the ceremony. Eventually, this setback led to their decline in Hong Kong. A few leaders were extradited, and the power of the societies was further eroded by local organized crime groups (Zhang 1984; McCoy 1973; Posner 1988).

In Taiwan, Ching members maintained low profiles and did not become involved in criminal activities. A Ching society member maintains that there is no relationship between Taiwanese crime groups and Ching societies in Taiwan:

> The criminal elements respect us. Most of us have nothing to do with those criminal groups. Maybe a few brothers are close to criminal organizations. What could have happened was that a former criminal element is recruited by us because he behaved very well after he dissociated himself from his gang. However, after becoming a Ching member, he falls back on his previous criminal way of life. . . . We never identify ourselves as Ching members to outsiders. So the

> criminal elements have no way to associate with us. I will say there is absolutely no relationship between organized crime groups and the Ching societies. (From an interview conducted for this study, my translation)

Ten months after the Hung societies made a dramatic move by announcing their intention to move into the mainstream society, Ching societies also attracted major media attention by conducting a highly publicized initiation ceremony. Powerful leaders of the societies attended the ceremony, and new members, including a political candidate, were recruited right in front of the public eye (*Sing Tao Jih Pao*, August 23, 1989, 40).

It is clear that secret societies in Taiwan are currently undergoing major reform. New members, many of them politicians, successful businessmen, or movie or television stars, are being initiated openly. Leaders of the societies are being treated as celebrities by the media. A few political candidates, seeking ways to bolster their reputations, publicize their affiliation with the secret societies and the endorsement of their campaigns by the societies. There is no doubt that, as most public posts are beginning to be assigned through free elections, the role of the secret societies in Taiwan politics is going to grow.

3

FROM SECRET SOCIETIES TO ORGANIZED CRIME

Following the Opium War (1840-1842), China was forced to cede Hong Kong to the British. After World War II, Hong Kong emerged as one of the most developed areas in Asia. Along with Taiwan, Korea, and Singapore, it is one of the "Four Little Dragons," a name that compliments its strong economy. The colony occupies 400 square miles and has a population of 5.5 million, of which 98 percent are Chinese. Almost all major banks of the world have branches in the colony, which now ranks as the world's third largest financial center (after New York and London) (*Business Week*, March 5, 1984, 50-64). It is also the third largest container seaport in the world. Because Hong Kong is a duty-free port, it attracts millions of tourists each year. As a transshipment port between the People's Republic of China and the rest of the world, Hong Kong has played an increasingly significant role in the world economy since China opened its door to the West in the late 1970s.

The colony will be ceded back to China in 1997. When British and Chinese officials met in the early 1980s to discuss the issue, the prices of stocks and real estate tumbled. Despite China's promise to let the colony maintain its social and economic systems for fifty years after 1997, Hong Kong residents remain skeptical. As a result, some of Hong Kong's largest enterprises have transferred their capital to overseas branches, and a few have decided to move their headquarters to other countries. Tens of thousands of business people and professionals have left the colony to settle in the United States, Canada, and Australia (*Wall Street Journal*, March 30, 1988, 14; *New York Times*, May 8, 1988, 15).

When the pro-democracy movement erupted in Beijing and Shanghai in May 1989, more than half a million Hong Kong residents demonstrated in support of the movement. After Deng Xiaoping's government crushed the protesters by sending troops into Tiananmen Square and killing hundreds of unarmed civilians, Hong Kong people's confidence in the Chinese government further eroded. The price of stocks plunged 22 percent in one day. When the Chinese government continued to execute dissidents and purge pro-democracy intellectuals, Hong Kong residents reacted by speeding up their flight from the colony. Between now and 1997, it is expected that many Chinese in Hong Kong will leave the colony (*Newsweek*, June 19, 1989, 27).

DEGENERATION OF SECRET SOCIETIES

The transformation of secret societies into organized crime groups can be seen most clearly in Hong Kong. Because many people involved in the study and control of organized crime believe that crime groups there will transplant to North America before the end of this century, a close examination of these groups is warranted here.

Secret societies in Hong Kong were diverted from political to criminal purposes early in their existence. When Hung societies were first established in Hong Kong, their goals underwent a dramatic change. Without a patriotic cause, members turned their attention from the survival of their country to the survival of themselves. By 1845, three years after Hong Kong was ceded to Britain, the colony's social order was so disturbed by the activities of the Triads (as the Hung were then sometimes called), that the British enacted the Ordinance for the Suppression of Triads and Other Secret Societies (the Societies Ordinance). It prohibited residents from joining the Triad societies, attending meetings, and possessing books or paraphernalia that are related to the societies (U.S. Department of Justice 1988).

A Triad member from China formed the first local (as opposed to transplanted) Triad society in the early twentieth century. Members were predominantly peddlers. The purpose of the society was to protect the territory of the members from other peddlers. Soon, at least ten similar societies were established, and individual conflicts escalated into group conflicts.

In the midst of repeated group fights for territory, a member proposed the unification of all societies into an integrated organization to avoid group confrontations. The first meeting of the societies was called the Conference of the Hung League. At the meeting, all societies agreed to add the word *wo* (peace) in front of the names of their groups. These societies later developed into the powerful branches of the notorious Wo group (Zhang 1984). Until now, most peddlers in Hong Kong are alleged to be Triad members (*World Journal*, October 25, 1985, 15: *China Times Weekly*, November 10, 1985, 71-72).

According to Zhang (1984), the development of Hong Kong Triad societies as criminal groups can be divided into three stages: the prewar period of 1930-1940, World War II, and the postwar period from 1945 to the present.

The first stage was also known as the Golden Period. At that time, there were about thirty Triad organizations, formed by peddlers and workers from both the private and public sectors. The organizations were registered as trade guilds, benevolent association, or athletic clubs that dealt with their members' employment, welfare, funeral, and other problems. As these Triad organizations rapidly expanded their influence in the labor field through increased membership, "bona fide labour associations were often forced to organize fighting sections of their own in order to oppose Triad infiltration into their particular spheres. Some of these associations became so obsessed with self-protection and retention of their employment monopolies that they, in turn, employed the Triad oath and ritual in order to bind their members more closely together and also, in some cases, to ally themselves with and obtain the general protection of one of the larger society groups" (Morgan 1960, 67). A nationwide labor strike occurred during this period, and in order to suppress the strike, British soldiers were dispatched to patrol the streets. By then, most residents relied on public water pumps in the streets for household water. During the strike, residents were afraid to come out of their homes because they feared harassment by British soldiers. Triad members exploited the situation by carrying water to the houses for a lucrative price. Later, these gang members also sold stolen food to the residents. During this short strike, criminal organizations in Hong Kong were thus able to establish a solid foundation.

The second stage of the evolution of the Triad societies occurred during the time of the Japanese occupation of Hong Kong. In order to maintain social order within the colony and to detect anti-Japanese activities, the Japanese rulers established the so-called Hing Ah Kee Kwan (Asia Flourishing Association) by mobilizing various Triad societies. As members of the association, Triad elements became informers and enforcers for the ruling Japanese troops. For their cooperation, the Japanese rewarded the societies by destroying all criminal records and allowing them to operate gambling and opium houses. Under the encouragement of the Japanese, the Triads were also involved in running prostitution rings for the Japanese soldiers who came to Hong Kong for recreation. The most notorious crime groups of that period were the Wo On Lok, Wo Hung Shen, Wo Laik Wo, Tung Shan Wo, and Fuk Yee Hing.

After the war, Hong Kong Triad societies continued their relentless expansion. But the groups in the postwar period were structurally and spiritually quite different from the prewar organizations. Structurally, each Triad group before the war had its *Hai Di* (membership record book). Whenever a senior member recruited a new member, he had to report the new recruit's name, birthplace, criminal specialty or occupation, and aliases to the administrative officer for recordkeeping purpose. Thus, during the prewar period, membership could be verified easily. In the postwar periods, however, all organizations abandoned the maintenance of the Hai Di. A person could become a member simply by the acknowledgment of a *tai lou* ("big brother"). As a result, the administrative bodies gradually lost control over the members. Group members committed criminal activities without the support or knowledge of the administrative bodies.

The breakdown of communication within the organizations had a profound effect on the loyalty of the members. During the prewar period members normally were loyal to and trusted one another, and they sacrificed themselves, if necessary, to protect other members from arrest or prosecution. In the postwar period members readily turned in their brothers to protect themselves.

After the war, the emergence of the 14K, the Ching societies, and the Tai Hwin (Big Circle) dramatically changed the nature of Triad societies in Hong Kong. The emerging groups, all transplanted from China, were more ruthless than the local groups. Since these outside groups started to establish a stronghold in Hong Kong, not only did street violence escalate, but the type of Triad activities also shifted from victimless crimes such as gambling and prostitution to predatory crimes such as extortion, robbery, and drug trafficking.

In 1956 the seriousness of the Triad problem finally became apparent. Many Hong Kong residents participate in the celebration of the Double-Tenth National Day of the Taiwan government. On that day in 1956, a group of 14K members was infuriated when an employee removed the national flags of Taiwan from the walls of a public housing project. Members of 14K raided the office of the employee and set the building on fire. Thousands of emotionally charged 14K and Wo On Lok members initiated a riot as the news of the raid broke out. Chinese Communist sympathizers were assaulted, and their property was destroyed. When the situation became uncontrollable, the British army intervened, a curfew was imposed, and thousands of Triad members were arrested. As a result of this episode, the British established the Triad Society Bureau to monitor and control the societies (Zhang 1984).

In 1967 the Cultural Revolution in China spilled into Hong Kong and resulted in a series of political disturbances. Law enforcement officials shifted priorities from controlling organized crime to scrutinizing radical political groups and preventing political riots. Consequently, peddling, illegal transport services, gambling, prostitution, narcotics trafficking, and many other illegal activities proliferated. Triad members and corrupt police officers worked closely in promoting many illegal operations. Corruption in both private and public sectors was so pervasive that the Independent Commission Against Corruption (ICAC) was formed in 1973 (Lethbridge 1985). The head of the Triad Society Bureau was convicted of corruption and the bureau was disbanded (*Far Eastern Economic Review*, May 15, 1986, 50-51). Many police officers were also indicted for taking bribes and providing illegal services (*South China Morning Post*, July 28, 1987, 13).

When local political disturbances subsided in the early 1970s, law enforcement authorities returned to combating Triad activities. The police established the Organized and Serious Crime Group. In addition, Fight Crime Committees were formed in many districts to control Triad problems at the local level.

A report by the Fight Crime Committee in 1976 declared that Triad societies existed largely in name only, having degenerated into loose bands of petty criminals. However, ten years later, the committee issued another report indicating that there were 70,000 to 120,000 Triad members in Hong Kong, and their involvement in illegal activities was extensive. The committee recommended to the Legislative Council the imposition of tough legal measures to curb the Triad problem. According to a U.S. Department of Justice report, the Criminal Intelligence Bureau of the Royal Hong Kong Police described the period between 1977 and 1983 as a "renaissance" for the Triad societies (U.S. Department of Justice 1988). Other sources suggest that there were now 160,000 Triad members in Hong Kong in 1988, constituting 3 percent of the total population (*Centre Daily News*, February 8, 1988, 4).

The reason the Fight Crime Committee underestimated the power of the societies in 1976 is unknown. However, later investigations showed that law enforcement agencies in Hong Kong were penetrated by Triad members in the mid-1970s. Several senior police officers of that period were later convicted for taking bribes from Triad societies.

Gang violence is vicious but seldom deadly, in part because of Hong Kong's strict ban on the private possession of firearms.

Chief Superintendent Brian Merritt of the Royal Hong Kong Police Organized and Serious Crime Bureau indicates that Triad societies are not organized crime syndicates. They are totally different from the Mafia in that the top leaders are often not involved in organized crime at all. While the senior Triad leaders arbitrate disputes and receive "gifts" from society members, middle-level officers may run their own criminal enterprises with no need to report to the chairman or "dragon head." Within the ring that runs criminal activity, there may be members of other Triads or people who are not Triad members at all. Nevertheless, membership in the Triad provides the protection of the society and access to people and activities with whom one can form criminal ventures (*Los Angeles Times*, July 19, 1987, 6).

According to the Fight Crime Committee, a typical progression into organized crime would involve the following stages:

1. recruitment into a youth gang involved in juvenile delinquent and anti-social behavior;
2. agreement to follow the leader of a youth gang who is a Triad member;
3. entry into a street gang, either before or after initiation into a Triad society, operated by an office-bearer;
4. involvement in organized crime, gang fights and settlement talks on behalf of the office-bearer;
5. at the same time, operating own minor rackets, such as street-level drug distribution, protection rackets or debt-collection;
6. formation of own gang and a need to support it by engaging in a wide variety of organized crime activities;
7. promotion to Triad office-bearer rank and involvement in prostitution, loan-sharking and criminal monopolies;
8. formation of "front" business to hide involvement in organized crime and going, in part, legitimate by investing illegal income in a wide variety of business concerns;
9. reaping large profits, evading tax, and making efforts to appear completely respectable. (Fight Crime Committee 1986, 16-17)

Triad societies in Hong Kong have been completely transformed to purely criminal organizations without patriotic or political aspirations. H.W.E. Heath, former commissioner of the Hong Kong Police Department, maintains that "in present day Hong Kong the Triad member is nothing more than a run-of-the-mill hoodlum masquerading in the name of a long-dead giant" (Morgan 1960, xi).

TRIAD SOCIETIES IN HONG KONG

Unlike the Hung societies, the structure of Hong Kong Triad societies is much simpler. Instead of eleven positions within the hierarchy, local Triad organizations here have only six positions, with each represented by a number that is significant in the Triad subculture (Zhang 1984; *CLEU LINE*, October 1985):

1. Shan Chu (a 489) is the head of each group. He is also known as Lung Tao or Tai Lou. For instance, the Wo group has only one Shan Chu who represents all the organizations who belong to the Wo group.
2. Yee Lu Yuan Swie or Fu Shan Chu (a 438) is the head of each organization and runs the organization. Some organizations may have more than one Yee Lu Yuan Swie.
3. Hung Kwan (a 426) is the organization's enforcer who leads the soldiers in actual combat. Most Triad officers are predominantly enforcers.
4. Pak Tse Sin (a 415) is the advisor on administrative, financial, military, and public affairs.
5. Cho Hai (a 432) is the organization's messenger who is responsible for liaisons with organizations of the same group. The Cho Hai is no longer an important position.
6. Sey Kow Jai (a 49) is the ordinary member. He is not entitled to participate in policymaking. If a Sey Kow Jai has a tenure of more than ten years and is recommended by senior members other than the Cho Hai, he may participate in policymaking and recruiting activities (Figure 2).

Besides these "official" positions, the organizations may have peripheral members not officially recruited, whose names are not registered with the organizations. Since proof of membership in any criminal organization is a crime, most members prefer to remain peripherals.

Upward mobility within the organization is rare, if not impossible. A Sey Kow Jai may be promoted to the position of Hung Kwan, Pak Tse Sin, or Cho Hai. A Hung Kwan, Pak Tse Sin, or Cho Hai cannot become a Shan Chu or Yee Lu Yuan Swei unless he has served as either acting director or supervisor of the organization. The two acting positions are assigned to two of the senior members (except the Sey Kow Jai) as adjunct positions.

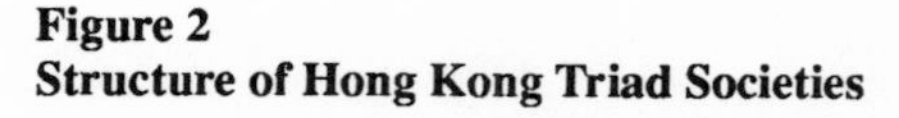

Figure 2
Structure of Hong Kong Triad Societies

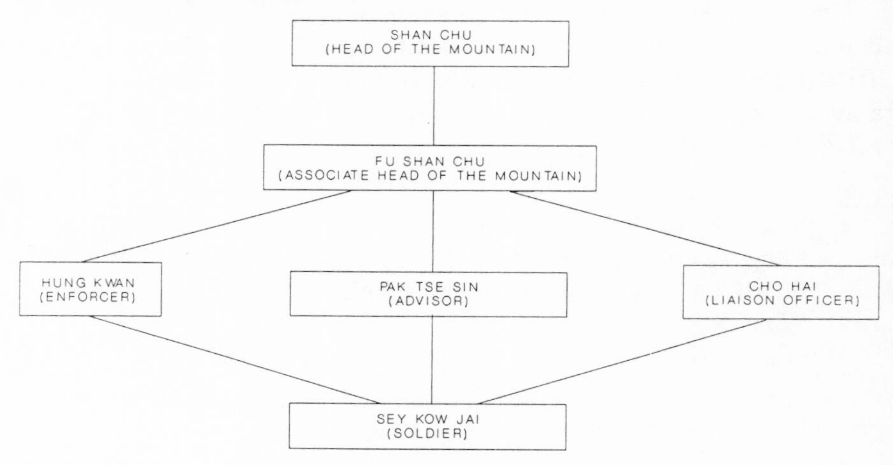

Triad organizations in Hong Kong comprise four major groups: the Chiu Chao, the Wo, the 14K, and the Big Four (Zhang 1984). Figure 3 lists all the Triad and non-Triad organizations active in Hong Kong.

The Chiu Chao Group

This group consists of four criminal syndicates: Fuk Yee Hing, Sun Yee On, Gain Yee, and Yee Kun. The Fuk Yee Hing is one of the oldest crime groups still operating in Hong Kong; its members are mainly the descendants of immigrants of Chiu Chao origin. When it was established in the early 1900s, it was known as the Yee Hing Company, a branch of a Hung society in China. The company handled financial matters for the parent organization in China.

Established in 1919, Sun Yee On emerged as a powerful organization in the postwar era. It was registered as a legitimate commercial association but in reality was heavily involved in protection rackets (*Centre Daily News*, February 8, 1988, 4). It is now a dominant force in Hong Kong and probably the best organized. Most police raids on Triad strongholds are targeted at this group (*World Journal*, September 6, 1987, 22). Sun Yee On controls brothels, bars, and nightclubs in a densely populated commercial district in Kowloon. Police arrested eleven Sun Yee On leaders, including the Shan Chu, in April 1987 for their membership in a Triad society and involvement in extortion. The case is significant because it was the first time a Shan Chu was convicted and imprisoned (*Sing Tao Jih Pao*, January 29, 1988, 28).

Figure 3
Hong Kong Triad Societies

Cantonese	Chiu Chao and Hakka	Mainlanders	Taiwan
Wo Group	Fuk Yee Hing	Ching societies	United
Wo On Lok	Sun Yee On	Big Circle	Bamboo's
Wo Shen Wo	Gain Yee		Chao Tong
Wo Shen Tong	Yee Kun		
Wo Yee Tong			
Wo Yung Yee			
Wo Hop To			
Wo Laik Wo			
Wo Shen Yee			
Wo Hung Shen			
Wo Kung Lok			
Wo Kung Ying			
Wo Yak Ping			
Wo Gee Ping			
The 14K			
The Big Four			
Tang Yee, Tung Shan Wo			
Tung Lok, Tung Yee			
Leun Ying Society			
Leun Yi Society			
Leun Kun Society			
Leun Kun Ying			
Ma Kow Jai			

The Wo Group

Before World War II, there were about thirty-six organizations in the Wo group. After 1945, some of the organizations disbanded and others merged; thirteen organizations now belong to the group. Some of the more powerful societies are the Wo On Lok, Wo Shen Wo, Wo Yung Yee, Wo Hop To, Wo Laik Wo, and Wo Shen Tong (Zhang 1984).

The Wo On Lok, previously known as the On Lok Tong, was the most powerful crime group before the emergence of the 14K. It played a leading role in the mass robbery and killing of Hong Kong residents on the eve of the Japanese invasion and in the organized crime riot in 1956.

The Big Four

This group comprises nine organizations whose names start with one of the following words: *tang*, *tung*, *leun*, and *ma*. The group is also known as the Leun group.

The 14K Association

The 14K is the most powerful Triad organization in Hong Kong. It has branches in Japan, Taiwan, Macao, Europe, and Southeast Asia. Locally, the group has eight branches, known as the *dui*. The association was established by a Kuomintang general in Guangzhou (Canton) to back up the party in the war against the Chinese Communists during the late 1940s. After the Kuomintang retreated to Taiwan, many 14K members flocked to Hong Kong. During its first two years there, the general prevented the association from becoming a criminal group. However, after his death, eight branches of the original eighteen were transformed into ruthless criminal groups that specialized in extortion and intimidation (Morgan 1960).

When the 14K first emerged in Hong Kong, it viewed itself as the legitimate representative of the Hung societies in China. The association openly acknowledged the Kuomintang in Taiwan, and its activities and slogans were politically oriented. During that period, the 14K was perceived as an outsider by the local crime groups. Conflicts between the 14K and local gangs were frequent, and there were at least thirty incidents in which one or more people were killed. In the official report on the Hong Kong organized crime riot of 1956, the 14K was called the "semi-official underground organization of the Kuomintang" (Zhang 1984). The 14k members are now in control of Yau Ma Tei and Mong Kok, two of the most lucrative commercial districts of Kowloon.

Other than the Chiu Chao group, the Wo group, the Big Four, and the 14K, a group of criminals from China are active in Hong Kong. These mainland Chinese criminals are known as Tai Hwin Jai, or Big Circle. According to some observers, the Big Circle is not an organization. It refers to either criminal elements who were recently smuggled into Hong Kong from China to commit crime, or to those criminals who were former Red Guard members and who entered Hong Kong illegally during the Cultural Revolution. Since Guangzhou is known as the Big Circle to Hong Kong residents, criminals who came from there are also called Big Circle. Criminal elements from China are mostly experienced fighters whose ruthlessness surpasses those of the Hong Kong local groups (*China Times Weekly*, May 19, 1985, 72). Besides these criminal groups, the Yueh Tung (criminals from Macao) and the Bamboo United's Chao Tong (an overseas branch of a Taiwan-based criminal organization) are the two groups that appeared on the Hong Kong crime scene only recently.

Hong Kong Triad societies are not well organized. More often than not, branches within a society will become involved in serious group conflicts to protect the interests of an individual branch. For example, many groups belonging to the Wo group have been constantly fighting with each other. Branches of the 14K have also battled furiously with each other for a prolonged period of time (*World Journal*, June 15, 1985, 6). In sum, Triad members nowadays are more concerned with individual financial gain than they are with any other values or norms. The spirit of loyalty and brotherhood exists only on paper and ceremonial oaths. As Brian Merritt of the Royal Hong Kong Police pointed out, the Triads "don't cooperate with each other. They do their own thing totally. There are still dragon heads and other office-holders, but nowadays the only thing the leaders control is promotion, and they occasionally officiate in initiation ceremonies for new members. They no longer have the power to tell their members what criminal trades they should go into" (*Asiaweek*, November 11, 1988, 53).

HEROIN, PROSTITUTION, AND GAMBLING

Major activities of the Triad societies are drug trafficking, prostitution, gambling, and extortion.

Drug Trafficking

Over the past several years, Hong Kong has emerged as the center for Southeast Asian heroin transshipment and money laundering. The amount of Number 4 heroin seized in Hong Kong increased from 12.4 kilograms in 1985 to 79.24 kilograms in 1986, 157.2 kilograms in 1987, and 161 kilograms in 1988. Because local heroin addicts consume only the smokable form (Number 3 heroin), the increase in Number 4 heroin seizures suggests that more heroin is being transported abroad via Hong Kong. In 1988, drug enforcement authorities there indicted nine major international drug syndicates and arrested more than forty major offenders (*World Journal*, November 22, 1988, 3).

Among Triad organizations, the Chiu Chao group plays a major role in drug trafficking. Because most overseas Chinese in Thailand are Chiu Chao, the group in Hong Kong has good connections with drug traffickers in Bangkok and Chiang Mai (McCoy 1973). According to Loo, "it is strongly suspected that the Chiu Chao shoulders the bulk of the heroin trade from Asia to other parts of the world" (1976, 33). The group also controls drug manufacturing in Hong Kong. Zhang notes that the "Chiu Chao group, among them Fuk Yee Hing and Sun Yee On in particular are very much involved in drug manufacturing. Whenever the police raided drug manufacturing factories, [they] found that eight or nine out of ten arrestees were Chiu Chao" (1984, 168; my translation).

Besides the Chiu Chao group, 14K members are also alleged to be involved in heroin trafficking. In Taiwan, police found that 14K members work closely with local crime groups in importing heroin from Thailand to Taiwan. Taiwan police arrested twenty-one 14K members in 1985 for smuggling fifteen pounds of heroin (*World Journal*, January 25, 1985, 4).

Triad activities in the Netherlands have also concerned Dutch social control agencies (Winterton 1981). According to authorities in the Netherlands, the 14K is one of the most active groups in heroin trafficking in Rotterdam and Amsterdam, the heroin trade centers of Europe. Power struggles over the drug trade between the 14K and a crime syndicate formed by drug traffickers from Singapore and Malaysia have resulted in several killings (Bax 1984; Weijenburg 1984).

Hong Kong Triads also dominate the heroin trade in Australia. Drug enforcement authorities there seized forty-three kilograms of heroin in a yacht that arrived in Sydney from Hong Kong, and they arrested thirty-three offenders in October 1988. The yacht was registered to an alleged 14K member (*World Journal*, October 24, 1988, 3). Seven months later, Hong Kong and Australian police arrested sixteen offenders in Sydney and

Hong Kong for smuggling eighty kilograms of heroin into Australia (*World Journal*, May 25, 1989, 7). The heroin was first moved from the Golden Triangle to China and then smuggled into Australia via Hong Kong and a small island near Australia by being hidden inside a truck. During the action, Australian police also confiscated $820,000 (Australian) and three handguns.

Besides Taiwan, the Netherlands, and Australia, Hong Kong crime groups are also involved in smuggling Southeast Asian heroin into the United States. American drug enforcement officials believe that New York-based Chinese crime figures visited Hong Kong often in the past few years and that they now play a significant role in the transshipment of heroin to America from Hong Kong. For example, a 14K member was arrested in New York City for smuggling thirty-three pounds of heroin from Thailand into the United States (*World Journal*, September 23, 1986, 20; April 22, 1987, 20).

Most Southeast Asian heroin imported into the United States comes directly either from Thailand or from Hong Kong. When Thailand and Hong Kong became major targets for drug enforcement authorities, travelers, air packages, and cargoes from these two areas were closely scrutinized for heroin smuggling. As a result, heroin traffickers moved their drug operations from the Golden Triangle to the Netherlands, South or Central American nations, and China before eventually smuggling it into the United States. Although there is increasing involvement in heroin trafficking by Chinese who live in China, Taiwan, America, Thailand, and South and Central America, people who are Hong Kong or American residents, or citizens who came originally from Hong Kong are considered to be the most active in heroin trafficking.

However, the extent to which the Hong Kong Triad societies are involved in international heroin trafficking is not clear. Except for Taiwan and the Netherlands, where 14K members dominate the heroin trade, there is little evidence to support the contention that Hong Kong Triad societies are responsible for the bulk of the heroin smuggled into the United States. Many Chinese have been arrested in the United States, Hong Kong, Thailand, and Canada for heroin trafficking, and thousands of pounds of heroin have been seized. However, only one defendant was suspected of being connected with Hong Kong Triad societies (United States Senate 1987). Robert Stutman of the Drug Enforcement Administration suggests that "while Triad members are involved, I don't think the Triads themselves control the trafficking in New York City" (*Asiaweek*, November 11, 1988, 53).

If Hong Kong Triads do not play a key role in the Southeast Asian heroin trade in New York City or other parts of the United States, who is responsible for the many hundreds of pounds of heroin smuggled into this country every year? I will discuss the role of local Chinese gangs' involvement in the heroin trade in Chapter 7, and a section of Chapter 9 will explore the roles of traffickers who are not affiliated to either Triads or gangs.

Prostitution

Triad organizations in Hong Kong are heavily involved in prostitution. Gangsters infiltrate various facilities, both legal and illegal, to promote prostitution. These facilities are generally brothels (including health clubs), illegal massage parlors (including sauna baths, finger massage parlors, and rehabilitation centers), one-girl studios, and boarding rooms. To give an idea of the extent of prostitution activities, there are one thousand so-called One-Phoenix Studios (a prostitute operating inside a studio) in Hong Kong, most located in a well-known red-light district, and more often than not, operated by two or more criminal organizations as joint ventures (*World Journal*, May 13, 1985, 5).

In order to stay competitive in the prostitution business, the 14K, Tung Shan Wo, Tang Yee, Sun Yee On, Wo Shen Wo, Wo Shen Yee, and several Leun organizations have special branches staffed by members known as the Ku Yeah Jai. The Ku Yeah Jai are mostly young, handsome males who specialize in recruiting runaway girls to work for the organizations as prostitutes. These branches have their own enforcers, limousines, and beautiful apartments. Loo notes that

> Young girls who have run away from home are known to be prime targets of the Triads. Furthermore, some girls may be raped or gang-raped to force them into prostitution. This practice is known as "sealing" or "stamping their property." After the girl has agreed to become a prostitute, she is usually sold to a call-girl center. A young and attractive girl can be priced anywhere up to H.K.$7,000. (1976, 30-31)

If she is not sold, the girl is allocated to one of the call-girl centers owned and operated by the organization. The organization helps attractive and talented young women to enter the entertainment world as actresses or singers. If they become successful as entertainers, the organization controls their activities and income (Zhang 1984).

Women who work in the various houses of prostitution are mostly native-born. A few come from China, Taiwan, the Philippines, and Thailand. Taiwanese women arrive in Hong Kong as either actresses or singers, the Filipino women as private maids, and the Thai women as tourists. According to sources from the Hong Kong vice squad, the average age of the prostitutes is falling; some of the girls are as young as thirteen. The 14K and Wo Shen Wo are the organizations most active in operating teenage prostitution rings (for example, *World Journal*, May 19, 1985, 7).

Gambling

Except for betting on horses and government-sponsored lotteries, Hong Kong organized crime groups are involved in all types of legal and illegal gambling. The two most prevalent types are illegal grand gambling dens and legal mahjong "schools."

Establishing a grand gambling den requires an investment of H.K. $50,000 to $3,000,000 (U.S. $6,500 to $400,000). Normally, the den has gangsters as internal investors, and nongangsters as external investors. The den's employees—such as public relations officers, the general manager, guards, the treasurer, dealers, assistant dealers, messengers, and marketing agents—are all Triad members.

Although the mahjong schools are the major form of legal gambling, they still require the support of criminal organizations. Every mahjong school is protected by a group of Triad members who are responsible for ensuring that gamblers do not create disturbances and that rival crime groups do not rob the school (Zhang 1984).

Other Activities

Besides drug trafficking, prostitution, and gambling, criminal organizations also try their hands at extortion, arson, contract killings, robberies, and fraud. A Sun Yee On member testified that about 80 percent of the restaurants have to pay a protection fee to Triad societies (*Centre Daily News*, December 1, 1987a, 4).

The Big Circle groups are active in robbery. Their main targets are jewelry stores. Normally, one of the local organizations will bring in criminals from China. The organization then provides them with housing, fraudulent identifications, weapons, and information on potential targets. Once the imported criminals have robbed several stores and the local organizations have rewarded them for their services, they will be smuggled back to China. Their temporary stay in Hong Kong may never be known to local police (*China Times Weekly*, May 19, 1985, 72).

Since the early 1980s, many jewelry stores have been victimized by the Big Circle. For example, in May 1985, several Big Circle people robbed a jewelry store in Kowloon and escaped with several million Hong Kong dollars worth of jewelry. Although the police had prior knowledge of the plans and had put the store under surveillance, the robbers were still able to carry out the crime. While the robbers were fighting their way out after the robbery, they wounded several police officers and several bystanders. According to officers at the scene, the robbery was not only well planned, but the robbers were well trained in weaponry as well (*World Journal*, May 3, 1985, 1). Four months later, the same jewelry store was again robbed by three gunmen alleged to be criminal elements from China (*Centre Daily News*, September 18, 1985, 5).

Two Big Circle criminals were arrested on October 13, 1987, while they were in the process of sneaking into Hong Kong. Police also confiscated four Chinese-made handguns and some explosives. According to the arrestees who have prior arrest records in China, several Hong Kong criminal elements arrived in China to hire them for the purposes of committing robbery. The Hong Kong crime group arranged for the transportation and paid the hired robbers H.K. $5,000 (U.S. $650) as a down payment. Both parties agreed that once the planned robberies were committed, the Big Circle would be paid H.K. $45,000 (U.S. $6,000), and that all the proceeds from the robberies would be retained by the local crime group (*Tin Tin Daily News*, October 14, 1987, 1).

HONG KONG POLITICS AND THE DIFFUSION OF TRIAD SOCIETIES

The political uncertainty in Hong Kong has led law enforcement authorities in the United States (President's Commission on Organized Crime 1984b; Grace and Guido 1988), Canada (*New York Times*, December 12, 1988), Australia (*Centre Daily News*, July 14, 1988, 3), New Zealand (*Sing Tao Jih Pao*, August 30, 1989, 34), the Philippines (*China Daily News*, July 7, 1989, 13), Taiwan (*Centre Daily News*, December 1, 1987b, 5), West Germany (*Center Daily News*, January 28, 1989, 5), and Britain (*South China Morning Post*, July 24, 1988, 7) to be concerned that Hong Kong Triad groups might transfer their operations to their countries. The President's Commission on Organized Crime (1984a) revealed that Hong Kong Triad groups were already involved in money laundering in the United States. It also alleged that a meeting was held in Hong Kong in 1983 between Chinese gang leaders from North America and Hong Kong Triad leaders. The commission assumed that the purpose of the meeting was to discuss the possible transfer of Hong Kong Triad groups to the United States and Canada.

Intelligence sources confirm that Hong Kong Triad members already control legal and illegal gambling, loansharking, and prostitution in the San Francisco area. A report by the Department of Justice concluded that "several Hong Kong OC [Organized Crime] leaders travel often to the U.S. and appear to coordinate their activities with American COC [Chinese Organized Crime] groups such as California's Wah Ching or New York's Tung On" (U.S. Department of Justice 1988, 29). To prove their allegation, authorities in San Francisco convicted a Wo Hop To leader for not revealing his criminal records in Hong Kong when he applied for residency status in the United States. His affiliation with the Triad society was discovered during a routine check by officials who examined his application to purchase a gambling club (*Sing Tao Jih Pao*, August 22, 1989, 22).

Likewise, there are indications that Triad members from Hong Kong are arriving in New York City. A police officer of the New York City Police Department reports that criminal elements from Hong Kong are being seen in the New York City area and are involved in joint ventures with local Chinese criminals. Two Hong Kong Triad members who operated a gambling club in New York City were slain by killers from Hong Kong in 1987 (*Centre Daily News*, February 21, 1987, 20; *South China Morning Post*, April 8, 1987, 3). Besides law enforcement authorities, a Chinese community leader in New York City is also convinced that Hong Kong Triad members have begun to operate in the New York metropolitan area.

Sources in Taiwan also indicate that 14K members are organizing a Triad society there. The society will have six branches, and each branch will be headed by a 14K senior member dispatched from Hong Kong (*Centre Daily News*, December 1, 1987b, 5). The 14K members are also alleged to have firm control over the illegal gambling industry in Taiwan (*Mei Wah Report*, January 25, 1989, 63-65).

No matter how much law enforcement agencies around the world are alarmed by the possibility of a mass exodus of Hong Kong Triad members, Hong Kong police officers are skeptical that such a move will ever occur. Brian Merritt of the Royal Hong Kong Police denounces the speculation as simply "nonsense." He argues that he sees no sign of diminished Triad activity in Hong Kong or any hard evidence to prove that Hong Kong Triad groups have increased their activities in the United States (*South China Morning Post*, June 8, 1987, 1).

The issue of possible transplantation of Hong Kong Triad societies abroad had caused so much concern by law enforcement authorities worldwide that it even drew the attention of China's leader, Deng Xiaoping. In order to calm down the already nervous tens of thousands of Triad members, Deng commented that among Hong Kong Triad members, there are "some Triad members who are not criminals, and some of them are even patriotic. I hope they reform themselves in the future" (Huang 1984, 72).

After a few years of theorizing about the possibility of this move, the U.S. Department of Justice altered its stand on this matter in its 1988 report on Asian organized crime. In the report, the department concluded that "most Triads and their leaders probably will stay in Hong Kong" (1988, 30). The conclusion stemmed from the assumption that China would not jeopardize its relationship with Hong Kong by taking unusual punitive or extralegal measures against local crime groups because, by doing so, it could frighten an already nervous group of investors.

This conclusion is not at all convincing. There is no assurance that harsh punitive measures against the vicious Triad groups would frighten investors. Hong Kong has long been troubled by the Triad groups, and their elimination could bring only positive reactions from residents and investors. Besides, Communist China is known for cruel, yet efficient, measures for eradicating criminal organizations.

Besides politics, there are other factors at work to drive Hong Kong Triads to expand their overseas operations. First, local Triad societies are profoundly affected by the presence of the Big Circle. Their ruthlessness and illusiveness had threatened the supremacy of the local Triad groups (*China Times Weekly*, May 19, 1985, 72). In the power struggle between the Big Circle and local crime groups, the latter groups are being outmatched. In order to save face, some of the Triad societies are being forced to seek new territory abroad.

Second, a generation gap has developed between senior members and new recruits in all Triad societies. The elders are more conservative and are content with stable incomes from prostitution, gambling, and extortion. The new recruits are eager to move into risky but more lucrative businesses such as drug trafficking. Because the Chiu Chao group monopolizes the drug trade in Hong Kong and Southeast Asia, new recruits to non–Chiu Chao Triad groups are being forced to establish their drug operations in Europe and North America.

Third, since the end of the left-wing political riots in 1967 and the establishment of the Independent Commission Against Corruption in 1973, police corruption has declined significantly in Hong Kong, and the police are now able to concentrate on organized crime activities. Triad members have come to the conclusion that their activities are no longer immune from detection or prosecution. Consequently, they have started to seek less threatening environments abroad (Huang 1984).

One of the countries to which they have turned is the United States. In the remainder of this book we will study the already established tongs and street gangs that are manifestations of Triad subculture here.

4

CHINATOWNS AND TONGS

Due to poverty, political instability, and accessibility to the outside world, inhabitants of the coastal areas of China have a long history of emigration. Approximately 30 million Chinese now live in areas outside China and Taiwan, congregating in Southeast Asia and North America. These so-called Overseas Chinese are mostly Cantonese, Fook Chow (Fujianese), Hakka, and Chiu Chao. They are conservative, hard-working, and proud of their Chinese heritage. They prefer to preserve their customs and values while adjusting to their host societies. In order to accomplish this goal, Chinese immigrants tend to establish their own communities and build networks of voluntary associations among themselves (Chu 1985).

In 1980, 96 percent of the Chinese population in the United States lived in metropolitan areas, compared with 75 percent of the total U.S. population. States that have large Chinese populations are, in descending order, California, New York, Hawaii, Illinois, Texas, and Massachusetts. All these states have one or more large Chinese communities that are commonly known as "Chinatowns." These communities are so well established that they have bilingual schools, social service agencies, post offices, clinics, libraries, and banks. Chinese residents rarely need to leave the communities to fulfill their needs.

Since the early 1970s, with the influx of Mandarin-speaking immigrants from Taiwan, China, and Vietnam, new Chinese communities have sprung up in Queens (*New York Times*, September 14, 1986, 7) and Brooklyn (*New York Times*, September 13, 1987, 74) in New York City; the southwest area of Houston; Monterey Park in Los Angeles; and Oakland in the San Francisco Bay area. Compared with residents in the traditional communities, residents in the newly established communities are better educated and wealthier, and they have encountered less difficulty in assimilating into American society (*New York Times*, February 20, 1988, L29).

THE POLITICAL ECONOMY OF CHINATOWNS

Chinatowns in the United States are social and cultural centers for Chinese immigrants. Regardless of the size and nature of a Chinatown, it is invariably the place most often visited by the Chinese. They go to enjoy authentic Chinese food; to buy Chinese groceries, vegetables, and newspapers; to rent Chinese videotapes; to go to Chinese theaters; to seek help from Chinese professionals; to meet friends; and to gamble. Most Chinese cultural centers, associations, banks, social service agencies, and clinics are located in or around Chinatowns. The services available in Chinatowns attract Chinese from diverse ethnic and socioeconomic backgrounds.

Chinatowns not only are social and cultural centers for the immigrants but also play a significant role in the economy. Most Chinatowns in large cities are major tourist attractions (Light 1974). Every day, buses bring people for sightseeing, shopping, and dining. Three types of businesses dominate New York City's Chinatown, located in the Lower East Side of Manhattan: restaurants, garment factories, and small stores that sell Chinese groceries, meat, and vegetables. Rents in the community are high (*New York Times*, June 1, 1986, C1; December 25, 1986, A1), and business competition is fierce.

Voluntary associations play an important role in Chinatowns (Kuo 1977). Family associations are organized by people with the same family name. A district association comprises people who came from the same district of China. For a Chinese immigrant, family name and province are two important means of identification. The third type of organization, the tong, recruits members without regard to surname or district affiliation. There are also professional associations such as the Association of Oriental Garment, the Chinese American Restaurant Association, and the National Chinese American Jewelry Association (*Chinese Business Guide and Directory* 1989).

Politically, community organizations in New York's Chinatown can be divided into three groups. The first group, led by the Chinese Consolidated Benevolent Associations (CCBA), consists of pro-Kuomintang traditional groups. The second group includes a small number of traditional associations that are supportive of the Communist government in China. The third group is made up of professional organizations that take a neutral political position. The power struggles within the community occur mainly between the first and third groups.

CCBA was established in 1883 (Liu 1981). The president of the organization is known as the "mayor of Chinatown." The main services of CCBA include counseling and referral of immigrants and settling disputes among community businesses. The organization is also the sponsor of the New York Chinese School, English classes for adults, and a day-care facility. In addition, it serves as a bridge between the city government or the Kuomintang government in Taiwan and the community.

CCBA is governed by an executive board consisting of nineteen representatives, seven of whom are permanent. The twelve nonpermanent members and the president are elected by a community council every two years. The council has eighty-four representatives from the sixty member associations.

Seven of these associations are permanent members. The Lin Yan Association, formed in 1890, comprises Toisanese, who are the first wave of immigrants. They came from the four poorest areas of Guangdong (Kwangtung) province. The members of the Leun Cheng Association (developed in 1900) are also Cantonese who came from areas in Guangdong other than the four poorest areas. As a rule, only these two organizations' leaders are eligible to be president of the CCBA. The rule was made to keep the often conflicting tongs from controlling CCBA, thereby preventing the organization from being implicated in tong wars.

Three permanent associations of the CCBA are tongs in nature. They are the On Leong Merchant Association, comprised of mostly Cantonese-speaking businessmen; the Hip Sing Association, formed by predominantly Toisanese-speaking working-class immigrants; and the Chih Kung tong, the overseas branch of the Hung societies.

The other two permanent associations are the East Coast Branch of the Kuomintang party and the Chinese Chamber of Commerce. The Kuomintang group is an intermediary between the community and the government of Taiwan. The Chinese Chamber of Commerce was formed by wealthy Chinese merchants and controls the economic aspects of Chinatown.

Besides these seven major associations, there are other organizations that exert a certain amount of influence on community affairs. They are the pro-Communist Tsung Tsin Association, Fook Chow Association, Tung On Association; the pro-Kuomintang Lee's Family Association, Gee How Oak Tin Association; and the politically neutral social service organization such as the Chinese-American Planning Council (formerly Chinatown Planning Council).

NEW YORK CITY'S CHINATOWN: A DISORGANIZED COMMUNITY

New York City's Chinatown is composed of predominantly poor, uneducated, working-class immigrants. By comparison, the wealthier and educated professional immigrants are more likely to settle in the Chinese communities of Hawaii and California. According to Kwong, "because of its large pool of manual labor and service jobs, New York's Chinatown tends to pre-select immigrants of working-class origin much more than other American Chinatowns. Chinese with professional and technical skills prefer California or Hawaii, where there are already established communities of Chinese professionals" (1987, 40).

In a disorganized community, according to Shaw and McKay (1942), residents are predominantly working-class with heterogeneous backgrounds. Because residents move out of the community as soon as they gain some financial security, mobility is high. Cultural values are attenuated, and social institutions, isolated and unstable, have inadequate resources. A disorganized community is "incapable of implementing and expressing the values of its own residents" (Kornhauser 1978, 63). This lack of cultural and structural control within the community leads to the emergence of a delinquent subculture. Once such a subculture arises, it persists as a semiautonomous system, with its own culture and closely knit structure.

Although New York City's Chinatown appears to be a homogeneous ethnic community, it has all the characteristics of a disorganized community. First, Chinatown residents are either newly arrived working-class immigrants or old immigrants who have failed to improve their socioeconomic status after years of hard work. They are mostly restaurant or garment factory workers. According to a survey, more than half of all Chinatown residents are living below the poverty level (*Sing Tao Jih Pao*, March 21, 1977). A recent study also shows that 30 percent of the Asians live in poverty, compared with 25 percent of non-Asians (Chinese-American Planning Council 1989). Second, Chinatown is a heterogeneous community. Residents come from China, Hong Kong, Taiwan, Vietnam, and other Southeast Asian countries, which have different cultural, political, legal, and economic systems. Within the community, residents speak at least ten major dialects and belong to more than one hundred fragmented organizations that are often at odds with one another. Third, the community has high population mobility because most residents move to Queens, Brooklyn, Long Island, upstate New York, or New Jersey once their financial status improves. Their vacant apartments are then rapidly filled by newcomers.

As a result, cultural values are weakened and become obsolete. The values of each subgroup of the community are not compatible with those of other subgroups or with those of the mainstream society. The norms and values of the Fook Chow, Chiu Chao, Cantonese, and Hakka coexist within the community and are followed closely in intragroup interactions. However, when people of diverse groups come into contact, there are no communal norms to follow. As a result, social interactions among residents of different ethnic origins are often filled with misunderstanding and tension. In addition, the isolation of Chinatown from the rest of the society makes American values and norms irrelevant within the community.

Structural disorganization within Chinatown is by no means less severe than cultural disorganization. Despite the existence of many family, district, and benevolent associations in the community, few have the resources to sponsor long-term social or cultural activities for their members or the residents. Those few organizations with adequate resources are normally inward-looking and provide help only to their members. Without financial support from the society or community, the associations are forced either to dissolve or to operate gambling houses to pay the rents and meet other expenses. Most associations choose to operate gambling houses and thereby transform themselves from benevolent associations to providers of illegal services.

Social service agencies in Chinatown are also unable to serve the community adequately. Viewed as left-wing radical groups by the predominantly right-wing traditional associations, they receive little support from the community. As a result, social service agencies and the traditional associations do not work together to promote the welfare of the residents. In some instances, the benefits of the residents are overlooked as the two groups vie for control in the community (*New York Times*, July 20, 1986, 12).

Internally, social service agencies are plagued by high employee turnover because of poor working environments and low pay. Qualified and experienced bilingual workers leave their jobs within the community once they find a job outside. Social service agencies are unable to use human resources from outside the community because American service providers cannot communicate with clients who do not speak English. In sum, social service agencies within the community are plagued by high employee turnover rates, inadequate funding, and little support from traditional associations.

Businesses within the community show little interest in the community affairs, perhaps because they are often victimized by local crime groups and distrustful of people with whom they could not identify. Business owners prefer to maintain low profiles and are reluctant even to identify themselves as owners of certain businesses for fear of extortion by gang members. As a result, most merchants are concerned only with their businesses, and their lack of support for the welfare of the residents further erodes the integration of the community. Takagi and Platt asserted that Chinatown is a "gilded ghetto" in which the interests of the residents have been neglected.

> Chinatown does not belong to its people. By this we mean that Chinatown is not a community of people with common interests; nor is it organized to meet the needs of its residents. It is, instead, a mass of people identifiable by race and organized from the most humble worker and employer in Chinatown to the downtown hotels, the airlines, the surrounding industries (fishing, poultry, meat, rice, and overseas trade), and to the Chamber of Commerce, each linked to the other, and each dependent upon the other to form the structure of the tourist industry. (1978, 2)

Chinatown is also politically fragmented. The associations are divided according to their political orientation in the conflict between the Kuomintang and the Chinese Communists. Conflicts among various groups have prohibited community residents from forming strong political organizations that could help qualified Chinese to run for public office. Besides, the associations themselves are fragmented internally. Within each organization, many factions are involved in power struggle, and the animosity among the factions often impaired the organization's ability to carry out long-term plans.

Because of the severe cultural and structural disorganization, not only individual and group relationships are tense and hostile, but social problems within the community are also exacerbated due to negligence and the lack of powerful advocate groups. Housing is one of the most urgent problems. Although hundreds of newcomers are arriving monthly, only a limited amount of housing is available in the Chinese community. A one-bedroom apartment costs around $700 monthly, plus $5,000 to $8,000 *fong tai chin* (key money) up front for getting the lease. Despite the high rents, apartments in Chinatown are small and poorly maintained. Many have no bathrooms or living rooms or both. A 1969 report on Chinatown housing showed that 42 percent of the apartments were overcrowded, 63 percent had not been painted in three years, 75 percent had absentee landlords, and 85 percent were infested with pests (Chernow 1973). Yet, most new immigrants are willing to pay the exorbitant price because they want to live close to their own people and their jobs.

Few recreational facilities are available in the community. For those who have to work until late in the evening, the only recreational activity is gambling. For young immigrants, community-sponsored activities are also limited. The only playground within the community is outdated and poorly maintained.

Final evidence of the disorganization of Chinatown is the high incidence of depression and suicide (*Centre Daily News*, March 31, 1986, 20). The mental health of the residents has long been neglected because Chinese immigrants are more concerned with their physical health than with their mental well-being and because the outpatient mental health programs in the community are ill equipped to provide adequate services. Faced with problems in housing, employment, and adjustment, and having few channels for discussing their problems and expressing their grievances, immigrants often become alienated from both the mainstream society and their own community.

THE EMERGENCE OF TONGS

The scene is thus set for the emergence of a delinquent subculture, and this subculture is most often associated with the tong. The word *tong* simply means "hall" or "gathering place." Tongs were first established in the United States in San Francisco by the first wave of Chinese immigrants, who were predominantly goldfield or railroad workers. The first two tongs were formed in 1845 (C. Sun 1962).

Prior to the emergence of tongs, Chinese communities in the United States were controlled by large family or district associations such as the Wong Family Association and the Four District Association. Immigrants whose surname is shared by only a few or who came from a small district were not accepted by the well-established associations and were left unprotected. In order to defend themselves, they banded together to establish the tongs (Gong and Grant 1930; Lyman 1977). Since the tongs were capable of recruiting members without restriction, they expanded rapidly. Soon the tongs were drawn into many decades of street battles known as the "tong wars." The secretive nature of the tongs (unlike family or district associations, tong members were hard to identify) and the strong alliance among them when they fought with elite organizations enabled them to overpower the family and district associations. As a result, the tongs became the most powerful associations in the Chinese communities, prompting members of family and district associations to join at least one tong for additional protection.

The tongs, like the family and district associations, provided many needed services to immigrants who could not get help from anywhere else. The tongs also acted as power brokers in individual and group conflicts within the community. Ten more tongs were established in San Francisco by the early twentieth century, and eventually more than thirty tongs were formed in the United States (U.S. Department of Justice 1988). In the following sections, the three most powerful tongs in the East Coast are briefly discussed.

Chih Kung Tong

Chinese workers in the United States who were Hung members first established the Chih Kung in the 1850s (Ong 1988). The political goal of the organization was to overthrow the Qing (Ch'ing) and restore the Ming, a goal initiated, as we have seen, by the Hung societies. In 1897, the Chih Kung was infiltrated by the Pao Wong Tang (Party for the Preservation of the Ch'ing Emperor), a propaganda organization formed by the Manchu government to persuade Chinese immigrants to abandon their antagonism toward the Qing emperor (Y. Sun 1977).

Sun Yat-sen realized that his nascent revolutionary movement would need the support of overseas Chinese organizations. To make himself acceptable to the tongs, he joined the Chih Kung in Hawaii in 1902 and was assigned as an officer. When he visited the United States and Canada later to seek support, he was well received by the tongs. Sun persuaded Chih Kung members to abandon their Pao Wong Tang membership. He also set up networks among the fragmented Chih Kung chapters around the world and rewrote the constitution of the organization, transforming it into a politically conscious group. By rewriting the tong's constitution, Sun did a remarkable job of making revolutionary ideas part of the Chih Kung philosophy and bringing various chapters under the control of the headquarters in San Francisco.

Later, the Chih Kung and Sun's revolutionary organization in Tokyo worked together to establish a financial support center that collected money from Chinese communities in the United States and wire it to China to aid the revolutionary army. The center's ability to provide desperately needed financial aid to the local soldiers played a pivotal role in Sun's victory over the Qing government (Fung 1947). After the revolution and the birth of the Republic of China, Sun proclaimed that the "overseas Chinese are the procreators of the revolution."

The Chih Kung renamed itself the Chung Kuo Hung Mun Chih Kung Tang (Chinese Hung Society Party of the Chih Kung) in 1945 and moved its headquarters from San Francisco to Vancouver, Canada. Although some leaders wanted to transform the organization into a political party, the Triad values of the group remained intact. Members still burned yellow papers and took oaths at initiation ceremonies (Pung 1987).

During the civil war between the Kuomintang and the Chinese Communists, the Chih Kung Tang called for peaceful negotiations between the two rival groups, albeit without success. In 1946, the Chih Kung Tang was infiltrated by members of the Kuomintang; the organization again changed its name, this time to Chung Kuo Hung Mun Ming Chih Tang (Chinese Hung Society Party of the People), and became a vehicle of propaganda for the Kuomintang. In 1981, the overseas group readopted its initial name—the Chih Kung tong.

Following the Communist takeover, the power of secret societies in China declined substantially. They were reorganized "as a nominally separate political party charged with the task of appealing to overseas Chinese on behalf of the Communist cause" (Lyman 1977, 88). The Chih Kung organization in China became one of these government-funded political parties that have little power (*World Journal*, December 11, 1988, 3). The Chih Kung in the United States and other parts of the world remains loyal to the Kuomintang. In the United States, the more active Chih Kung chapters are located in New York, Boston, Chicago, Washington, D.C., Kansas City, Detroit, Baltimore, and San Diego.

On Leong Merchant Association

Since the 1960s, both the On Leong and the Hip Sing have abandoned the name *tong* and have renamed their associations because the word *tong* reminds people of the infamous tong wars, which are described later in this chapter. On Leong was formed in 1894 in Boston by a Chih Kung member. Ten years later, the headquarters was established in New York City (Pung 1987), and it is now located at the corner of Mott and Canal streets. Territories include Mott and Bayard streets (see Figure 4 for the location and territory of the Chinatown's associations). Members are mainly merchants in these territories. The association has chapters in Boston, Philadelphia, Pittsburgh, Providence, Cleveland, St. Louis, Detroit, Minneapolis, Washington, D.C., Baltimore, Miami, Houston, New

Figure 4
Territory of the Adult Organizations in New York City's Chinatown

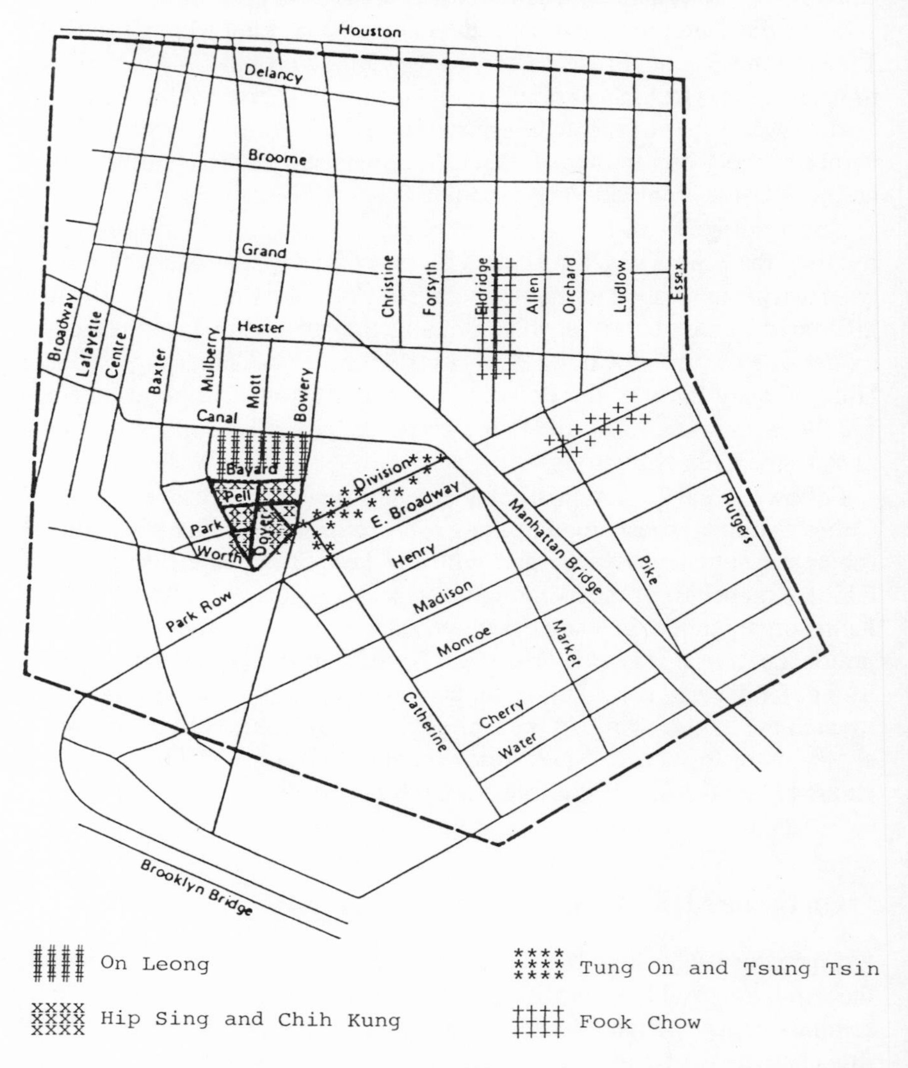

Orleans, Richmond, and Atlanta. Nationwide, there are 30,000 to 40,000 members (*World Journal*, April 23, 1988, 19).

In the mid-1970s, Eddie T. C. Chan, a sergeant with the Hong Kong Police Department, arrived in New York City. Chan was alleged to have been involved in extensive corruption while he was in the British colony. Soon after his arrival, he opened a few restaurants and a funeral home in the community. Regardless of his affiliation with Triad societies in Hong

Kong, he was extorted by the Ghost Shadows. Later, as a successful businessman, he was elected president of the On Leong. During his tenure with the organization, he also became the vice-president of a Chinatown bank and the president of the Chinese American Welfare Association (a nationwide advocate group located in Washington, D.C.). Through his connection with the then Queens borough's president, he came into contact with many American local and federal politicians (Meskil 1989).

Law enforcement authorities charged that the On Leong leader was closely affiliated with members of the Ghost Shadows, a gang active in the territory of the On Leong. He was alleged to be the man behind the shootings of disgruntled Ghost Shadows in Chicago by gang members from New York City. He was also accused of ordering gang members to kill a gang leader who extorted him. Besides, Chan was also implicated in the fraudulent activities carried out by the Continental King Lung Group, an investment company established by him. A Triad member in Hong Kong identified him as the "Dragon Head" (Crime Boss) of New York Chinatown's underworld (President's Commission on Organized Crime 1984b). He repudiated the charges (*World Journal*, October 26, 1984, 1). However, when he was subpeonaed by the President's Commission on Organized Crime to testify at the commission's hearings, he fled the United States.

Hip Sing Association

The headquarters of Hip Sing, the other major tong, is on Pell Street; it controls Pell Street, Doyers Street, and the Bowery. The tong operates a credit union that provides loans and financial services to its members. The association has branches in Washington, D.C., Philadelphia, Chicago, Minneapolis, Atlanta, Oakland, Boston, Kansas City, San Francisco, Pittsburgh, Denver, San Diego, and Seattle (*World Journal*, August 24, 1989, 24).

Benny Ong (or Eng), the leader of the Hip Sing, is a powerful figure in the community. He is also the leader of the Chih Kung tong. He maintains good diplomatic relations with both the People's Republic of China and the Republic of China (Taiwan). The two Chinas solicit his influence on their behalf in the United States.

Little is known about Ong, except that he was imprisoned for murder in 1936, and was then paroled eighteen years later. He had been arrested for assault, robbery, gambling, and drug offenses before his conviction for murder. In 1976, he was again sentenced to prison for bribery. He was alleged to be the man behind the Golden Star massacre in New York's

Chinatown (discussed later in this chapter). He denied the allegation, however, and the case was never solved (Meskil 1989).

There are other associations that allegedly resemble the tongs in terms of their affiliation with criminal elements and extensive involvement in gambling operations. They are the Kam Lum Association, Tung On Association, and Tsung Tsin Association. Little is known about these organizations, and they are rarely scrutinized by law enforcement authorities (Daly 1983; U.S. Department of Justice 1988).

TONG STRUCTURE AND CULTURE

Tongs have similar structures. When Sun Yat-sen regrouped the Chih Kung tong, he set up an organizational model for other tongs to follow.

Most tong headquarters have a president, a vice-president, a secretary, a treasurer, an auditor, and several elders and public relations administrators. Each tong branch has a ruling body that includes the president, secretary, treasurer, auditor, and several staff members. Figure 5 illustrates the structure of the Hip Sing Association.

Figure 5
Organizational Chart of the Hip Sing Association

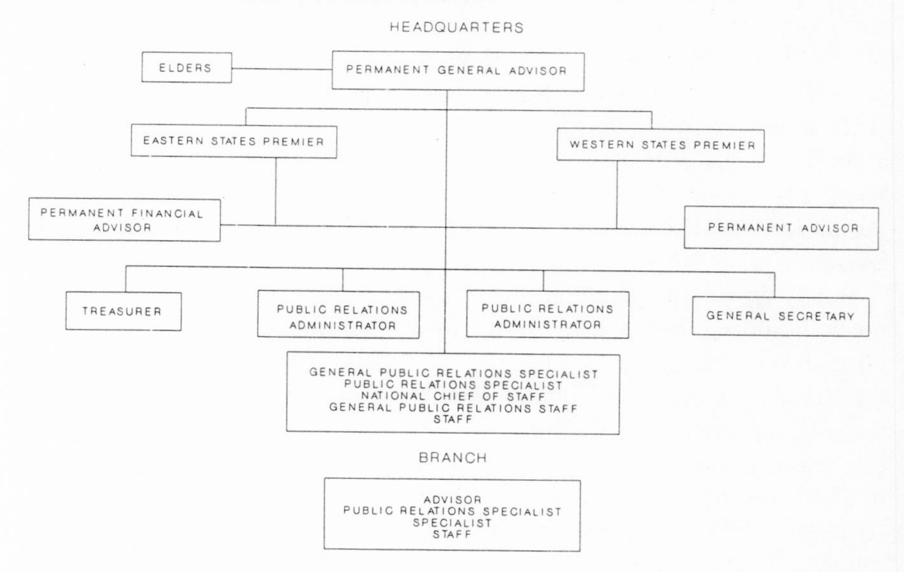

Source: Adapted and translated from Centre Daily News, September 16, 1985, p. 20; World Journal, August 24, 1989, p. 24.

Most tong members are legally employed or have their own businesses. These members pay their fees regularly, visit the associations occasionally to meet people or to gamble, and attend the associations' banquets and picnics a few times a year. They are not involved in the tongs' daily affairs or in decision making. Only the officers and employees are involved with the organizations on a daily basis. They control internal and external affairs, and some are intermediaries between the tongs and Triad societies or street gangs.

Many gang members also joined the tongs. Although young tong members who are themselves gang members have little to say in the tong's affairs, they control street-level and illegal activities within the tong's territory. Specifically, gang members act as protectors of the gambling places operated by tong members, are involved in demanding protection money from the stores that are located within the tong's vicinity, guard the territory from invasion by other gangs, and lay a hand on almost all illegal activities that are carried out within the territory. As the power of the Chinese gangs has grown rapidly in the 1970s and 1980s, tong elders cannot control their young tong members anymore.

The tongs adopted the norms and values of the Triad subculture. Members are required to go through the Triad initiation ceremony when recruited, take the thirty-six Triad oaths of loyalty, and bow to the god of the Triad societies. They memorize Triad poems and slang and are urged by leaders to internalize the Triad norms of loyalty, righteousness, patriotism, and brotherhood. Although law-abiding members, who constitute the majority, may become familiar with Triad philosophy for a short while during the initiation ceremony, core members of the tongs are committed to Triad norms and values on a long-term basis.

In their work on tong wars, Gong and Grant have made a valid point about the inner working of the tongs, that "always underlying tong activities are certain clever and powerful men whose names are never mentioned" (1930, 148). It is safe to say that their observation is still valid after six decades. Community residents and a tong member interviewed for this study all clearly indicated that most community associations, including the tongs, are fragmented. Within each association, there are many factions. A senior member who does not identify with a particular faction is most likely to be elected president, a result of compromise among the factions. In other words, the person who occupies the highest position could be a puppet. He is selected because he is isolated and is acceptable to the many factions. Those who are more powerful and more ambitious are least likely to be elected as formal leaders. Nevertheless, they are the ones who pull the strings. Because of their anonymity, few people outside of the association know who they are and how they control the daily activities of the association.

POLITICS, GAMBLING, AND TONG WARS

The tongs are involved in many community affairs. This section examines some of their major activities.

Tongs as Anti-Communist Groups

Tongs have never participated in American politics. However, they are deeply involved in Chinese politics. Their position in Chinese politics, in turn, lures them into political activities within the Chinese communities in the United States. In the preceding section, the significant role of the Chih Kung tong in Sun Yat-sen's anti-Manchu movement and during the period of civil war between the Kuomintang and the Communist party was discussed. Here, I will focus on the role of the tongs in Chinese politics since 1949, the year the Communist party came to power in China.

For the past forty years, the tongs in various parts of the world, especially those in the United States, have closely identified with the Kuomintang for three reasons. First, the Kuomintang considers Sun Yat-sen as the national hero, and his doctrines were adopted as guidelines for making national policy. Since many senior Kuomintang officers were former members of the Tung Mun Hui, the close relationship between the organization and the Chih Kung tong during the revolution invoked the tong's sympathetic attitudes toward the Kuomintang. Second, the successful operations of the Overseas Chinese Committee of the Taiwan government facilitated communication between the immigrants and Taiwan. Every year, the committee arranges for tong leaders and thousands of overseas Chinese to go back to Taiwan to celebrate National Day, and with the collaboration of the CCBA and the tongs, sponsors various celebration activities in the United States. As a norm, the committee and the Taiwan consulate in New York would send delegates to participate in the tongs' anniversary celebrations. The committee also works closely with the CCBA to provide proper political guidance to the tongs. Third, the lack of formal diplomatic ties between the United States and the Chinese Communists in the years before the Carter administration have deterred the tongs from establishing relationships with the Beijing government (*New York Times*, February 22, 1971, B2). With such close ties to the Kuomintang, it is only natural that the tongs are committed to keeping the Chinese Communists' influence away from the Chinese communities in the United States. The tongs are also involved in protecting their supremacy in Chinatown affairs by keeping the Chinese-American Planning Council from replacing CCBA as the most influential organization within the community (*New York Times*, July 20, 1986, 12).

The Institutionalized Gambling Industry

From the perspective of American law enforcement, the tongs, regardless of political and benevolent activities, are criminal organizations that control street gangs and are involved in many illegal activities. According to an intelligence report (Attorney General of California 1972), the tongs today are involved in heroin smuggling, in prostitution, opium smoking, gambling, protection rackets, and in extortion and blackmail. The President's Commission on Organized Crime (1984b) also alleged that the tongs control the street gangs and are responsible for crimes within the Chinese community. The U.S. Department of Justice (1985) likewise suggested that the tongs engage in gambling, loansharking, extortion, police and political corruption, and narcotics trafficking.

Oddly enough, although the tongs are accused of this wide variety of criminal activities, no office-bearers of the tongs have been arrested or indicted for any felonies since the 1950s. The criminal justice system has little evidence to prove that the tongs, as organizations, are involved in all these illegal activities. Before 1965, when there were a substantial number of opium users and single males in the community, the tongs did operate opium and prostitution houses. However, as the population of the community changed after the liberalization of immigration, these illegal services were not in demand.

The tongs' role in the promotion of gambling activity within the community is better known. There are two types of gambling clubs in the Chinese community, low-stake and high-stake. Low-stake gambling clubs are operated by family, district, and other associations in basements or upper stories of the associations' offices. These clubs are normally open to members and members' friends and relatives only. Gamblers know each other well, and most of them have jobs. Gambling activities do not start until late in the afternoon and slow down after midnight. Winnings or losses for the average gambler are a few hundred dollars. The most popular games are mahjong and thirteen-card poker.

The commission, 5 percent of the bets, goes to the house, which is the association. The association pays rent and utility bills from the commissions and hires people to run errands for the gamblers, such as buying food, beverages, and cigarettes. Most family, district, and merchant associations operate one or more of these clubs. Except for some minor conflicts among players, these clubs are normally tranquil and do not attract the attention of the street gangs.

High-stake gambling clubs are normally physically separated from the associations. These gambling clubs are located in core areas of Chinatown and are heavily guarded by Chinese gang members. For an outsider, it is hard to tell the existence of these clubs because there are no signs to indicate that the places are gambling clubs. The only sign on these gambling places is a small sheet of paper with two Chinese characters *hoy pei*, meaning "in action."

Unlike the low-stake gambling clubs where gambling activity is a way for members to socialize with one another, gamblers in the high-stake gambling dens neither know nor care much about socialization. The clubs are open seven days a week around the clock, and gambling activity reaches its peak after midnight. Inside these clubs, besides mahjong and poker games, pai gow and fan tan games, run by professional dealers, are available. The commission, also 5 percent of the bets, goes to the shareholders of the house. More often than not, the shareholders, about ten to twenty persons per house, are all members of the tong that controls the area where the gambling club is located. They each invest from $3,000 to $4,000. Robbery, extortion, and murder occur often in these gambling dens because so much money is involved; and the people who hang around them are mostly heavy gamblers, the unemployed, illegal aliens, and gang members.

Normally, if a tong has a vacant basement or hall to rent, it puts an announcement in the organization's bulletin. Tong members who are willing to rent it talk to the senior officers. The organization does not put any restrictions on how the place can be used, and if the tong members who rent it want to set up a gambling operation, the tong may provide support.

According to law enforcement authorities, gambling in New York's Chinatown is such a lucrative business that the "more prosperous parlors on Mott Street gross more than $500,000 weekly, and estimates of the total weekly takes for the dozen or so dens in Chinatown run about $3,000,000" (Rice 1977, 63). A police lieutenant revealed that a gambling den located on Division Street made $247,000 a month and paid a gang leader $3,400 a week for protection (Bresler 1981). For example, a recent raid on the On Leong's gambling place in Chicago resulted in the confiscation of more than $300,000 in cash (*World Journal*, April 24, 1988, 3).

Since the establishment of a legal gambling industry in nearby Atlantic City, New Jersey, in the late 1970s, many Chinese gamblers have been lured there. Casino operators have employed many aggressive and innovative marketing tactics to expand their Asian customer market. Extraordinary bonuses are being offered to Chinatown gamblers; famous entertainers from Hong Kong are being invited to perform to the Chinese audiences on major holidays; and limousines are being arranged to pick up heavy gamblers from the Chinese community. Consequently, the gambling industry within the community had declined substantially in the 1980s.

Tong Wars: Past and Present

One aspect of tong culture that has received much attention is the power struggles and street fights that have come to be known as tong wars (Gong and Grant 1930; Dillon 1962). The fiercest of these occurred between 1894 and 1913 in San Francisco. The war occurred either between the tongs and the powerful family associations or among the tongs.

Most tong conflicts were provoked by members, and later escalated into group conflicts. The reasons for the conflicts were diverse. Tong wars occurred because a tong recruited a rival tong's members, invaded rival tong's territory, fought over so-called "sing song girls" (Chinese prostitutes), or showed no courtesy to rival tongs. However, according to a Chinese ambassador's report to his government in the 1930s, narcotics and gambling were the major reasons behind the tong wars.

> Narcotics and gambling are the causes of the tong wars. The tongs are generating unlimited amounts of income from operating opium and gambling dens. The tongs are so rich that a tong would spend tens of thousands of dollars for a building, and a tong's annual expenditures could be more than a million dollars. The tongs are well organized, their leaders very dignified. Each has about twenty to thirty branches, with ten to twenty thousand members. The tongs recruit a bunch of thugs (hatchetmen) to run opium and gambling dens, and to revenge and kill when the situations call for action. If a thug kills a person, the tongs will reward him with several thousand dollars; if he is killed, his family will receive a subsidy of ten thousand dollars. A hatchetman's subsidy is higher than a senior government official's. A group of hatchetmen is similar to a regular army, and the tongs resemble the warlords. (Liu 1981, 658; my translation)

Whenever there was a tong conflict, the tongs involved in the conflict announced their intention to go to war with the other party by posting a *chun hung* (declaration of war) on the walls of the community. Soon after the *chun hung* were displayed, the associations mobilized their salaried soldiers known as the "hatchetmen" or the "highbinders" to kill the rival's street soldiers. Ordinary members of the tongs were ignored by warring street soldiers. Officials of the rival tongs disappeared from the public scene, and the head of the hatchetmen and his followers took over the tong's affairs. Normally, an incident would last for weeks, months, or even years, spreading from the West Coast to the East Coast or vice versa. During the warring period, famous killers such as the Fish Duck, Hong Ah Kay, and Little Pete became household names among the Chinese community people (Gong and Grant 1930; Lee 1989).

After 1913, conflicts among the tongs were arbitrated by the Wo Ping Woey, a peace association formed by leaders of the tongs and large family and clan associations to alleviate tong rivalry. However, some conflicts still got out of hand, and tong murders continued (Lyman 1977; Liu 1981).

Nevertheless, efforts at reconciliation continued. In 1930, community leaders in New York City's Chinatown formed a Peace Committee. The CCBA and the Kuomintang itself became active in settling disputes. After the Communist takeover of China in 1949, the tongs, instead of fighting among themselves, banded together to prevent Chinese Communists from infiltrating the communities. In 1960, the On Leong and Hip Sing formally signed a treaty and announced that the two tongs would coexist peacefully. Since then, they have never been involved in open disputes. As a courtesy, the two organizations send delegates to each other's annual convention and celebration.

Nevertheless, fatal confrontations may still erupt if a new tong encroaches on the territory of a well-established one. The formation of a new tong creates tension among the existing ones. If the new tong is also involved in illegal activities, such as gambling and loansharking, the existing tongs consider it a serious threat. According to a Hip Sing member interviewed:

> The traditional associations do not want to lose face by engaging in well-publicized conflict. They are always willing to solve any dispute behind closed doors. However, some emerging associations are struggling very hard to become prominent within the community. They want to become members of the elite group. If they do not respect the traditional groups while they are on their way up, then that could mean trouble. If the intrusion would only cause the old groups some financial loss, then the situation is not that bad. The traditional groups are not financially deprived, they do not care much about losing some

income. But they are very sensitive to other groups' willingness to pay deference and respect. Some emerging associations think they can do whatever they want and do not have to care about the elite groups. (my translation)

The Golden Star incident is a good example of a modern-day tong war. In December 1982, two to four masked gunmen fired into a crowd of patrons inside the Golden Star Bar in New York's Chinatown, killing three and wounding eight others (*New York Times*, December 24, 1982, A1). The bar was a hangout for members of the Kam Lum and the White Tigers street gangs. Police believed that the shooting was the work of the Flying Dragons gang and that it occurred to prevent the merging of the Kam Lum and White Tigers. Later investigation showed, however, that the clash was between two tongs, the well-established Hip Sing and the newly formed Kam Lum.

The leader of the Kam Lum was a former Hip Sing member. He dissociated from the Hip Sing and organized the Kam Lum because of a disagreement with the Hip Sing leader who had recruited him. The Kam Lum was located on East Broadway, and the tong claimed East Broadway, Division Street, Chatham Square, and Market Street as its territory. The tong also recruited former Flying Dragons members who were ousted by their gang, which was associated with Hip Sing. The Kam Lum quickly became a threat to the two elite groups, the On Leong and the Hip Sing. Within a few months, they had a headquarters, gambling hall, and street gang; they also filed the preliminary papers for the creation of a savings-and-loan bank to lure Hong Kong investment dollars. Sooner or later, there would be a third powerful tong in Chinatown, and people in the Hip Sing and On Leong did not relish the idea of another rival group. Worst of all, the Kam Lum did not pay deference to the Hip Sing, although they managed to extend their respect to the On Leong. According to Daly (1983), the Kam Lum leader's lack of respect for the Hip Sing and his active recruitment of former Flying Dragons members antagonized Hip Sing leaders.

After the massacre, young members of the Kam Lum occupied Pell Street, the domain of the Hip Sing and the Flying Dragons, for four hours. Fortunately, the Flying Dragons, under instructions from Hip Sing leaders, stayed inside, and another explosive confrontation was avoided. However, after the incident the power of the Kam Lum faded.

A few months later, Michael Chen, the leader of the Flying Dragons, was shot to death execution-style in front of the Hip Sing headquarters on Pell Street (*New York Daily News*, March 15, 1983b, 4). Although the case was never solved, it is assumed that his death is related to the most recent tong conflict.

Three months after the Golden Star Massacre, thirteen gamblers were slain inside a Seattle Chinatown gambling club. The victims had been robbed, hog-tied, and shot in the head at least once at close range (*New York Daily News*, February 20, 1983, 3). The fourteenth victim survived, despite being shot in the head, and pointed out the murderers to the police. According to police investigations, two of the three gunmen were Hop Sing members, and eleven of the fourteen victims were Bing Kung people (*World Journal*, February 25, 1983, 3). The Hop Sing and the Bing Kung are two of the most powerful associations in Seattle's Chinatown, and they are not friendly toward each other. Although all three offenders have been sentenced to death or life imprisonment, the real motive behind such mass killings is still unknown.

Thus, tong conflict is by no means over. The elders of the elite tongs may settle disputes among themselves peacefully, but younger members who are affiliated with street gangs may prefer to solve their conflicts through violence. These gangs are described in the next four chapters.

5

THE DEVELOPMENT OF CHINESE GANGS

This chapter discusses why and how Chinese street gangs emerged from street-corner groups to organized criminal gangs in San Francisco, Los Angeles, Monterey Park, and New York City, where Chinese gangs are deeply entrenched in the ethnic communities. New York City deserves our utmost attention because it is there that most Chinese gangs congregated and established their headquarters. Besides, in New York City street gangs are still closely affiliated with adult organizations and many former gang leaders are being initiated into the adult organizations as core members with the potential to become ultimate leaders.

There is a striking resemblance between Chinese gang members nowadays and tong hatchetmen of the late nineteenth and early twentieth centuries. Both groups are closely associated with the tongs and the community gambling industry and fiercely involved in territorial fights, and they all adhere to Triad subcultural norms and values. We can see the mirrors of modern Chinese gang members in tong hatchetmen active several decades ago.

SAN FRANCISCO: THE BIRTHPLACE OF CHINESE GANGS

The first wave of Chinese immigrants, mostly laborers from Guandong (Kwantung) province in China, arrived in California in the mid-nineteenth century to work in the goldfields. After the Gold Rush, these workers were hired to build the transcontinental railroads. During that period, most Chinese laborers congregated in San Francisco's Chinatown (Nee and Nee 1986). Since then, the community has expanded into one of the largest ethnic enclaves in the United States (*San Francisco Chronicle*, November 18, 1986, 1).

Chinese street gangs first appeared in San Francisco in the late 1950s. The first juvenile gang was known as the "Bugs" and was formed by American-born Chinese. Members were heavily involved in burglary and were easily identified by their mode of dress, which included high-heeled "Beatle"-type boots (Loo 1976).

In 1964, young immigrants organized the first foreign-born Chinese gang, which was known as the Wah Ching (Youth of China). The main goal of the gang was to protect members from American-born Chinese (Thompson 1976). After the immigration laws were changed a year later, the Wah Ching rapidly evolved into a powerful gang by recruiting members from among the new arrivals. Initially, the gang had its headquarters in a coffee house in Chinatown. Before the gang became a predatory group, Wah Ching leaders sought help from San Francisco's Human Rights Commission and the Chinese Consolidated Benevolent Association to alleviate the problems young newcomers were encountering. Not only did these institutions fail to respond to the youths' cries for help, but the coffee house where they gathered was forced to shut down.

Following the closing of the coffee house, certain community associations hired Wah Ching members as lookouts for their gambling establishments. They were responsible for protecting the gambling dens from police raids, and they ran errands for gamblers. As members of the gang became familiar with the gambling operations, they demanded and received higher salaries from the associations.

Later, Wah Ching became part of the Hop Sing tong, and the gang converted itself from an ordinary street gang into the youth branch of the well-established adult organization. The Suey Sing tong also formed a youth group which they called the Young Suey Sing, or Tom Tom, gang. The rivalry between the two tongs resulted in street fights between their gangs (Attorney General of California 1972).

One of the Wah Ching leaders, unhappy with the Hop Sing's control over the gang, left the gang in 1969 to form the Yau Lai (or Yo Le), which later became the Joe Fong Boys. The gang claimed complete independence from the power hierarchy of Chinatown (Joe 1981).

Besides working as lookouts for the gambling casinos, members of Wah Ching and Joe Fong Boys started to prey upon Asian people. Most store owners paid the gangs regularly to avoid being disturbed. The stores of those businessmen who refused to pay the gangs were often vandalized or destroyed (Loo 1976).

As the Wah Ching and Joe Fong Boys proceeded to become the most dominant gangs in San Francisco's Chinatown, street violence broke out. Gang leaders, members, and innocent bystanders were killed in the struggles. Between 1969 and 1973, eighteen murders were associated with Chinese youth gangs in San Francisco. For example, on March 1, 1970, Glen Fong, nineteen, a brother of Joe Fong, was killed by ten shots from a .30 carbine at the door of his Chinatown home; he was then president of the Wah Ching. In May 1973, Anton Wong, twenty-four, the new leader of the Wah Ching, was shot dead in the streets of Chinatown (Emch 1973; Robertson 1977).

Gang violence continued unabated thereafter. Between 1973 and 1977, there were about twenty-seven gang-related murders. One of the most vicious took place in September 1977 at the Golden Dragon Restaurant. In order to avenge a shootout, three Joe Fong Boys armed with guns entered the restaurant to attack the Wah Ching. The gunmen recklessly opened fire on the customers. Five people were killed and eleven seriously wounded, but none of the victims were gang members. Six months later, the case was solved when one of the gunmen confessed to the killing and testified against his accomplices. As a result, ten Joe Fong members were found guilty (*San Francisco Examiner*, May 10, 1987, B1).

Besides the Wah Ching, Joe Fong Boys, and Young Suey Sing, Chinese gangs such as the Hop Sing Boys, the Kit Jais, the Asian Invasion, and the Local Motion are active in the San Francisco area. The single largest Chinese gang in California now is the Wah Ching. The California Bureau of Organized Crime and Criminal Intelligence (BOCCI) upgraded the gang from a street gang to an organized criminal group in the early 1980s. BOCCI estimates that the Wah Ching has six to seven hundred members and associates, about two hundred of whom are "hardcore." It considers the Wah Ching the foremost organized crime group in California (Kaplan, Goldberg, and Jue 1986).

The leader of the Wah Ching is a "businessman" who appears to be closely affiliated with the Sun Yee On group in Hong Kong (U.S. Department of Justice 1988). He is also alleged to be associated with Hong Kong 14K members active in the entertainment business. He was subpoenaed, along with several other Chinese crime figures, by the President's Commission on Organized Crime to testify at its hearings in New York City in 1984, but he refused to appear.

LOS ANGELES AND MONTEREY PARK: THE HOMES OF TAIWANESE AND VIETNAMESE GANGS

The Los Angeles County Sheriff's Department conducted an Asian Criminal Activities Survey, with questionnaires mailed to forty-six municipalities and nineteen Los Angeles County Sheriff's Stations. The completed questionnaires showed that "46 percent are experiencing an increase in Asian crime; 23 percent are encountering reports/rumors of extortion of Asian owned/operated business; 45 percent have encountered incidents of violence involving Asian suspects and/or victims; and 40 percent are aware of Asian organized crime or Asian gang activity in their jurisdiction" (Los Angeles County Sheriff's Department 1985, 1-2).

In Los Angeles, the most powerful Asian street gangs are the Wah Ching, the Bamboo United, the Four Seas, and the Vietnamese gangs. The Wah Ching was formed in 1965, a year after the group was established in San Francisco. Chinese high school students were constantly being picked on by a Mexican American youth gang at that time. When some of the Wah Ching from San Francisco moved to Los Angeles, they established the Los Angeles Wah Ching by recruiting immigrant students who needed protection from the Mexican gang. Following the developmental pattern in San Francisco, some Los Angeles Wah Ching split to form the Los Angeles chapter of the Yau Lai (now extinct) in 1969. Since then, the two groups have become perennial rivals (Attorney General of California 1972). The Wah Ching was recruited by the Hop Sing tong, and the Yau Lai is aligned with the Bing Kung tong.

Despite the formation of these gangs, conflicts between Chinese and Mexican youths did not subside. In February 1985, Chinese teenagers shot and wounded five Mexican youths in Los Angeles's Chinatown (*World Journal*, February 17, 1985, 3). In another incident, a gang fight broke out between Chinese and Mexican high school students on a campus in Alhambra, California. During the encounter, a Chinese student was stabbed in the chest (*Centre Daily News*, October 29, 1985, 11).

In the Los Angeles area, Chinese gangs are also active in Monterey Park, known as "Little Taipei" (*New York Times*, January 13, 1985, A1). Within several years, the Asian population of Monterey Park grew from 20 percent to more than 38 percent, and the percentage of whites declined to less than 35 percent. According to the local police chief, "the Asian gangs are struggling for control of the lucrative criminal enterprises in the Los Angeles and San Gabriel Valley, including gambling, illegal alien-smuggling, extortion, protection and narcotic distribution rackets" (President's Commission on Organized Crime 1984b, 465-66).

Because law enforcement authorities in Taiwan made massive arrests of underground figures in the late 1970s and early 1980s, hundreds of criminals from Taiwan sought refuge in the United States at that time. Most of them came to Monterey Park because the Chinese there are predominantly Taiwanese immigrants. However, the leaders among these criminals were reluctant to work in restaurants, a job many newcomers are forced to take during their transitional period in the United States. Without stable incomes, they found it difficult to recruit followers. As a result, Monterey Park is sarcastically referred to as the place where one can find a hundred "big brothers" but only one "little brother."

In the beginning, these crime figures from Taiwan attempted to operate high-stake gambling clubs, but with so few Chinese in Monterey Park able to afford to gamble heavily, the leaders changed their operations, shifting from high-stake poker games to modest mahjong games. The more affluent gang leaders are involved with wealthy Vietnamese criminals in loansharking operation. In general, however, criminals from Taiwan, reluctant to become involved in drug trafficking and street violence, maintain a low profile in Monterey Park (*Mei Tung News*, May 23, 1988, 5).

Two Taiwan-based gangs and a few Vietnamese gangs are in control of criminal activities within the Chinese community in Monterey Park. In the following section, these gangs are examined briefly.

Four Seas

High school students established the Four Seas gang in 1955 in Taiwan. It was disbanded in 1962 but reemerged as new leaders solidified the gang's financial foundation by operating gambling houses and prostitution rings (Jin 1984). Members are mostly from the second generation of the Chinese who fled to Taiwan from China.

After Four Seas members arrived in the United States (sometimes illegally), they became active in collecting debts, operating gambling houses and nightclubs, and investing in legal businesses such as restaurants and trading companies (*World Journal*, December 1, 1984, 24). Three Four Seas members were indicted, along with a Bamboo United leader, for kidnapping a Chinese woman and demanding a ransom of $1 million (*New York Times*, January 13, 1985, A1).

Bamboo United

Bamboo United was established in 1956 in a suburban area of Taipei, Taiwan. The authorities disbanded it in 1958, but it endured and developed into a major street gang in 1960. At that time, it expanded its influence from the suburbs to the commercial districts of Taipei.

In 1981 leaders began to operate underground dancing halls and to infiltrate the lucrative entertainment business. By 1983, the gang had recruited many new members, and it grew from the initial eight branches to twenty-five (*World Journal*, June 4, 1985, 4). Unofficial sources suggest that there are over 10,000 Bamboo United members in Taiwan (Jin 1984). An overseas branch was established in Hong Kong (*World Journal*, March 25, 1985, 5). The gang has not established a tong in the United States, but it has a substantial number of members who are active in Los Angeles, San Francisco, Houston, Dallas, and New York (for example, *New York Times*, August 3, 1986, 26). The gang also has members in the Philippines, Saudi Arabia, and Japan.

The development of Bamboo United has been closely related to the criminal career of Chen Chi-li, one of its highest leaders. Chen was born in 1943 and came with his parents to Taiwan when the Kuomintang retreated from China. His father was a prosecutor, and his mother a legal clerk. He joined Bamboo United when he was fourteen. In 1965 he received a college degree in engineering, a significant accomplishment at that time. After graduation, Chen served in the army as a lieutenant and upon discharge worked as a commercial painter. He led his young followers in vicious gang fights with rival gangs and emerged as the most powerful leader of the organization. He was arrested and indicted in 1970 for aggravated assault and incarcerated for two and a half years. Upon release, Chen was sent for three and a half years to Green Island, a place where chronic criminals are disciplined and punished harshly (Lau 1988).

After his release, Chen turned his attention to business and became successful within a relatively short time. He claims that he completely dissociated himself from Bamboo United from 1976 to 1980. Later, he reemerged as the leader of the gang because government officials asked for his help in preventing non-Kuomintang politicians from exploiting the masses in street demonstrations (Committee to Obtain Justice for Henry Liu 1985).

Since its involvement in the assassination of a Chinese-American writer who immigrated to the United States from Taiwan, the gang has become known internationally. The writer, Henry Liu, was shot to death at his home in Daly City, California, by two Bamboo United members in 1984. Liu had written a critical biography of the then president of Taiwan and was in the process of writing a book about the dark side of politics in Taiwan.

According to various accounts (for examples, June 1985; *New York Times*, April 21, 1985, E2; *World Journal*, June 4, 1985, 4), Chen Chi-li, Swei Yi-fung (another Bamboo United leader), and Vice-Admiral Wong Shi-lin, head of the Taiwan Defense Ministry Intelligence Bureau, met in July 1984. Wong criticized some of the overseas Chinese, Henry Liu in particular, for their betrayal of Taiwan. Chen suggested that something had to be done to traitors such as Liu and boasted that he controlled Bamboo

United members in the United States. Wong urged Chen to "teach Liu a lesson" when the opportunity arose.

Chen initially ordered Bamboo United members in Los Angeles to carry out the mission, but to no avail. Chen and Swei were then trained for a short period at the Intelligence Bureau and were given pictures and addresses of Henry Liu and other information about him. Chen and Swei arrived in the United States in September 1984.

It is not clear what Wong meant by teaching Henry Liu a lesson, but Chen was determined to kill him. After Chen's arrival in the United States, Wu Tun, the enforcer of Bamboo United, joined him. Chen and Wu went to Liu's curio shop at the Fisherman's Wharf in San Francisco to attack him there but changed their minds when they found the area well patrolled. They then asked Tung Kwei-sen, another Bamboo United leader in Taipei to join them. When Tung arrived, they set up a plan to kill Liu in his home. After following Liu a few times, Wu and Tung sneaked into his home and shot him to death. Within a few days, Chen, Wu, and Tung flew back to Taiwan.

Four weeks after the assassination, Taiwanese police and military personnel carried out a nationwide raid on criminals. Chen Chi-li was the first person to be arrested. Hundreds of underworld figures, including Wu Tun, were also arrested. With the help of Bamboo United members in the Philippines, Tung Kwei-sen fled to Manila.

While the government in Taiwan was denying any involvement in the killing of Henry Liu, a magazine in Taipei broke the news that three Bamboo United leaders were responsible. Officials reacted immediately. They claimed that when Chen Chi-li was interrogated, he confessed to Liu's murder. Furthermore, they revealed that some Intelligence Bureau officers were also implicated. Chen and Wu were convicted in a public trial in Taipei, and both were sentenced to life imprisonment. Wong Shi-ling was convicted in a separate trial and also sentenced to life imprisonment.

After Tung Kwei-sen fled to Manila, he was alleged there to be involved in a mass murder. He later traveled to Thailand and from there to Brazil, where he was arrested. He was subsequently extradited to the United States to stand trial for Henry Liu's murder. He was convicted and sentenced to fifteen years imprisonment.

Liu's murder and the subsequent trials and hearings were well publicized worldwide. Countries with a substantial number of Bamboo United members, particularly the United States, became concerned about the gang. Two months after the defendants in Liu's case were sentenced to prison in Taipei, the leader in Los Angeles was arrested for kidnapping a

Chinese woman in Monterey Park. Three months later, seven Bamboo United leaders and members were arrested in California, Texas, and New York for murder, drug trafficking, gun smuggling, and gambling (*New York Times*, September 17, 1985, A1). These two incidents crippled the organization's far-flung criminal activities in the United States.

Vietnamese Gangs

In Southern California, as of 1980, approximately 110,000 Vietnamese refugees are concentrated in Los Angeles, Santa Ana, Anaheim, Westminster, and Garden Grove. According to law enforcement authorities, Vietnamese gangs such as the Frogmen, the Catalina Boys, the Thunder Tigers, and the Pink Knights are active in those areas (Los Angeles County Sheriff's Department 1984). These gangs are formed by Vietnamese and Vietnamese-Chinese from South Vietnam and generally labeled as the "*Viet Ching*" (Vietnamese Youth).

Vietnamese gangs are now rapidly expanding on both the West and East coasts (Badey 1988). Their criminal specialties are predatory crimes such as robbery and extortion. Over the past several years, many Vietnamese or Vietnamese-Chinese businessmen have been victimized by them. Unlike Chinese gangs that are better organized and closely affiliated with adult organizations, the Vietnamese gangs are loosely knit and have no connections to their community organizations. In other words, they are not tied to their communities and have no gang territory. The fact that they are not structured and not embedded in the communities allows them to be extremely mobile, thus alluding any law enforcement efforts to track them.

Another unique characteristic of the Vietnamese gangs is their patterns of criminal activity. Law enforcement authorities have noticed that Vietnamese criminal elements are engaged in regional or nationwide crime sprees, committing a series of robberies from city to city or even state to state. For example, they will rob or extort merchants in various cities in California, drive to Texas, Louisiana, Mississippi, and Florida, and commit more crimes, and eventually show up in Boston, Chicago, and New York, looking for more victims (*New York Times*, November 25, 1985, 14; United States Senate 1986; *World Journal*, January 14, 1987, 3).

Wherever these so-called "roving bands" go (Badey 1987), they team up with local Vietnamese criminal elements, who provide them with information about potential victims and logistical support. Restaurants, gambling clubs, massage parlors, and nightclubs in New York City are constantly robbed by Vietnamese gangsters from out of town. For example, six Vietnamese youths armed with four Uzi machine guns robbed a Chinese nightclub near New York City's Chinatown. Since many victims are themselves leaders of the Chinese underworld and they have never seen the offenders before, investigators theorized that the crime was carried out by outsiders, with the support of Vietnamese gang members active on the outskirts of Chinatown (*Sing Tao Jih Pao*, August 21, 1989, 24).

Vietnamese gangs are normally heavily armed, and they do not hesitate to use their weapons. Their mobility, ruthlessness, and complete isolation from both their community and the mainstream society have earned them a reputation of being extremely dangerous. They have instilled fear upon not only the businessmen, but also criminal elements of Chinese origin. Consequently, Chinese crime groups are actively recruiting Vietnamese gang members to work as street muscles.

NEW YORK CITY: THE "RED FLOWER TEMPLE" OF CHINESE GANGS

The number of Chinese gangs in New York City surpasses any other American city. There, not only local gangs are active in the Chinese communities of Manhattan, Queens, and Brooklyn, but out-of-state gangs such as the Wah Ching and Viet Ching are also occasionally seen. Besides, crime groups from Taiwan, Hong Kong, and China have always viewed the city as the place to establish their "beachhead" if they are going to transplant to the United States. To use the Chinese underworld slang, the city is the "Red Flower Temple" (the place where Hung members set up their first nationwide meeting) where members of the subculture come to meet one another. Figure 6 shows the emergence and persistence of Chinese gangs in New York City within the past thirty years.

The development of Chinese street gangs in New York City may be divided into four stages: emergence, from 1960 to 1968; transformation, between 1969 and 1973; crystallization, 1974-1982; and diffusion, from 1983 to the present. Figure 7 compares the uniqueness of the four developmental stages.

Emergence, 1960-1968

Before 1965, Chinese youths in New York City, most of whom were native-born, attended schools near Chinatown in which the enrollment was 95 percent black and Hispanic, with the remaining 5 percent Chinese and white. Chinese students were constantly picked on at school and nearby

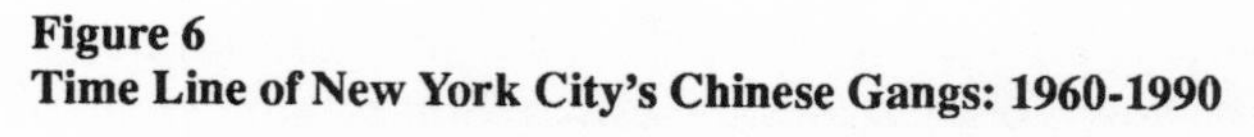

Figure 6
Time Line of New York City's Chinese Gangs: 1960-1990

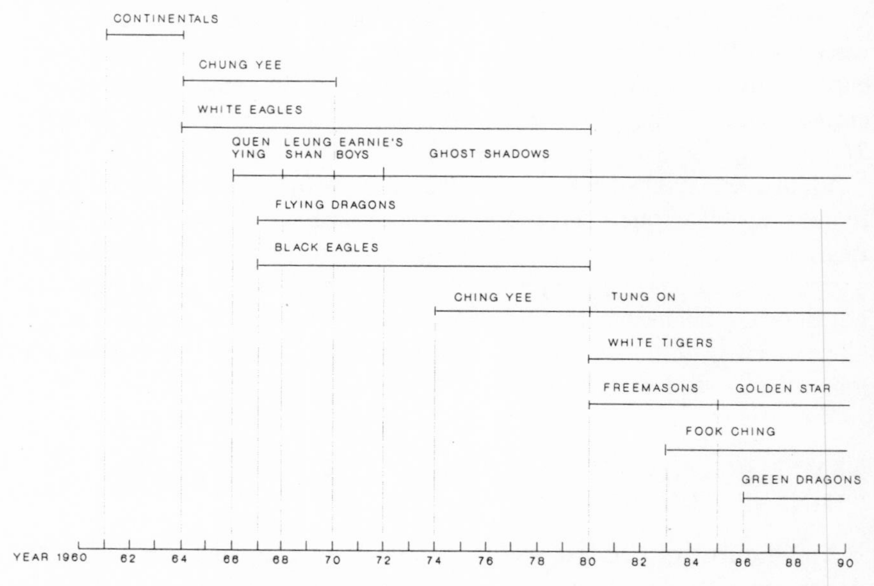

playgrounds by members of other ethnic groups (*New York Times*, January 15, 1964, 33).

When the Chinese youths found that neither their parents nor school officials could protect them from these students, they banded together to protect themselves. The first Chinese street gang, the Continentals, was formed in 1961 by native-born Chinese high school students. The gang had as many as one hundred members. It fought against not only the Puerto Ricans and the blacks but the Italians and whites as well.

Although they defended themselves against racial discrimination and were involved in certain delinquent activities such as gambling and truancy, the Continentals did not commit any street crimes. As native-born Americans, they were part of American youth culture and somewhat alienated from the surrounding Chinese establishment. They did not feel ostracized by the larger society, a feeling that is deep-rooted in tong members and foreign-born Chinese youths. Unlike Chinese gangs that emerged later, the Continentals were not affiliated with tongs because of the cultural gap between them. According to Chang:

> A great majority of Continental gang members were close to their native culture, but also well adjusted to Western culture. . . . They were a gang as early as 1961 and while they were not hired by anyone

> to protect anything, the aggression initiated by Italian and Puerto Rican gangs necessitated their formation. While they were children of the streets, the streets were not their lives. Their survival did not depend on a robbery or a theft. They were, in their own way, romantic anti-heroes. . . . They were generally in school, at home, and in work. (1972, 13-14)

In 1964, an On Leong leader organized a youth group made up of foreign-born teenagers. The group was called the On Leong Youth Club, and its major activity was practicing martial arts under the leadership of a tong member. The tong leader's real motive for forming the club was unknown. Some sources indicate that he established it to promote his reputation within the community. Other accounts, however, claim that he was a dedicated community leader who wanted to provide a gathering place for the adolescents so that they would not run wild in the community (*Mei Wah Report*, October 6, 1985, 16-21). The club later transformed itself into the first foreign-born Chinese youth gang known as the White Eagles.

Unlike the Continentals, the White Eagles were closely related to the community but alienated from school, family, and American society. Their major concerns were not racial conflicts at school but racial harassment and disorderly conduct by non-Chinese visitors in the community. Their self-appointed mission was to protect the community from outsiders by ensuring that non-Chinese tourists would not make discriminatory remarks about the Chinese and would pay their bills. According to a former White Eagles member:

> In the early 1960s, we found that Chinatown residents and businessmen were often being humiliated and exploited by other minority groups, and yet they did not have the guts to fight back. We saw outsiders come to Chinatown, enjoy their meals in the restaurants, say bad things about the Chinese, and often refuse to pay their bills. What we did was to make sure no outsiders would come here and verbally abuse our people; and if they do, we will beat them up. If someone tries to get away from a restaurant without paying his bill, we will first knock him down and then take the money from his pocket and turn it over to the restaurant owner. (From an interview conducted for this study, my translation)

In the same year that the White Eagles was formed, the Chung Yee was also established. Unlike the Continentals, who had difficulty recruiting

Figure 7
Comparison of Various Developmental Stages of New York City's Chinese Gangs: 1960-1990

	Emergence 1960-1968	Transformation 1969-1973
1. Active Gangs	Continentals Chung Yee White Eagles Quen Ying Flying Dragons Black Eagles	White Eagles Ghost Shadows Flying Dragons Black Eagles
2. Members' Ethnicity	American-born China and Hong Kong immigrants	Mainly Hong Kong immigrants
3. Major Activities	Group fights with other ethnic groups; protection of Chinatown; adolescent social activities	Extorting and robbing businessmen in the community; guarding gambling places; fighting with rival gangs and American-born; involving in the community political affairs
4. Uniqueness	Gangs were unorganized street corner groups or martial arts clubs, involved only in nonutilitarian activities; gang fights were spontaneous and non-fatal; the gangs were not implicated in community affairs	Gangs were institutionalized by the adult organizations to guard the gambling dens; nonaffiliated gangs started to terrorize the community through extortion and robbery; turf battles were often fatal; the gangs were implicated in the community political affairs

Crystallization 1974-1982	Diffusion 1983-1990
White Eagles Ghost Shadows Flying Dragons Black Eagles Ching Yee Tung On White Tigers Freemasons	Ghost Shadows Flying Dragons Tung On Fook Ching White Tigers Golden Star Green Dragons Viet Ching
Mainly Hong Kong immigrants	Hong Kong, Taiwan, China, Korea, and Vietnam immigrants
Extorting and robbing businessmen inside and outside the community; guarding gambling places; involving in intergang and intragang power struggles; many gang members were killed in public places	Extorting and robbing businessmen and pedestrians; guarding gambling places and massage parlors; investing in legitimate businesses; many gang members were killed in nonpublic places
Gangs and tongs became closely affiliated; intergang and intragang violence erupted often and many youths were killed; gangs became crystallized within their territories; innocent bystanders were often victimized by street violence among the gangs	Gang activity spread to Queens and Brooklyn; many nonaffiliated gangs were formed; Vietnamese-Chinese became prominent in the community; gang leaders became involved in heroin trafficking and operating legitimate businesses; shootouts on the streets decreased, but more victims were being murdered in nonpublic places

new members because of the small number of native-born Chinese, both the White Eagles and the Chung Yee were able to gain members from among new immigrants from Hong Kong.

By 1965, the White Eagles and the Chung Yee had become the two dominant powers on the streets of Chinatown. These two groups not only fought against non-Chinese who caused trouble within the community but also started to drive the native-born Chinese off the streets. There was, and still is, deep-rooted hostility between the Jook Sings (American-born Chinese) and the Jook Koks (foreign-born Chinese). Jook Sing and Jook Kok are "words for pieces of a bamboo plant: Jook Sing, a piece of the stalk—hollow inside, but impenetrable, walled-off at both ends—American born, neither Chinese nor American, cut off from both cultures. Jook Kok, describing the Hong Kong-born, was the branching point—open only at one end to Chinese culture" (*New York Times*, December 1, 1976, B1). The frequent violence between the Jook Sings and the Jook Koks in the mid-1960s marked a shift away from conflict with other ethnic groups and toward internal disputes. Before the Continentals were disbanded, considerable tension existed between them and the Jook Koks. One former Continentals member, when asked why he had so much hatred for the foreign-born youths, said:

> Whenever I saw this guy's [a Jook Kok] face, it made me feel all sorts of hatred. I was here all my life on Mott Street. Here comes this group from I don't know where and they had the audacity to say, "You have that side of the street and we have this side." The street was always open. You could walk anywhere without this hassle. Then these people came and said, "We have this street and you can't walk on it." It was so ridiculous. I look at those guys and I said, "You really got balls. There ain't no way this is coming down on us." And they would get uptight and say, "You don't know who you are or what you are." So for two years we had a lot of skirmishes between them and us. (Sung 1977, 31)

Within the next few years, other new gangs appeared. By 1966, the Quen Ying, the predecessor of the Ghost Shadows, had emerged around Henry Street on the outskirts of Chinatown. In 1968, the Quen Ying changed its name to Liang Shan. The year after the Quen Ying was formed, the Flying Dragons came into existence under the auspices of the Hip Sing. In the meantime, some of the younger members of the White Eagles left the group to form the Black Eagles. This gang, in comparison with the older White Eagles, was more aggressive, more violent, and more determined to bring disaster to the community. According to a former Black Eagles member:

> Chinatown is a shithouse, and when one walks into shit he becomes shit. The establishment has betrayed us. Why are there no schools for the Chinese? For training? Why is there no new housing? We need new business. Damn the restaurants and laundries. They say "get an education." But for what? To work in a restaurant? In a laundry? Take a walk down any street. Every ten steps there is a coffee shop, fifteen steps a restaurant. But the big shots cry, "The kids are always fighting; they rob, they steal . . ." but they created the problems. They have had thirty years to prepare training programs for immigrants. They didn't do it. It's their fault; it's the establishment's fault. We've got to bring it back to the community. Sure the Jook Sings get out and find jobs. We're left here with this shit. If I had the power I would end that establishment. I would form my own. (Chang 1972, 15)

Thus, by 1968, there were five street gangs in Chinatown—the White Eagles, the Chung Yee, the Liang Shan, the Flying Dragons, and the Black Eagles. During the emergence stage, the gangs were in essence martial arts clubs headed by a Kung Fu master who was a core member of a tong. Gang members were invovled in nonutilitarian activities such as practicing martial arts; driving away American-born young Chinese from Chinatown streets; and protecting the community from rowdy visitors.

Transformation, 1969-1973

During this period, the streets of Chinatown were dominated by two gangs: the White Eagles and the Black Eagles. Street violence escalated as knives and guns became increasingly available. Police statistics show that arrests of Chinese youths under age twenty-one rose considerably after 1969, a result of the increase in assaults and weapons charges. In 1970 the first arrest of a Chinese youth for murder occurred when a Black Eagle stabbed a seventeen-year-old White Eagle to death on the streets of Chinatown (*New York Post*, August 6, 1970).

A political youth group known as the I Wor Kuen (Righteous Harmonious Fist) was established in 1969. Composed mainly of native-born college students and former gang members, the group espoused Chinese communism and allied itself with the Black Panthers and the Young Lords, militant black organizations. The group was at odds not only with the right-wing elite groups such as the Chinese Consolidated Benevolent

Association (CCBA) and the tongs, but also with the foreign-born youth gangs (*New York Daily News*, September 14, 1970, 4). The I Wor Kuen held several demonstrations against the tourist buses that routinely flowed into the community. The group was outraged because the tourists came to Chinatown primarily to "stop only for twenty minutes, pay off the bus companies, and crowd Chinese people off the sidewalks while photographing them as curiosities" (Chevigny 1970, 12).

The predominantly pro-Kuomintang Chinatown residents in general, and the foreign-born youth gangs in particular, were unnerved by the I Wor Kuen. In February 1971, a group of fifteen foreign-born youths, armed with guns and knives, raided a billiard hall in Chinatown believed to be a hangout for the radical group. They wounded seven youths inside the hall (*New York Post*, February 24, 1971, 11).

During this period, the pro-Kuomintang traditional associations became concerned not only with young militant groups such as the I Wor Kuen but also with some community organizations that seemed sympathetic to the Communist government in Beijing (*New York Times*, February 22, 1971, B2). According to the traditional associations, the late 1960s was a time of turmoil and uncertainty. The associations' authority within the community was being challenged by the pro-Communist young militant groups and emerging community associations, and was also being shaken by the restless foreign-born gang members who acted violently on the streets of Chinatown. The violence and street-gang fights made the tongs look powerless and affected the economy of the community by frightening the tourist trade.

By this time, the gangs had transformed themselves completely from self-help groups to predatory groups. They terrorized the community by demanding food and money from business owners and they robbed the gambling establishments. When the youth gangs started to shake down merchants and gamblers who were tong members, the tongs finally decided to hire the gangs as their street soldiers. That way, the tongs ensured their members against robbery or extortion by the street gangs and also solidified their position within the community. Any effort by the left-wing associations to take over Chinatown would be brutally put down by the tongs' armies (Spataro 1978).

Thus, during the transformation period, the White Eagles and the Flying Dragons became closely associated with the On Leong and Hip Sing's gambling operations. Gangs that were not institutionalized by the tongs were heavily involved in street crimes in areas not controlled by the tongs. Instead of fighting with fists and knives, gang members started to carry guns and use them readily (*Mei Wah Report*, June 14, 1988, 162-68).

Crystallization, 1974-1982

In the mid-1970s, some gangs in Chinatown became inseparable from certain tongs. Gang members lived in apartments rented to them by the tongs and ate in tong restaurants. Gang membership became a full-time occupation for the youths, who detached themselves almost completely from school and family. But with all the security that gangs provided, members still had to protect themselves not only from rival gangs but also from rival factions within the same gang, as their gang conflicts reached an all-time high (U.S. District Court, Sentencing Memorandum, 1986). Although gang members were offered membership and jobs by the tongs, they were too powerful to be fully controlled by them. As a result, the community continued to experience increases in extortion and robbery (*New York Times*, January 19, 1974; U.S. District Court, 1985a).

While the Ghost Shadows were extorting and robbing on the outskirts of Chinatown, members of the White Eagles were busy shaking down merchants and gamblers on Mott and Bayard streets, even though they had been hired by the On Leong to protect these same people. The On Leong became increasingly annoyed. The final straw came when a White Eagle publicly humiliated an On Leong elder in 1974. On Leong decided to rid themselves of the White Eagles and did so by first cutting off the gang's money and firearms and then hinting to the Ghost Shadows that they should take over the tong's territory (*Mei Wah Report*, October 6, 1985, 16-21). The Ghost Shadows made their move in November 1974.

The Ghost Shadows' takeover of Mott Street (the On Leong's main street) was one of the most significant events in the history of New York City's Chinese gangs. According to Nickey Louie, a Shadows leader, that was "the most terrifying experience" of his group. The gang leader revealed how the incident occurred:

> We set up Thursday as the day. We even had an insider man to check out all the hangout spots of the Eagles. At 12 midnight we started out with twenty guys; none of the top Eagles were where we thought they'd be. Only a few of those on the fringe were around. We worked them over pretty good. No guns were used. . . . By then, because we "hit the grass and scared the snake," they quickly grouped together their best men. But since we started the war first, of course we didn't soften up. During that week, almost every minute was a shoot out. Until that night, a couple of my guys drove a car down Mott Street. They were attacked from both sides. They lost control of the car and smashed into a curio shop. Cops were already all over Mott Street,

> so some of the Eagles got arrested right on the street. After this, you can say the Eagles were dissolved, either they got arrested or they escaped. (*Canal Magazine*, December 8, 1978, 1)

In fact, the Ghost Shadows had picked the right time to make their move. According to other sources, none of the core members of the White Eagles were in New York's Chinatown because they had formed a soccer team and had gone back to Taiwan to participate in a grand tournament (*Mei Wah Report*, October 6, 1985, 16-21).

After the skirmish, the Ghost Shadows were in control of the most lucrative spots in Chinatown. The White Eagles retreated to Elizabeth Street, just a block away from the Shadows' territory. The Flying Dragons were on Pell Street, Doyers Street, Division Street, and Bowery Street, the domain of Hip Sing. Once the gangs settled down on their respective turfs, they returned to their protection and extortion businesses.

Because of public pressure and close surveillance by law enforcement agencies in 1975, the gangs maintained a low profile. Some started to extort retail businesses in Queens, Brooklyn, and Long Island (*China Tribune*, January 18, 1976). Still, Chinatown remained the battleground of the youth gangs. Conflicts between the Eagles and the Ghost Shadows were far from over. In March 1975, the Ghost Shadows shot and wounded a member of the Black Eagles. A week later, an Eagle spotted a Ghost Shadow near Little Italy and shot him to death as he was trying to run away. The murderer was convicted and received a life sentence (*China Tribune*, June 18, 1976).

In late 1975, an internal struggle between the older and younger factions of the Ghost Shadows erupted. Younger members were especially incensed with the way the leaders distributed money to them. They accused the senior members of embezzling the group's money. Tensions mounted when a meeting that was to settle the disagreements only generated more hostility. The older faction, after assuring support from the On Leong, went to Mott Street in January 1976 to shoot members belonging to the younger faction. Although no one was hurt, the event signified the beginning of a continuing power struggle among various factions within the Ghost Shadows. In the aftermath of the confrontation, the older group occupied Mott Street, and the younger group controlled Bayard Street, another lucrative area nearby.

The most violent year in the history of Chinatown was 1976. Intergang and intragang wars erupted often in the streets of Manhattan's Chinatown. Merchants were terrorized by gang members who were involved heavily in theft, robbery, and extortion. Merchants who refused to pay put their lives in jeopardy. Official statistics also show that the complaint rates for violent crimes within the Fifth Precinct reached an all-time high in 1976 (K. Chin 1986). The Fifth Precinct established its Chinatown Gang Task Force that same year.

In early 1976, conflict between the Ghost Shadows and the Flying Dragons broke out. A Ghost Shadow was shot and killed inside the Flying Dragons territory. The murder brought together the two rival factions of the Ghost Shadows. In March 1976, the Shadows spotted a Dragon at the Co Luck Restaurant in Chinatown. Two armed Ghost Shadows entered the restaurant and opened fire, killing a thirty-nine-year-old woman who was dining with her family and friends, and wounding five others. The Flying Dragons member was wounded slightly in the arm (U.S. District Court, Sentencing Memorandum, 1986).

While the local gangs were fighting fiercely to protect their turfs, the police found that the number of Wah Ching members from San Francisco increased dramatically. Because the Wah Ching did not have their own turf, they were unable to collect protection money from the stores or gambling houses. Without regular sources of income, the Wah Ching became heavily involved in robbery. In 1976 eleven Wah Ching members were arrested in a series of violent incidents (*Chinese Journal*, June 5, 1976, 24).

In August 1976, while the Wah Ching were attempting to move into the core areas of Chinatown, gang leaders announced a news conference at the Chinese Consolidated Benevolent Association's meeting hall. At the meeting, Nickey Louie of the Ghost Shadows, Michael Chen of the Flying Dragons, Paul Ma of the Black Eagles, and Ah Hung of the Ching Yee (a less powerful group formed in 1974 and later renamed Tung On) declared that they would end the street fighting and look for jobs. The gang leaders also revealed that they had invited the Wah Ching to participate, but the latter had declined.

Local newspapers reacted favorably to the announcement, but law enforcement authorities remained skeptical, not believing that the gangs would dissolve themselves. Why the gang members suddenly decided to abandon their criminal way of life was unclear. According to some sources, the news conference was held to impress the New York City government of the fact that more funds needed be funneled into the community's various social service agencies. Others alleged that the local gangs were primarily attempting to present a united front to the invading Wah Ching.

The peace lasted only one month. Official sources indicated that violence broke out between the Shadows and the Black Eagles because the Black Eagles, despite the agreement, went into Shadows territory on

Bayard Street and were determined to remain. In September 1976, Paul Ma, the Black Eagles leader who attended the news conference, was shot and wounded along with his wife and three other Eagles on Ghost Shadows territory. Three Shadows were arrested for the shooting (*China Post*, September 10, 1976). A few weeks later, a Ghost Shadow was killed by three Black Eagles. Several days following that, a Black Eagle was shot to death inside a Chinatown theater (*New York Daily News*, October 17, 1976).

Asked why the gangs were unable to maintain peace among themselves, Ghost Shadows leaders provided the following explanation:

> Initially, when we and the other gang leaders got together and decided to cooperate and reform, we really wanted to do so. The reason was that we are adults now and do not want to be gangsters anymore. However, there are some people who do not want to see the gangs come together and emerge as a powerful group. These people are afraid of us exposing their involvement in illegal activities. So they intentionally provoke conflicts among the gangs. Of course, we are also to be blamed for not being able to keep our tempers and our faith in one another. (*China Tribune*, May 19, 1977, 1; my translation)

Before 1976 street violence was primarily the manifestation of power struggles among the gangs. Thereafter, however, intragang killings increased. They originated with the Ghost Shadows. Nickey Louie was again accused of pocketing the gang's money and abusing his power. Louie held a meeting to reconcile the differences between the two hostile factions, but his attempt failed, and the Shadows were divided into two warring and suspicious camps.

Louie struck first. He and his associates shot a leader of the other faction. That faction fought back and attempted to kill Louie a few times between late 1977 and early 1978. In another incident, Louie was shot at in a Chinatown barber shop (U.S. District Court 1985b). He recalled later how he was shot:

> That night the door of the barber shop was locked. I was playing mahjong with three other guys, with my back facing the long corridor. Suddenly they looked at me with astonishment on their faces. I realized something was wrong. I turned my head and saw a .38 caliber pointing at my right jaw. At that moment I heard five shots. The first bullet went through my face. I stood up without thinking and that's why the second and third shots got my back and my right arm. I swung

> the gun away from me with my right hand and therefore the fourth and fifth shots missed. I grabbed the muzzle and that man pulled the trigger three times but I heard only clicks. That's it. So I wildly threw him against the wall. By that time, I felt a rush of faintness. Hot blood bursting from my nostrils. I couldn't stand it any longer. I rushed out through the back door and headed straight to the Fifth Precinct. (*Canal Magazine*, December 8, 1978, 1)

After the incident, Louie left for Chicago and spent some time there. He returned to New York City in 1980 and formed the White Tigers in Queens by recruiting former Shadows members. The new gang's major goal was to recapture Mott Street from the Shadows.

In December 1980 the Tigers held a series of meetings to devise a plan for taking over Mott Street. A meeting was set up between the Tigers and the Shadows in a Chinatown restaurant while armed members of the gangs stood guard on the streets. The negotiations broke down when the Shadows refused to capitulate and cede the territory the White Tigers sought. As the Shadows left the restaurant, a White Tiger attempted to shoot the Shadows, but his gun jammed and the Shadows escaped unharmed. Two Tigers were arrested by police officers who happened to be in the vicinity (U.S. District Court, Sentencing Memorandum, 1986).

In 1976 when the Ghost Shadows' factional problem began, the Flying Dragons also experienced an internal struggle. Two of its factions got into a violent confrontation at an ice-skating rink; gunfire broke out, seriously wounding two gang members and hitting a white youth (*China Tribune*, December 1, 1976, 1).

By the end of 1976, despite their internal problems, the Chinese gangs not only were "rumbling" in Chinatown but were also spreading their operations to other parts of Manhattan. The police became aware that Chinese restaurant owners outside Chinatown were being harassed by gang members for extortion money. In December 1976 unidentified youths alleged to be Black Eagles members murdered a couple who owned a midtown Manhattan restaurant. The owners were the victims of reported extortion by gang members prior to their murders (*China Tribune* December 11, 1976, 1).

Leaders of both gangs experiencing internal difficulties were arrested in 1977. In January, Flying Dragons leader Michael Chen was arrested for killing a Ghost Shadow inside a theater in Chinatown (*China Tribune*, February 2, 1977, 1). The charge was later dismissed. Five months later, Nickey Louie was taken into custody for assaulting two Chinese youths in the community. He hit the youths with an iron pipe when they refused to join his gang.

The arrests of the two leaders, however, did not deter Chinatown gang members. Street violence continued within the community, reaching an explosive stage when Man Bun Lee, a former president of the CCBA who publicly requested that law enforcement officials get tough with the gangs, was stabbed five times in front of his restaurant on Mott Street by a hired assassin. Lee survived the attack. His assailant was later arrested on the West Coast and found guilty of the assault. The real motive behind the attempted murder was never known. But for all its mystery, the incident brought a clear message to the community: no one who antagonizes the gangs is safe.

In the late 1970s, while the Ghost Shadows went through their fierce internal struggle, the Flying Dragons solidified their power base within the area of Pell Street, Doyers Street, and East Broadway. Compared with the Ghost Shadows, the Flying Dragons were better organized and much more sophisticated in executing criminal activities. While the On Leong never had complete control of the Ghost Shadows, the Flying Dragons were closely scrutinized by the Hip Sing.

Before 1982, the gangs victimized only the Chinese or people of other minority groups. At no time had the gangs intentionally assaulted non-Asians. They always tried to avoid bothering whites, knowing that whites would report the crime and testify in court. However, in July 1982 six Ghost Shadows kidnapped, raped, and killed a white woman from Virginia. The woman was picked up by the Shadows in a bar near Chinatown and taken to the gang's apartment on Mott Street, where she was gang-raped and strangled to death. The victim's body, wrapped in a blanket, was dumped near Chinatown. All the defendants were convicted and received maximum sentences. The case was the first successfully prosecuted gang-related murder, the first in which a Chinese took the witness stand to identify a Chinese gang member, and the first in which a gang member became a witness and testified against the gang (Leng 1984).

The involvement of the Shadows in the murder of the white woman, in addition to their internal conflicts, caused the group's downfall. Many Shadows either were arrested or were killed by rival gangs in the ensuing years (*New York Daily News*, November 21, 1982, 5). The Flying Dragons, however, were very much in control of their turf, and their ability to prevent the White Tigers from taking over East Broadway and the surrounding areas boosted their reputation enormously.

Within this period, after many fierce power struggles, the more powerful gangs became crystallized and settled down in their respective territory.

The less powerful gangs either dissolved or left the core areas of Chinatown to find new territories of their own in other places.

Diffusion, 1983 to the Present

In the 1980s, new gangs such as the Fook Ching, the White Tigers, the Tung On, the Green Dragons, and the Golden Star arose in the peripheral areas of Chinatown and in the outer boroughs of Queens and Brooklyn, following the emigration patterns of Chinese businesses and residents.

During this time, a considerable number of Fook Chow people (Fujianese) came to the United States from southern China and Hong Kong. The Fook Chow are a closely knit group with strong ethnic identity. Because of their close ties, their economic power grew rapidly, and they are now considered to be the most powerful group within the Chinese community after the Cantonese.

The Fook Ching (Fook Chow Youth) gang comprises adolescents of Fook Chow origin. When the gang was in its embryonic stage, it was closely affiliated with the Fook Chow Association, the largest district association of the Fook Chow people. The adult organization was supportive of the gang and provided its members with lawyers in several court cases. However, as the gang became increasingly enmeshed in street violence, the association decided to withdraw its endorsement. Starting in 1983, the Fook Ching were responsible for a series of predatory and violent crimes (for example, *China Times*, February 22, 1984, 1), and, as a result, law enforcement agencies raided the gang's apartments in Chinatown and Brooklyn.

The Fook Ching gang then attempted to establish its turf on East Broadway, one of the fastest growing commercial areas in Chinatown. However, the Tung On and the Flying Dragons were determined to keep the Fook Ching away from that lucrative street. The Tung On and the Dragons assaulted many Fook Ching members. The Fook Ching pressed on, however, and became active in Queens, Brooklyn, and Long Island (*Centre Daily News*, January 8, 1986, 20).

After the Golden Star incident (described in Chapter 3), the White Tigers became the dominant gang in the newly established Asian community in Flushing, Queens. Local police officers and community leaders indicate that most Chinese businesses in the area are extorted or robbed often by the gang (*China Daily News*, March 7, 1985, 20). Besides Queens, the northern area of Chinatown is also the scene of White Tigers activity. Of the gangs that do not have a base in Chinatown, the White Tigers are considered to have the best connections with criminal elements there, primarily because the gang was established by former Ghost Shadows members (U.S. District Court 1986).

The Tung On gang is a relatively new but rapidly growing Chinese gang. It was formed by former Ching Yee members and controls the new commercial areas on Division Street and East Broadway, the territory of the Tung On Association. In 1983, when the gang was rising, its members were in constant conflict with the Kam Lum, a gang also active on East Broadway (*China Times*, February 22, 1984, 1).

The notoriety of the Tung On reached its peak when two factions of the gang were involved in a shootout on their turf in May 1985. Seven people were wounded, including a four-year-old Chinese boy who was shot in the head as he walked along the street with his uncle (*New York Daily News*, May 22, 1985, 3). The gun battle marked the first time a child had been harmed by the gangs' reckless shooting. In April 1987, three Tung On members were ambushed while walking along East Broadway. In that incident, a six-year-old girl was struck in the back by a stray bullet (*Centre Daily News*, April 11, 1987, 20).

The Golden Star, formed by former Kam Lum members, has been constantly attempting to encroach on the Tung On's territory. In January 1988, a Golden Star member was shot execution-style while he was sitting inside his car (*World Journal*, January 17, 1988, 25). Later on, the gang became closely affiliated with Vietnamese youths active on Canal Street along Lafayette and Centre streets.

The Green Dragons, a Queens-based gang composed of former Fook Ching members, was responsible for killing two young Fook Ching members in January 1987. The two victims were kidnapped by twelve Green Dragons at a skating rink in Queens after the Fook Ching youths had a skirmish with girls who were associated with the Green Dragons. The two victims, aged fifteen and seventeen, were attacked by the gang outside the skating rink and brought to the Green Dragons apartment in Queens, where they were beaten again. Later, the victims were executed, and the bodies were dumped in a nearby river. The Green Dragon who pulled the trigger was a fourteen-year-old Korean youth (*New York Times*, June 28, 1987, 30).

As Chinese businessmen began to congregate in the Flushing, Elmhurst, and Jackson Heights areas of Queens, the extortion activity of the Green Dragons also increased. Since there are few gambling places in Queens to collect protection fees, the White Tigers and Green Dragons have to rely on extortion or robbery as their major sources of income. As a result, extortion or robbery-related violence has erupted often in Queens over the past two years. For example, a Green Dragon was shot to death by an employee of a restaurant that was extorted by the gang (*World Journal*, January 5, 1988, 20). A few days later, the restaurant was attacked by two gunmen. Fifteen months later, the owner of the restaurant was slain when someone fired several shots from outside (*Centre Daily News*, May 5, 1989, 21). In several other incidents, store owners or managers were being killed or shot at by young Chinese offenders (for example, *New York Daily News*, July 24, 1989, 15).

The Future: Legitimation?

The federal Racketeer Influenced and Corrupt Organizations (RICO) statute began to be used against Chinese gangs in 1985 with considerable success. In February of that year, twenty-five Ghost Shadows were indicted in federal court in New York City (*New York Daily News*, February 19, 1985, 3). Seventeen members were arrested during the initial raid, and two more were apprehended later (*Centre Daily News*, November 21, 1985, 20). Six are still at large and are believed to have fled the country. The arrested Shadows all pled guilty to most of the charges, and all received long prison terms. Some local law enforcement authorities in New York pointed out that although the Flying Dragons were responsible for most of the Chinatown gang violence and "have a history of violence that is much more savage than the others," the Ghost Shadows were targeted because law enforcement officials were not able to build a strong case against the Dragons (*New York Newsday*, February 20, 1985).

Seven months after the indictment of the Shadows, thirteen United Bamboo members were indicted by the federal court in Manhattan for major drug dealing, gambling, extortion, bribery, kidnapping, and murder for hire. Twelve of them were arrested in related actions in Texas, California, and Nevada (*New York Times*, September 17, 1985, A1). Bamboo members refused to plead guilty, and the case went to trial. Most defendants were found guilty by the jury and were sentenced to lengthy prison terms.

Notwithstanding these convictions, gang-related violence persists. Since 1985, besides the shootouts and killings on the streets of Chinatown, there has been an increase in homicide cases in which the victims were shot at close range in their offices or cars, or the victims were abducted and executed and their bodies were dumped in remote areas. Unlike the killings on the streets, these homicides have not been solved by the police.

Those Chinese gang members who were active in the early 1970s and who remained closely connected with their groups have become the leaders. They have also moved on, however, to operating legitimate businesses such as restaurants, entertainment companies, travel agencies, and nightclubs. They are also involved in money laundering, drug trafficking, prostitution, and racketeering. Through their connections with influential figures within the community and their new roles as successful businessmen, they have become "respectable" members of the community. Some have even become officers of tongs or other community associations. From these observations, we can predict that Chinese gangs will enter the "legitimation" stage soon. At that stage, gang members, especially gang leaders, will try to invest their illegal gains in legitimate businesses and transform themselves into successful businessmen and community leaders. They will totally dissociate themselves from predatory crimes and illegitimate businesses, leaving those activities to their young followers.

The comprehensive look at the development of Chinese gangs in this chapter indicates how they developed and evolved into criminal organizations. In the next chapter, we discuss why this evolution occurred, and in the following chapter we examine the specific criminal activities of the gangs in detail.

6

SOCIAL SOURCES OF CHINESE GANG DELINQUENCY

Social factors pertinent to the rise of Chinese gang delinquency can be categorized as causative and intervening. The causative factors are school problems, family problems, and the lack of employment opportunities. These causative factors, together with the isolation and disorganization of the Chinese communities, alienate immigrant youths from their communities and the larger society. Freed from both internal and external control, adolescents can easily drift into delinquency (Matza 1964). However, affiliation with and internalization of Triad norms and values are critical intervening factors. If a group of Chinese delinquents is not exposed to these subcultural norms and values, the group will not develop into the type of street gang that flourished in American Chinatowns.

Immigrant youths are called "transplanted children" (Sung 1979). They are uprooted from their childhood environments and transplanted to a completely different, perhaps antagonistic, society. Those who grow up in a secluded and fragmented Chinese community are likely to feel alienated from both the community and the society, and they thus have only school and family to count on for support. However, instead of functioning as bonding agencies, both school and family can be sources of frustration and disappointment for immigrant youths.

SCHOOL

Asian American students have achieved enormous success in the American school system (*Newsweek on Campus*, April 1984, 4-14; *New York Times*, January 30, 1986, 75; January 29, 1988, A35). Asian Americans constitute only 2 percent of the total population, but in 1986, five of the top ten candidates for the Westinghouse Award (an award to high school students for achievement in science) were Asians. Ten percent of the freshmen enrolled in Ivy League schools are Asian Americans, and about 25 percent of the students at the University of California at Berkeley are of Asian descent. A survey showed that Asian American high school students' average score on the Scholastic Aptitude Test is thirty-two points higher than the average score of white students (*World Journal*, May 19, 1988, 3). Thus, they have been labeled the "model minority."

Educators are amazed by the success stories of these students. What they overlook is that most of those Asian students who excel in school were born here or came to the United States before they were teenagers. Those who arrive here as teenagers are most likely to do poorly in school. Although the dropout rates for Asian American high school students in New York City in the class of 1987 was 12.7 percent (*New York Times*, June 21, 1988, A1), the lowest of all ethnic groups, those Asian students who do drop out are predominantly foreign-born, poor newcomers.

The chance for their children to acquire a good education is one of the most important motives for parents to bring their families to the United States. School systems in Hong Kong, Taiwan, and China are very competitive, and no more than one in four high school graduates is accepted into a college or university. When they come here, however, parents are convinced that their children will be admitted to a college.

But first their children have to get over the hurdle of the language barrier (Sung 1987). In order to learn the language, older students are forced to start in lower grades with much younger, native-born classmates. Such arrangements are demoralizing and humiliating for the newly arrived youths (*New York Times*, November 16, 1969). When they need help with school work, they cannot turn to their parents because the latter may not speak English at all. Some schools have developed special programs to teach English to foreign-born students, but these programs can help only those who speak either Cantonese or Mandarin. Students who understand neither are, in effect, excluded; some young immigrants who are of Hakka, Fujian, Chiu Chao, or other ethnic groups are not able to communicate in either Cantonese or Mandarin (*Centre Daily News*, March 21, 1986, 19).

Along with their language problem, young Chinese immigrants have problems socializing with other ethnic groups in schools. Their difficulties with English encourage other students to ridicule them. To make matters worse, American-born Chinese scorn the foreign-born for their inability or unwillingness to become assimilated into the culture, while the foreign-born, in turn, view the native-born as neither Chinese nor American (*New York Times*, December 1, 1976, B1).

A close examination of the emergence of Chinese gangs in San Francisco, Los Angeles, and New York City in the mid-1960s indicates that the gangs were formed in schools where racial tensions were high. Only at a later stage did the Chinese gangs begin to come into contact with adult groups, move their hangouts to the communities, and change their patterns of activity.

In short, going to school can be a frustrating experience for Chinese immigrants who find themselves unable to compete with younger students, belittled by other ethnic groups, and held in contempt by native-born Chinese. As a result, they tend to congregate with others who share their problems.

FAMILY

For Chinese, the family is the most important social unit. It provides members with a sense of identity and security, and it functions as the most powerful informal source of social control. Chinese may sometimes show little concern for their community or society, but they always have great respect for senior members of their immediate or extended families. In Chinese societies, the father is the authoritative figure and the role model; the mother has a domestic, subordinate role with primary responsibility for the children and household duties. When a child lacks discipline, the parents are usually the first to be blamed.

However, in its adjustment to the new environment of the United States, the Chinese family changed dramatically. For one thing, some Chinese immigrant families are not intact. They generally consist of only the father and several of the older children; the mother and younger children remain in Hong Kong because travel is prohibitively expensive for the entire family. Also, immigration visas for certain family members may take longer to be approved. The family may not be reunited for many years, and some families never are. According to a gang member, his family was dispersed after he, his father, and a brother immigrated to the United States:

> My father came to the United States first. About fifteen years ago, my big brother and I arrived here. My mother and a few brothers and sisters are still in Hong Kong. My father has been working as a kitchen helper for the past twenty years. My brother and I went to high school for a few years, and then both dropped out. We now live in a small one-bedroom apartment in Chinatown. My father sends money back to Hong Kong once in a while. I am not sure when my mother and the rest of the family are going to come; maybe they will never come. (From an interview conducted for this study, my translation)

Even when both parents are present, more often than not they both have to work. It is not uncommon for the father to work in a restaurant and the mother in a garment factory. Both may work ten hours a day, six days a week. When the youngsters encounter problems, they are unable to get help from their harried parents (K. Chin, Lai, and Rouse 1990). Sung (1979) found that 32 percent of the Chinese high school students she interviewed did not see their fathers from one day to the next, and 17 percent did not see their mothers from one week to the next. She also discovered that fathers who held professional positions in their homelands could not find similar employment after immigration, and a substantial number of them resorted to working in restaurants because they lacked proficiency in English. The downward mobility of the fathers not only lessened their status in the eyes of their families but also left the youngsters without good role models. Some immigrant families are virtually led by their bilingual children because the parents are unable to communicate with people outside the community.

Not only are parents incapable of disciplining their children because they have to work hard and lack the language proficiency to help their children with schoolwork, but they are also uncertain how to raise their children in a new environment where child-rearing practices are vastly different from those of their homeland. Most immigrant parents tend to discipline their children harshly and expect them to be quiet and family-oriented. Parents are normally shocked and dismayed over their children's demand for autonomy in making decisions as to how they should dress, behave, and socialize. As a result, the relationship between parent and child in the immigrant families are often filled with uneasiness and conflicts.

In Chinese societies, when a family is in need of emotional or financial help, it normally turns to extended family members. The Chinese are reluctant to talk about their personal or family problems to people who are not related by blood. "Never reveal your family problems to an outsider" is a rule that is strongly upheld. As a result, social service providers play a minimal role in family crisis intervention. Extended families form a network in which a family is well protected and supported. However, when a Chinese family immigrates to the United States, it is cut off from its extended families. When parents are unable to provide emotional or financial support to the children, the children have no other family members to turn to. When the children are in trouble, parents have no relatives from whom they can obtain help.

A final source of stress for Chinese families is the shortage of adequate housing. As we have mentioned, families are often crowded in one- or two-bedroom apartments that have no living rooms or kitchens. Congestion within the household may drive adolescents to the streets (R. Chin 1971).

OPPORTUNITY STRUCTURE

Chinese teenagers who drop out of school, like other minority dropouts in the United States, have few opportunities for employment. Even if they are willing to do menial work, their language problem is a major block to finding jobs within the mainstream society. They must look for work in the Chinese community, where most jobs do not require any knowledge of English. However, the most likely positions for young Chinese without an education, technical skills, or work experience are unskilled ones as waiters, kitchen helpers, or cooks. These jobs not only pay poorly, but also require long hours of work under appalling conditions.

Chinese employers, knowing that newcomers are ill equipped to seek jobs outside the community, take advantage of them. Employers within the Chinese communities normally provide no benefits—no insurance, sick leave, overtime pay, or vacations. Restaurant workers often work almost all year long, getting only one day a week off without pay. Turnover rates are high for restaurant workers; immigrants circulate from restaurant to restaurant, never knowing how long their present jobs might last. Young immigrants nowadays are reluctant to work in Chinese-owned restaurants and thus have no legitimate career to pursue.

CRIMINAL ROLE MODELS

When young immigrants fall behind in school or suffer ridicule from native-born students, they drop out. And when they cannot bring their problems to their parents because the parents either are working long hours or are themselves poorly educated, young dropouts seek support and understanding from peers with similar problems. Finding comfort with them, they hang around coffee shops or arcade stores within the community. Or they may start hanging around the gambling clubs to run errands for the house and the gamblers. Their association with the adult groups is a crucial turning point for them; they are transformed from detached and alienated delinquents to paraprofessional criminals. For a loosely knit group of street-smart youths to develop into a street gang, the association they are affiliated with has to be a Triad-influenced tong organization. Without the transmission of Triad norms and values to the youth group by core tong members, and a tong territory in which the youth group can flourish, the delinquents will remain simply a group of marginally connected criminals, as is the case with many youth groups that hang around the gambling establishments of family and district associations. Although there are many such youth groups in Chinatown, they have never developed into street gangs.

As we have noted previously, most adult organizations in the Chinese community have their own gambling parlors. To function properly, a gambling parlor needs young people to run errands, maintain order, and protect the club from outsiders. As a result, gambling dens have many wayward youths hanging around most of the time. Members of the traditional adult associations, especially core members of the tongs, can identify with the alienated youths because they themselves have a strong feeling of being victims of prejudice by their own community and society. Thus, the tong elders and street-corner youths have more in common: alienation from the progressive community organizations and American society, and a history of being feared by law-abiding Chinatown residents.

As far as tong elders are concerned, hiring the alienated youths to work in the gambling establishments is a way to prevent them from becoming involved in predatory crimes within the community. Not only are the youths being saved, but the community is being spared the youths' depredations. According to a community leader,

> Why tongs are willing to be affiliated with gangs? Because if a tong decides to expel all gang members from the association, they are not going to disappear. Other tongs would have recruited them anyway. In this case, a tong without a gang will be overpowered by the rival tongs. The gangs are in a sense the "nuclear weapon" of the tongs. They help maintain a balance of power among the community adult organizations. No organization could strike the other party without fear of being retaliated. (From an interview conducted for this study, my translation)

However, the relationship between tong elders and the youths is not purely an employer-employee relationship. In order to solidify the youth groups' connections to the tongs, leaders of the youth groups are recruited into the tongs through a Triad initiating ceremony. This way, tong officials can control the gang kids through the gang leaders who are also tong officials. As tong officials, gang leaders then initiate their followers into the tongs. As a result, the relationship between tongs and gangs becomes indistinguishable because of the gang leaders and members' dual membership. Members of the tongs and the gangs become "brothers" of one big "Triad family." In other words, Chinese gangs are linked to the tongs in subtle ways. The gang leaders serve as middlemen between the tong elders and the street soldiers. For this service, they receive from the tong money that they distribute to their members. In addition, the leaders relay the elders' messages to other members.

Some tong leaders never make direct contact with the leaders of the gang. Instead, the tong's youth activity coordinator acts as middleman between them and the gang. Usually, the youth coordinator is also in charge of the tong's gambling activity. The tong may also have another youth coordinator to sponsor the organization's basketball and soccer programs for young tong members. Other tong leaders, however, flaunt their links with the gangs and are not secretive about their close affiliations with gang members.

Law enforcement authorities are convinced that the Chinese street gangs function as the enforcers of the adult Chinese organizations. A former detective suggests that the tongs use the gangs in specific ways. First, if the tong has a problem with someone, it uses its gang members to intimidate the other party. Second, the tong uses the gang members to collect debts. Third, tong members who are shareholders of the gambling dens hire the youths to protect the dens from outsiders.

Apart from regular financial compensation for gang members, tongs in New York City are also alleged to be instrumental in helping fugitive members to flee the city and resettle in other places where the tong has chapters. Most fugitive Ghost Shadows seek refuge from arrest in Chicago, Boston, and Houston, while members of the Flying Dragons go to Washington, D.C., and Atlanta. Police theorize that the elusiveness of gang members strongly indicates tong involvement in the relocation of "hot" members.

From the gang members' perspective, tong elders are the only people in the community to turn to for jobs. In addition, the gambling dens are the only places for them to earn money. Gang leaders revealed the importance of the gambling establishments for their survival. In a 1977 interview, gang leaders revealed their feelings about being employed by the gambling clubs.

> We hope the community can create jobs for us. If we are employed, we won't be committing crime. Many people blame the gambling places [for hiring kids as guards], but we think the places at least offer us a job. If all gambling dens shut down, a lot of us are going to loose our jobs. (*China Tribune*, May 19, 1977, 1; my translation)

The following is a true story of a young immigrant who was hired by a gambling parlor and later initiated into a gang. The teenager arrived in the United States alone. He worked as a store clerk in his uncle's grocery store, and was upset with his job that paid very little but required long hours of hard work. He was also disappointed with the poor living conditions. One day, while he was sitting in a park thinking about his unfortunate circumstances, he met a friend who was a gang member. With his friend's recommendation, he found a job with a gambling club. All he had to do was to stand in front of the club and make sure that only regular gamblers were admitted. His new job paid three times better than his old one.

A few months later, he subdued a rowdy gambler who was creating a scene inside the gambling den. A few days after the incident, the friend who introduced him to the job accompanied him to meet a man in his mid-thirties. Also present were several other gang members. The man, who appeared to be the mentor of the gang and the operator of the gambling place, praised him for his courage and martial arts skills. The man announced that he was promoted as a "Third Brother," a person who is in charge of the street kids. He will no longer need to guard the place. He then went on to become a core member of the gang and was involved in extortion and street violence (*World Journal*, March 28, 1977).

However, the good intentions of the tong elders often backfire. With the moral and financial support of the tongs, the gangs grow into powerful criminal organizations, and once that happens, tong elders lose control of the gangs. Without the sanction or knowledge of the tong elders, gang members begin to extort money from businesses, rob business and gambling establishments, and become involved in street violence. Even some of the tong elders are brutalized by the gangs. Nevertheless, tong elders continue to initiate gang leaders into their organizations, associate themselves with gang members, let gang members guard their gambling establishments, and allow the gangs to hang around their organizations. Thus, the gangs exist because the tongs not only initiate the groups but also sanction their existence. It would difficult, if not impossible, for the gangs to develop as cohesive units if the tongs decided to withhold their support.

According to Cloward and Ohlin (1960), the development of a criminal subculture in a community needs two types of environmental supports. First, there needs to be an integration of offenders at various age levels. Second, there should be an integration of carriers of conventional and illegitimate values. From what we have discussed above, it is clear that within the Chinese communities where criminal gangs flourish, there is an integration of offenders at various age levels. Teenage gang members follow their gang leaders who are in their late twenties or early thirties, and the leaders in turn are closely associated with certain tong members whose age could range from mid-forties to late seventies. Furthermore, a small number of Chinese community leaders are the carriers of conventional and illegitimate values. These high-profile leaders, viewed by community residents as representatives, speak for the community, symbolize the community's political orientation, and appear in the community media almost on a daily basis. However, these are the same people who act as mentors of the gang members, drug traffickers, and providers of illegal services such as gambling and alien smuggling.

A CAUSAL MODEL OF CHINESE GANG DELINQUENCY

Sociologists such as Sellin (1938), Sutherland (1947), Cohen (1955), Miller (1958), and Wolfgang and Ferracuti (1982) have stressed the importance of learning and internalizing subcultural norms and values in the process of becoming deviant. When a person is associated with and internalizes subcultural norms and values that are at odds with those of the dominant culture, that person will become a deviant.

Contact with Triad subcultural norms, however, is not the only reason for gang delinquency among the Chinese. Thrasher (1927) and Shaw and McKay (1942) proposed that the most important cause of gang delinquency is social or community disorganization (Kornhauser 1978). Hirschi (1969) further theorized that social disorganization leads to loss of control of the youths by family, school, and other social institutions. As a result, young adolescents without any social bonds and commitments are free to become involved in delinquency.

My contention is that although social disorganization plays an important role in delinquency among Chinese adolescents, becoming a gang member invariably involves learning and internalizing Triad norms and values, transmitted by the tongs. Thus, if a Chinese boy is freed from social bonds, he may become a delinquent. However, for him to become a gang member, he has to come into contact with the values and norms of the Triads. Based upon the discussions on Chapter 4 and this chapter, Figure 8 illustrates a causal model of Chinese gang delinquency. Thus we can see that the structure of Chinese communities has contributed significantly to the development of street gangs. In the next chapter we will come to understand how the nature of Chinese communities also determines the kinds of activities street gangs become involved in.

Figure 8
Social Disorganization and Triad Subculture as Causes of Gang Delinquency

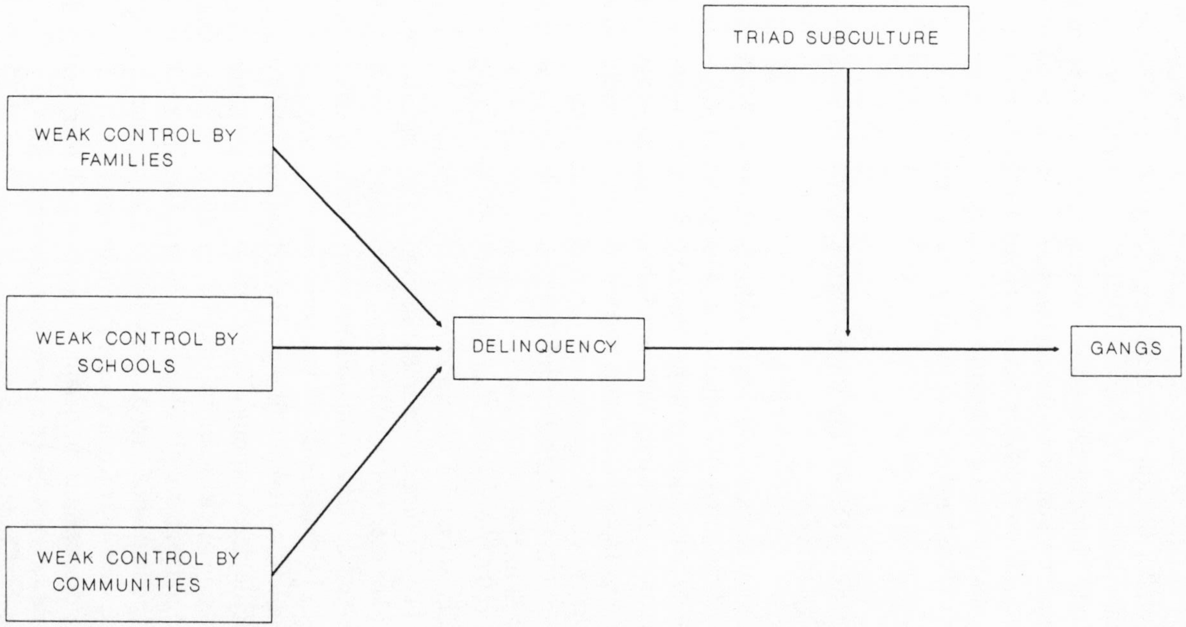

TRIAD SUBCULTURE

WEAK CONTROL BY FAMILIES

WEAK CONTROL BY SCHOOLS

WEAK CONTROL BY COMMUNITIES

DELINQUENCY

GANGS

7

CRIMINAL PATTERNS OF CHINESE GANGS

Once Chinese street gangs develop into institutionalized criminal organizations, they become involved in certain standard activities, which they carry out in predictable ways. For Chinese gang members, ganging is simply a way of *win saik*, meaning making a living. Thus, gang activities are primarily utilitarian ones such as protection, extortion, robbery, prostitution, and drug trafficking.

PROTECTION AND EXTORTION

The booming economy and the gambling industry in the Chinese communities have provided Chinese gangs with ample criminal opportunities. There are many businesses to be extorted, as well as considerable numbers of gambling houses that need protection. Thus, protection and extortion are the most prevalent crimes in the Chinese communities (Allen and Thomas 1987).

Of the businesses in the community, gambling clubs need the gangs' protection the most. In order to operate smoothly, the clubs must rely on gang members to protect the clubs and its customers from the police, intruders, and the gangs themselves. The task of guarding gambling establishments includes the following responsibilities:

1. If law enforcement officials raid the gambling den, gang members alert the operators as quickly as possible.
2. They ensure that only regular gamblers are admitted.
3. They maintain order inside the club.

4. They prevent invasions by rival gangs. If the den is robbed, they take certain retaliative actions.
5. They run errands for gamblers (buying food and drinks) and accompany the winners back to their homes.

To perform these jobs, a few members are dispersed in the streets where the gambling place is located. Three or four members guard the entrance, while some stay inside. Street leaders in the gang's nearby apartments oversee the entire operation. Members carry beepers to communicate with one another.

Despite protection of gambling places by the gangs, they are by no means tightly guarded. Police from the Public Morals Division often strike the houses (for example, *New York Post*, September 17, 1986, 13), and robberies by rival gangs are not uncommon (for example, *Centre Daily News*, June 18, 1985, 20). Sometimes, a club is shaken down by the very gang that guards it.

Other types of operations that require protection are the nightclubs and massage parlors (actually prostitution houses) owned by Asians and catering to Asian patrons. These businesses need gang members to protect them from members of other gangs.

Gangs supplement their primary activity of guarding gambling dens and adjacent streets with another criminal activity: systematic extortion of Chinese businesses. Police estimate that at least 80 to 90 percent of Asian businesses have to pay one or more gangs regularly or occasionally. Only those merchants who are close to the hierarchy of the tongs are said to be able to avoid paying the gangs.

Techniques of Extortion

The extortion techniques that gangs employ vary. According to police officers, prosecutors, and victims interviewed by the author, there are two major forms. First, gang members will explicitly demand money. Normally, gang members approach a new business during its opening ceremony and ask for *li shi* ("lucky money"). After the owner pays, they show up again later and tell the owner who they are, how the racket works, and that it is going to be easier to pay than to refuse. On some other occasions, gang members will tell the owners that they need money for food, or to help their "brothers" who have been arrested. There are times when gang members will ask businessmen to "invest" in their business or give them a "loan."

Second, money is not asked for but expected. For example, the gang members will try to sell festival-related goods such as firecrackers or plants to business establishments for an inflated price. Sometimes, gang members may simply tell the store owners that protection from the gang is provided to their businesses.

In order to carry out the crime, gangs employ several common practices. First, a group of youths may enter a restaurant during lunch or dinner time, and each of them occupies a table. They tell the manager that they are waiting for friends. They sit for hours, and their rowdiness is meant to intimidate customers. Otherwise, they may fight with each other, smash the dishes, or insist on remaining in the store after closing hours. An experienced manager knows what the disruptive youths want.

Second, young men may go into a restaurant and order the finest dishes on the menu. When they leave, they write "Shadows" or "Dragons" on the back of the bill and do not pay.

Third, some gang members dine in a restaurant but refuse to pay the bill. While they argue with the manager about it, two or three fellow members walk in and pretend to be customers. They appear to be sympathetic to the manager and chastise the youths who refuse to pay. When the "show" is over, a gang member calls up the manager, demands protection money, and tells the manager that if similar incidents happen in the future, his gang will protect the restaurant. This technique is known as *hei bai lian* (literally, black and white faces), meaning that while members play the role of the "bad guys," leaders will act as the "good guys" who ask money from the frightened victim.

The fourth method is called *tai jiau tsi* (literally, "carrying a sedan chair"). Gang members will try to flatter a potential victim by calling him "Big Brother" and act as though they are his loyal followers. If the businessman is unaware of the gang's tactic and associates himself with the gang, he may find out that it is too late for him to get rid of the label "Big Brother." As a "Big Brother," the victim has no other real benefits except to provide financial support to the gang.

The fifth approach is known as *wo di* (literally, "undercover"). A gang member will infiltrate a business by seeking a job there. During his tenure, he will collect information regarding who the owner is, where he lives, when the business will accumulate the maximum amount of cash, and other matters. The gang member will provide the information to his associates to draw up an extortion or robbery plan.

In order to deter owners from reporting extortion to the police, gang members may offer an IOU slip to the proprietor after receiving protection money. And they never take money from the cash register themselves to avoid being indicted for a predatory crime.

Most of the time, the owners negotiate about the amount of payment, but they do not bicker about whether they are going to pay. When the gang gets a victim paying, a schedule is arranged: several hundred dollars monthly for large stores; less than a hundred dollars per week for modest businesses. In order to signify their Triad background, gang members sometimes demand the amount of money that is associated with Triad oaths and legend.

> Because of the Triad mystique and intimidation factor, many of the gangs use certain symbols in the perpetration of crimes in order to accentuate the terror factor in the victim and community and to suppress resistance or subsequent testimony. For example, the amount demanded as a ransom payment in a kidnapping plot may be some denomination which includes the integers 3, 6 or 1, 0, 8. These numbers are highly significant in Triad lore since they represent the thirty-six sacred oaths of one secret society and the 108 monks of the Shaolin monastery who founded the movement. (U.S. Department of Justice, 1985, 20)

The gang usually has designated collectors and keeps records of its income from extortion.

When retail businesses refuse to pay, gangs may vandalize, burglarize, rob, or set fire to their shops. The owner then usually relents and cooperates. In some instances, gangs have beaten, shot at, or killed business and retail store owners. For those who do pay, the amount demanded by crime groups escalates rapidly, or another gang will show up soon with the same demand. When businesses are no longer able to meet the gangs' demands, they either close down, move to another area, or report the crime to the police. Usually, most business owners try to satisfy the gang by paying them the first few times. Only when they find out that they have to pay more than one gang or that their payments increase rapidly will they turn to law enforcement authorities for help.

Types of Extortion

Extortion in the Chinese communities may be classified into four types. The first and most prevalent type is monetary extortion, in which monetary gain is an end in itself. The offender and victim may not know each other prior to the incident, and the offender may carry out the extortionate act without the conspiracy of another party or the knowledge of the tong they belong to. Regardless of how the victim reacts to the offender's demand, he or she is unlikely to be physically assaulted by the offender in this type of extortion.

The second type is symbolic extortion, which is used as a display of power to indicate control over a territory. Monetary gain is not the major goal; gang members usually demand only free food or other small items such as cigarettes. Otherwise, they ask for heavy discounts from restaurant owners. These types of extortion occur almost on a daily basis and the victims are normally small business owners or peddlers who do business in the core area of a tightly controlled gang territory.

The third type is revengeful extortion. Offenders extort the victims because of something the victim did to the gang previously, or the gang is hired by the victim's adversary to extort the victim as a form of revenge. Because monetary gain is not the motivating factor, victims are likely to be robbed, beaten up, or killed even if they do not resist the perpetrators. Extortion is used simply as a cover for revenge.

The fourth type is instrumental extortion, which is used to intimidate the victim into backing down in certain business or personal conflicts. In this type of extortion, the victims are also vulnerable to assault and harassment. The extortionate act is, more than anything else, a message sent to the victim by his rival through the gang members. Gang members may rob or extort money from the victims for their own sakes. Conflicts pertaining to business territories and business or gambling debts usually result in instrumental extortion activity.

Extortion and Territory

Through extortion, the gangs assert their firm control over certain territories. For example, under the firm control of the Ghost Shadows on Mott and Bayard streets, merchants have to be concerned only with the Shadows. Likewise, business owners on Pell and Doyers streets are unlikely to be approached by gang members who do not belong to the Flying Dragons. Figure 9 illustrates the territory of the Chinese gangs in New York City's Chinatown.

When two or more gangs claim control of a specific area, or when the area is occupied by a weaker gang, store owners within that territory have to pay more than one gang (*World Journal*, October 23, 1985, 16). As of now, Canal Street and East Broadway, the rapidly expanding streets of Chinatown, have no single powerful gang that can claim exclusive sovereignty. Consequently, some of the store owners in those areas have to pay

Figure 9
Territory of the Gangs in New York City's Chinatown

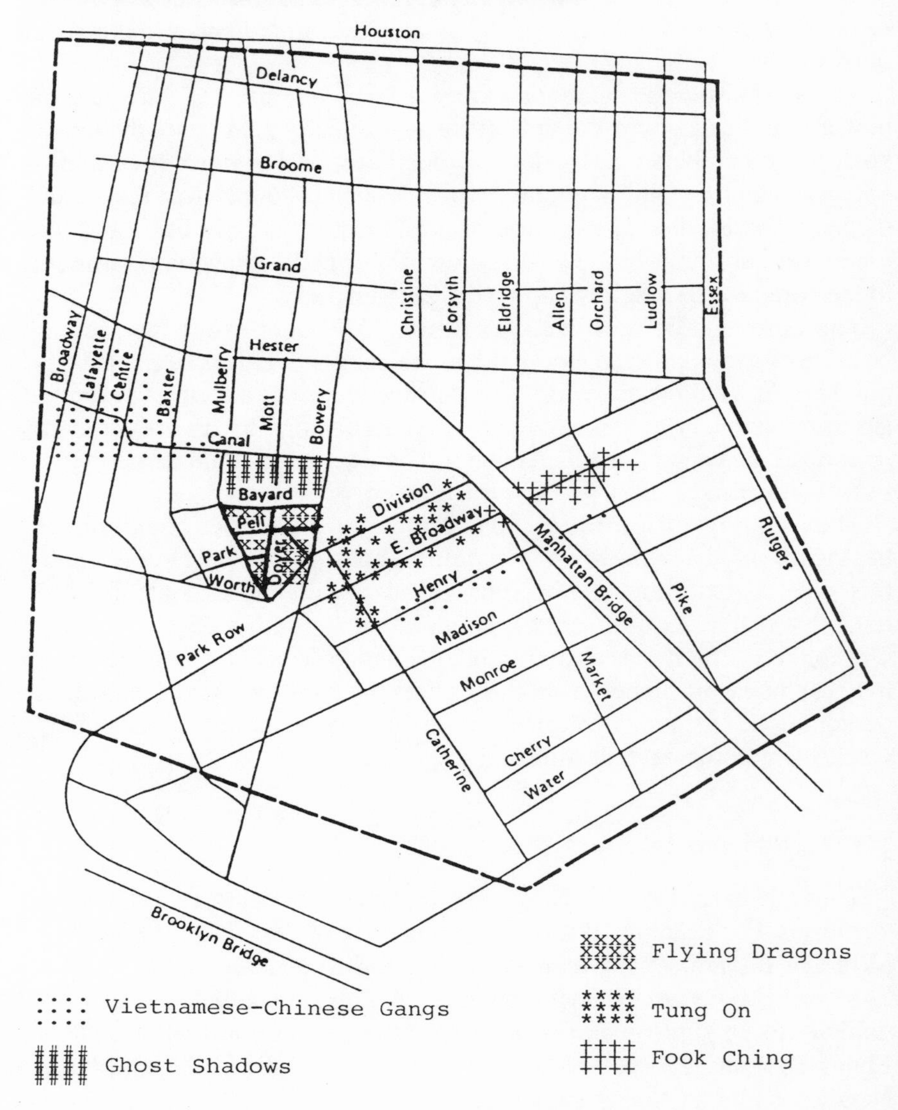

as many as five gangs simultaneously (*World Journal*, October 23, 1985, 16).

The same is true for the Chinese communities in Queens and Brooklyn. Although the White Tigers, the Green Dragons, and a Taiwanese gang are the three most active gangs in these newly established communities, more powerful gangs from Manhattan's Chinatown occasionally invade the area to commit extortion. When two or more gangs are active in a particular area and attempt to extort from the same victim simultaneously, street violence erupts as a result of the power struggle.

Before 1980, most extortion activities were confined to Manhattan's Chinatown. Only occasionally would gang members venture outside Chinatown to extort money from Asian business owners in lower or upper Manhattan. However, beginning in 1980, the gangs rapidly spread their extortion activities to other parts of Manhattan, Queens, Brooklyn, Long Island, New Jersey, and Connecticut. Unlike extortion activities within New York City that are mostly spontaneous and cost the victims fairly small amounts of money, out-of-state extortion is well planned, and gang members tend to demand a rather large amount. For instance, a New Jersey Chinese businessman was forced to pay $36,000 by a group of Fook Ching members (*Centre Daily News*, August 16, 1985, 20).

Since 1984, Chinese businessmen in Queens and Brooklyn have been frequently extorted by Chinese gang members. Unlike gangs in Manhattan's Chinatown, gangs there have no protection money to collect from gambling establishments. As a result, the only likely source of funds is extorting or robbing stores in the community. The lack of knowledge about the gangs by local precincts also contributes to the rapid increase in extortion. In addition, business owners in Queens and Brooklyn are not protected by tongs or other traditional organizations as are business owners in Manhattan's Chinatown.

ROBBERY

Robbery is another type of predatory crime often committed by Chinese gang members. Unlike protection and extortion activities that are sanctioned by the gang as a group, robberies are committed by members independently of their gang.

Gambling places in Chinatown are often robbed by a bunch of criminals. Few victims in any of these cases are willing to report the incident to the police. Because most gamblers carry a considerable amount of cash with them, a successful robbery will normally net several thousand dollars.

Gang members invariably choose the hours between midnight and dawn for robberies because this is the time of peak activity at high-stake gambling clubs. Gang members sneak into the club as gamblers. If they learn that the street thugs guarding the establishment are not around, they pull out their weapons and announce a robbery. Should the gamblers be slow in reacting to the robbers' demands, they are ruthlessly pistol-whipped. The robbers not only take all the cash on the tables but also frisk everybody for additional money and jewelry. Some of the smaller gambling houses are not protected by gangs, which makes them more vulnerable than the high-stake gambling places. However, these types of gambling places rarely attract the attention of perpetrators because there is not much money to be gained.

Jewelry stores in the community are the next most popular targets. Most jewelry stores in Chinatown are equipped with security doors and are tightly guarded, but well-dressed youths are able to gain entry as customers.

Since the mid-1970s, Chinese restaurants have been robbed frequently by young gunmen. Because these restaurants accept only cash, they have substantial amounts on hand at all times. Robbers usually carry out their actions just when the restaurants are about to close and when they have the most cash (*World Journal*, December 8, 1984, 20).

As mentioned above, some robberies occur because the owner refuses to pay protection money to the gangs. Sometimes robbery is an inevitable result of a prolonged extortion history. Gang members who regularly extort a particular victim may just decide to rob the victim in expectation of gaining a huge sum of money.

Moviegoers are also victimized by robbers inside Chinatown theaters. Indeed, these robberies have occurred so often that only a handful of young people are now willing to patronize these theaters.

As more and more Chinese- or Korean-owned massage parlors opened in Manhattan and Queens in the 1980s, New York Chinese gangs turned their attention to these businesses. In 1985 alone, masked Chinese gunmen robbed several massage parlors and in some instances wounded or killed the operators or the guards (*World Journal*, July 29, 1985, 1).

According to Triad codes, extorting and robbing acquisitive businesses is a way to redistribute wealth in an unjust society. Gang members thus tend to exploit businesses whenever there is an opportunity.

PROSTITUTION

Prostitution has long been one of the illegal enterprises of Chinese criminals, especially during the period between 1880 and 1924. At that time, Chinatowns were municipal vice centers frequented by both white and Chinese patrons. When the demand by white patrons for commercial sex diminished, the vice industry was replaced by the tourist trade (Light 1974).

However, since the 1970s, the influx of unattached Chinese immigrants and Vietnamese refugees caused the demand for Asian prostitutes to rise significantly. At first, this need was met by Korean women who worked as prostitutes in the massage parlors managed and owned by Koreans. However, since the patrons are mainly Chinese, they became increasingly active in the prostitution business. In 1985 there were at least twenty massage parlors in New York City, and new parlors are appearing in other cities with large Chinese populations. In Texas, Asian prostitutes are active in the so-called modeling studios (*China Times Weekly*, May 12, 1985, 65-67; *World Journal*, March 20, 1989, 24). Besides the massage parlors, there are also many nightclubs operated by Chinese and Koreans where commercial sex is available in a more subtle way. The nightclubs hire young Asian women as bar girls to drink or dance with the customers. If the customers want to take the girls out, they can do so after business hours.

Although women who work in massage parlors are still predominantly Korean (*China Daily News*, June 23, 1989, 10), women from Taiwan are being imported to work in them as well. Management arranges with travel agents in Taiwan to find women willing to work as prostitutes. They give the women visas and air tickets and $7,500 to $12,500 as a bonus for signing a contract to work for one year in the United States. The women come into the country with tourist visas that enable them to stay for six months, with an option to extend them for another six months. Once they arrive, management withholds all their travel documents.

There are two regular routes of the movement of the prostitutes. First, they arrive in Houston from Mexico, then fly to California, Seattle, Vancouver, Chicago, New York, Philadelphia, Washington, D.C., Virginia, and Montreal. The second route starts in Montreal and then goes through Toronto, Chicago, New York, Philadelphia, Washington, D.C., Houston, Dallas, Los Angeles, San Francisco, Seattle, and Vancouver. In order to provide customers with new faces year round, the girls are rotated often. They stay in a massage parlor for just a few weeks and then leave for the next designated city. Depending on the individual, the girls have to pay the house 30, 40, or 50 percent of whatever they get from the customers. In turn, the house provides lodging and food to the girls for free.

The extent of Chinese gang involvement in the operation of prostitution rings is not clear. However, one murder case illustrates that some of the gangs are at least providing protection for the massage parlors. In September 1985, police found the burned body of a young Vietnamese Chinese on Long Island. The victim was shot in the head execution-style, and his body was burned before being dumped. Investigators believed that the twenty three-year-old victim had been executed by Chinese gang members when he and his partners were in the process of robbing a massage parlor (*Centre Daily News*, October 12, 1985, 20). Police have suspected that some tong members also invest in and manage these illicit businesses. However, when police penetrated a few prostitution rings and arrested several people who managed the parlors and were responsible for importing women from abroad, they found that none of the offenders was associated with the gangs or tongs (*Centre Daily News*, December 22, 1988, 18).

DRUG TRAFFICKING

Before 1980, Chinese in the United States were importing only small quantities of heroin. After 1983, the amount of Southeast Asian heroin (China White) in the United States increased dramatically. Law enforcement officials estimated that Chinese crime groups were responsible for about 20 percent of the heroin imported into this country (President's Commission on Organized Crime 1984b), and 40 percent of the heroin in New York City was found to be of Southeast Asian origin. Chinese involvement in heroin trafficking continued to increase rapidly in 1986 and 1987 (*World Journal*, January 6, 1988, 36). In 1987 alone, law enforcement authorities solved more than twenty major drug trafficking cases involving the Chinese, and they seized two hundred kilograms of high-quality heroin.

There were indications that Chinese gang leaders were beginning to be involved in the heroin trade. For examples, a twenty-two-year-old Ghost Shadow member and his girlfriend were executed in their apartment in July 1987. The couple was suspected of being major heroin traffickers, and the killings were believed to be the result of their mishandling of the drug (*New York Newsday*, September 29, 1987, 7). Paul Ma, the former leader of the now extinct Black Eagles, is believed to be a major heroin importer in the New York area. Police have charged that he is using his occupation in a nightclub in downtown Manhattan as a front for his heroin business (*Centre Daily News*, May 4, 1988, 24). David Tong, shot to death gangland-style, was a major cocaine trafficker in the San Francisco area. Tong was a former leader of the Wah Ching. Although Tong was only twenty-five years old when he was killed, he had been active in the Chinese underworld for more than ten years. In order to stay ahead of his competitors, Tong marked down the price of his drug well below the market price, and his unorthodox way of marketing offended his rival dealers (*World Journal*, November 4, 1987, 3).

The arrest of gang leaders for heroin trafficking began in 1987. Paul Tang, forty, nicknamed Dice, was arrested for selling several pounds of heroin to undercover drug agents. Tang was closely associated with the

On Leong and was implicated in the shooting of dissident Ghost Shadows members from the balcony of the Chicago On Leong (*World Journal*, November 13, 1987, 24; *New York Newsday*, February 14, 1988a, 5). He had been the mentor of the Ghost Shadows for many years.

The first arrest of an active gang leader for heroin trafficking occurred in March 1988. Michael Yu, nicknamed Fox, the second highest leader of the Flying Dragons, was arrested along with thirty-nine young men and women for importing 100 pounds of heroin. None of the others arrested are members of the Flying Dragons. Most of them are young female immigrants from China (*Centre Daily News*, March 5, 1988, 24). The heroin, sent from Hong Kong in packages via the postal service, arrived in New York through Oakland, California, and the women who received the packages turned them over to the gang leader. The women were paid $8,000 to $10,000 per package.

A year later, Johnny Eng, nicknamed Machine Gun Johnny, the thirty-four-year-old highest leader of the Flying Dragons, was arrested in Hong Kong for heroin smuggling. Drug enforcement authorities in New York also indicted him for two major drug-related crimes. The first case has to do with the importation of approximately 160 pounds of heroin into the United States, hidden in Chinese tea boxes and mixed with Chinese herbal medicine to dilute the smell of the drug. In the second case, the gang leader was charged for the seizure of 180 pounds of heroin in Boston by authorities. This time, the drug was concealed inside a bean sprout washer (*World Journal*, August 26, 1989, 28).

Besides the leaders of the Ghost Shadows and the Flying Dragons, a leader of the Tung On gang was also taken into custody for heroin trafficking. The gang leader, Stephen Wong, nicknamed Tiger Boy, whose brother Clifford Wong is the leader of the Tung On Association, was accused of operating a heroin smuggling ring that had close ties to traffickers in Hong Kong (*New York Newsday*, June 2, 1989, 6).

In addition to the leaders of the three most powerful gangs, the Fook Ching gang as an organization is also active in the heroin trade. The gang is believed to have good connections with heroin producers and dealers in Southeast Asia (*Centre Daily News*, April 13, 1989, 24).

It is clear that only recently gang leaders have started to play an important role in the heroin business. They tend to hire people who are not part of the gang to work for them. They traveled frequently between the United States and Hong Kong, establishing their networks with drug producers and dealers in Southeast Asia. It is not clear, however, what role certain core tong members and gang members play in the gang leaders' drug businesses. Drug enforcement authorities assume that gang leaders' involvement in heroin trafficking probably has little to do with their gangs.

GANG VIOLENCE

Prior to the Chinese involvement in large-scale heroin trafficking, violence within the Chinese community was generally a manifestation of intergang and intragang tensions. Gang fights are reckless, vicious, and fatal, a result of the gangs' possession of powerful handguns. Since many gang shootouts occurred in the crowded streets or restaurants of Chinatowns, innocent bystanders have been shot at or killed.

Intergang Violence

There are many pretexts for intergang violence. Some fights escalate from simple disputes between two gangs in public places. Since gang members normally carry guns with them, any altercation could result in a wild shoot-out. Since the early 1970s, many gang members were being killed in parties, bowling alleys, billiard halls, restaurants, and nightclubs where rival gang members normally come to encounter each other (for example, *China Daily News*, October 13, 1987, 16). In some instances, fighting over a public phone or a billiard table has triggered a bloody shootout. In these incidents, more often than not, innocent bystanders have been hurt or killed by stray bullets.

Some shootings occur because gang members enter a gang territory without notifying the gang that controls it. It is alleged that if gang members want to watch movie in the territory of another gang, they must let the other party know in advance as a courtesy. It is not uncommon that gang members have been killed in the dark while watching movies in Chinatown theaters. Territory-related violence also occurred on the streets. There are certain areas in Chinatown that border two gang territories. As a result, these areas have experienced the most street violence in the past. For example, the intersection of Mott Street (claimed by the Ghost Shadows) and Pell Street (maintained by the Flying Dragons) has been the spot where Shadows and Dragons are often involved in reckless shootings (for example, *World Journal*, December 27, 1986, 24). Since the Vietnamese Chinese established their territory along Canal Street three years ago, the street had become the war zone between the Vietnamese and Chinese gangs. The Flying Dragons and the Tung On are most likely to come into conflict along East Broadway and Bowery Street where the domains of the gangs overlap (*Centre Daily News*, November 9, 1987, 24).

When two or more gangs try to control a certain block, gang fights are likely to take place in that area. So far, no particular gang is in complete control of the lucrative areas along Canal Street, East Broadway, Henry Street, and the outskirts of Chinatown. As a result, intergang violence has erupted in these areas as well.

Unlike Chinatown where many street gangs and adult associations are deeply entrenched and most streets already belong to a youth or adult group, Chinese communities in Queens and Brooklyn are not completely controlled by any particular group because the areas are spread out and still in their developing stage. These factors, coupled with the fact that young kids there are not supervised by any adult group, make these areas extremely prone to intergang violence. Within the past several years, we have observed that intergang violence had spread to these emerging communities from Manhattan's Chinatown. In Queens and Brooklyn, many young Chinese congregate in bowling alleys, billiard halls, skating rinks, nightclubs, or restaurants on weekend nights. These public places are the most likely battlegrounds for Chinese gangs in these two boroughs.

According to a district attorney who specializes in prosecuting Chinese street gangs, intergang violence ranges from well-planned assassinations to spontaneous street battles. In a few cases, gangs have carefully planned a hit and have succeeded. Most intergang shootings, however, are planned but accidental. Gang A, for example, happens to get word that Gang B members are eating at a restaurant, and the leaders of Gang A send younger members to try to shoot Gang B members there. The leaders are never present when the shooting happens. They stay at the gang's apartment waiting to hear the outcome. Some incidents are completely accidental; younger members of groups that are at war happen to run into each other and they start shooting. In some situations, such as dances and movies, gang members know that they might run into each other, so they all carry guns.

Not all intergang conflict results in street violence. More often than not, rival gangs do try to negotiate with each other before they attack the other party, a procedure known as *kong su* (Chinese gang slang for "negotiation"). Representatives from the rival gangs may agree to talk to each other on neutral turf, normally a nightclub or restaurant located outside Chinatown. We do not know how many intergang conflicts have been solved through the processes of *kong su*, but a few intergang killings have occurred in the nightclubs of midtown Manhattan because rival gang members were unable to come up with a peaceful solution (*World Journal*, January 14, 1988, 24).

Intragang Violence

Gang members fight not only with rival gangs but also with their own members. The larger a gang is, the more likely that it will develop internal factions. The more closely a gang is associated with an adult organization, the more likely that personal conflict among adults will be manifested in the young members. Intragang disputes are as frequent and tumultuous as intergang clashes. In New York City, the Ghost Shadows, the Flying Dragons, and the Tung On are the three gangs most often involved in intragang warfare.

The distribution of money is almost always the ground for intragang conflict, as other leaders of a gang attempt to get rid of a selfish leader who attempts to pocket most of the illegal gains from protection and extortion rackets. According to the sentencing memorandums prepared for the indictment of twenty-five Ghost Shadows leaders and members, leaders have repeatedly conspired with other leaders or members to kill a leader who they thought was not distributing the money. As a result, from 1976 to 1980, several Ghost Shadows leaders were the targets of their own gang members. And the Tung On's intragang struggle in May 1985 resulted in the wounding of seven people, including two innocent bystanders.

Most intragang violence involves tong members, who conspire with gang members to assassinate the leaders. Michael Chen, the Flying Dragons' most charismatic leader, was believed to have been killed by a rival faction of his own gang, with the support of tong members. In September 1987, a Flying Dragon was shot to death by an adult tong member in the core area of the gang's turf (*Centre Daily News*, September 21, 1987, 24). Likewise, a Ghost Shadows leader was slaughtered outside a gambling place protected by the Shadows. The gunman was a well-known mentor of the gang who also is a member of the On Leong (*World Journal*, September 9, 1985, 20). The gang leader was attacked when he challenged the authority of the On Leong member publicly. In sum, one can conclude that gang leaders or members are often severely punished by their own members or mentors when they fail to pass on money or are too arrogant in dealing with tong members who are mentors of the gang.

Some statistics are available on the incidence, type, and location of Chinese gang struggles. Gang-related assaults and murders occur at any time of the day or night. In New York City, most incidents take place in the major commercial areas of Chinatown such as Mott Street, Bayard Street, Pell Street, Doyers Street, Division Street, the Bowery, and East Broadway; other assaults occur in Queens, Brooklyn, and other parts of

Manhattan. The most likely places for gang members to kill each other is on the streets or in theaters, restaurants, offices, bars, massage parlors, and dance halls. Guns are the preferred weapon (K. Chin 1986).

The Changing Patterns of Gang Violence

Along with the dramatic increase in heroin trafficking by the Chinese, the patterns of gang violence have changed over the past four or five years. As stated above, before 1986 most street violence was the result of intergang or intragang conflicts. A few other fatal incidents occurred because the victims refused to capitulate to the gangs' extortion. Most of these violent acts were spontaneous, erupting in public places such as in a restaurant or on the streets.

However, starting in 1986, murder cases involving Chinese victims became more unpredictable and secretive. Most victims were being killed inside their cars, offices, or homes. More often than not, they were either shot in the head at close range or fired at several times by gunmen who burst into their offices or homes. For example, a wealthy owner of a seafood company and his associate were shot to death by several gunmen in his office in Chinatown (*New York Times*, November 5, 1987). In other incidents, a few Chinese males in their mid-twenties have been shot in the head inside their cars or apartments (for example, *World Journal*, August 16, 1987, 24). None of these cases seem to be the result of robbery or extortion, and law enforcement authorities have had little success in solving these cases.

The theory behind these killings is that the victims have been killed as a result of their involvement in heroin trafficking. Some of them were attacked because they embezzled the drug money or the drug. Some may be killed because of their roles in the heroin trafficking rings among the Chinese. The roles of the gangs in these slayings are unknown; however, police theorize that gang members are being hired to carry out the assassinations.

The other disturbing development in the patterns of gang violence is that victims of extortion are being brutally gunned down by gang members. Prior to the 1980s, only one couple was killed because they refused to pay the gang. However, in the past two years, at least four victims were shot to death by gang members because they resisted the gang's demand. The offenders are members of the emerging gangs in Queens and Brooklyn who are not affiliated with any adult organizations.

Having discussed how and why Chinese street gangs developed and having discussed their criminal activities, we now need to look at the characteristics of the gang members and of the gangs as groups to ascertain why the gangs persist and to determine the directions in which they are likely to develop in the future.

8

GANG CHARACTERISTICS AND SOCIETAL REACTIONS

Several decades after Thrasher's seminal work on gangs in Chicago, there are still many debates pertaining to the definition and characteristics of street gangs. For example, are the personalities of gang members similar to those of other adolescents or delinquents, or are they more pathological and violent? Do gang members commit more crimes than nongang delinquents? Is gang delinquency primarily a minority, immigrant, or working-class phenomenon, or simply the result of differential treatment by law enforcement authorities and sensationalization by the media? Are street gangs loosely knit or well organized? Are the gangs hierarchical organizations or age-graded groups? How cohesive are the gangs? How are gangs related to adult crime groups? Are the gangs likely to evolve into organized crime groups when members mature? (Klein and Maxson 1987; Spergel 1989).

Two paradigms attempt to describe the nature of street gangs. The first paradigm, espoused by law enforcement authorities, the media, and researchers who use official data, views street gangs as cohesive hierarchical organizations comprised of chronic and violent delinquents. The gangs are closely related to adult organized crime groups, and most members, as career criminals, will proceed to become members of the adult crime groups.

The second paradigm, put forth by ethnographers, suggests that street gangs provide members with a sense of security and companionship. Street gangs, in this view, are not purely criminal-oriented groups. The members are not necessarily more deviant than nongang delinquents, and for the most part they drop out of gang life when they grow up and become involved in conventional activities.

In this chapter, we will analyze how well these paradigms fit Chinese street gangs. What exactly are the characteristics of Chinese gangs? Are certain norms and values unique to them? How are they different from other ethnic gangs? By exploring these issues, along with the reaction of Chinese communities and law enforcement authorities to the gang problem, we will attempt to explain why gangs endure in Chinese communities.

Sources provided in this chapter are the synthesis of interview materials with law enforcement authorities, community leaders, and crime victims; personal observations; law enforcement reports; and newspaper accounts.

DEMOGRAPHIC CHARACTERISTICS

Sex

Gang members are all male. Although young females do hang around with members or live in the gangs' apartments, they are not initiated into the gangs. Except for carrying guns for their boyfriends, the girls are not involved in criminal activities.

Age

According to a report prepared by the Fifth Police Precinct, members' ages range from thirteen to thirty-seven (New York City Police Department 1983). The mean age for the 192 registered gang members is 22.7. Most members are in their late teens or early twenties. Because the report included active, inactive, suspected, and imprisoned members, the sample may overrepresent seasoned members. Those who are new members may not yet be known to the police.

Generally, for the well-established gangs, the leaders are in their late twenties or early thirties; street leaders are in their early twenties; and ordinary members are teenagers. In a Chinese gang, the younger the member, the more likely it is that he will be called upon to carry out violent crimes or be involved in spontaneous street violence.

Country of Origin

In the 1960s and 1970s, most gang members were young immigrants from Hong Kong. A few were American-born or Taiwan-born. Twenty-four out of the twenty-five Ghost Shadows indicted in 1985, for example, were born in Hong Kong. Since the late 1970s, the Ghost Shadows and the Flying Dragons have recruited many Vietnamese-Chinese. A Ghost Shadow member testified in 1984 that over 50 percent of his associates are Vietnam-born Chinese (President's Commission on Organized Crime

1984b). Occasionally, non-Chinese Vietnamese may be recruited temporarily from out of town to carry out certain violent or predatory crimes, but they are not considered members. In the 1980s, many young immigrants from Fujian (Fukien), China, are being recruited by gangs such as the Fook Ching, the Tung On, and the Green Dragons. Recently, some Korean youths were inducted into the Queens-based White Tigers and Green Dragons (*World Journal*, June 30, 1987, 22). So far, Chinese gangs have not recruited anyone who is of non-Asian origin. Most gang members, with the exception of a Queens-based Taiwanese gang, speak the Cantonese dialect.

Generally speaking, the Ghost Shadows, the Flying Dragons, the White Tigers, and the Golden Star are comprised mainly of Hong Kong-born and Vietnam-born Cantonese. Tung On members are predominantly Hakka youths from Hong Kong and China. Fujian adolescents from China dominate the Fook Ching and Green Dragons.

Other Characteristics

According to a district attorney, most gang members are school dropouts, although a few remain in school while maintaining active membership in a gang. Chinese gang members do not have dress codes, although some prefer to wear black—black leather jackets, black shirts, black pants, and black Kung Fu shoes without socks. Most of them spike their hair, have tattoos on their arms or chests, and carry beepers.

Chinese gang members have both English and Chinese names, and a nickname known only to their peers. Most nicknames derive from the second word of the given name (Chinese given names generally have two words) and attach the word "Ah" at the front or "Jai" at the end. Some of the nicknames are rather nonthreatening, such as "Fish Eyes," "Mongo," "Applehead," "Stinky Bug," and "Lobsterhead."

A couple of gang members' profiles are provided here to illustrate the characteristics of Chinese gang members. Michael Chen, a former leader of the Flying Dragons, was born in China and came to the United States in the mid-1960s after a temporary stay in Hong Kong. As a teenager, he attended schools near Chinatown but dropped out within a few years. He came from a poor family. Chen was arrested for homicide in Queens in 1976, but the charge was dismissed. A year later, he was indicted for a double homicide in a Chinatown theater, and again the charges were dismissed. His nickname, "the Scientist," stemmed from his cleverness in using electronic devices to keep track of rival gang members. Chen was also flamboyant, wearing silk clothes and owning three European sports cars. He lived in an apartment on Pell Street with his girlfriend. Before he was murdered, Chen owned a nightclub, a meat market, and a paper supply house (*New York Daily News*, March 15, 1983b, 4).

Another notorious gang member was Andy Liang, born in Fujian Province, China, who immigrated to the United States in the early 1980s with his family when he was a teenager. The family lived in Chinatown and Liang's parents worked in a restaurant and a garment factory to raise four children, of which Liang was the only son. Liang became a Fook Ching member after he dropped out of school and was arrested a couple of times for robbery, extortion, and a weapons charge. Later, he left the Fook Ching and joined the Tung On. His twelve-year-old youngest sister was abducted and killed in 1986. When police investigated the murder, Liang's association with the Tung On became the major focus. Although law enforcement authorities later discovered that the girl was strangled to death by a psychotic killer who lived next door, Liang gained enormous publicity throughout the investigation (*New York Daily News*, February 19, 1986, 5; *Centre Daily News*, March 10, 1986, 1).

A few months after his sister's death, Liang was chased by three Flying Dragon members on East Broadway and was shot several times. He survived the attack and again became the best known gang member in Chinatown (*New York Daily News*, April 10, 1987, 5). With another street leader of the Tung On, Liang organized an extortion ring that terrorized the area of East Broadway, Division Street, Catherine Street, and the Bowery.

In 1988, while Liang was in the office of a wealthy businessman in Chinatown, he was shot more than fifteen times and pronounced dead on the scene. The businessman testified that he shot Liang in self-defense when Liang demanded $3,600 from him and threatened him with a gun (*New York Times*, June 12, 1988, 34). The businessman was initially charged with second-degree murder, but he was acquitted when the judge found that there was insufficient evidence to indict him for the murder (*World Journal*, July 25, 1989, 24).

STRUCTURAL CHARACTERISTICS

Size

The sizes of the gangs vary. Each gang has, on average, about twenty to fifty hard-core members, a few inactive members, and some peripheral members. When conflicts among the gangs are intense, they may seek reinforcements from other cities. Law enforcement authorities estimate a total of two to four hundred active Chinese gang members in New York City.

Organization

The structure of the gangs also varies. The Ghost Shadows have four or five leaders at the top, the so-called *tai lou* ("big brother") who oppose one another. Under them, are several "lieutenants," or associate leaders, in command of the street soldiers. At the bottom of the hierarchy are the street soldiers, who guard the streets and commit most of the extortion, robbery, and street violence. They are known as the *ma jai* ("little horse").

Leaders maintain direct contact with certain tong elders and receive payment from them or from operators of the gambling houses. The leaders are the only liaisons between the tongs and the gangs. Leaders are rarely involved in street violence, although they give the orders. Whenever a leader wants somebody harassed or assaulted, he instructs the street leaders or members to carry out the assignment. The leader may provide the hit man with guns and pay him as a reward after he fulfills the "contract." Usually, the leader monitors the action from a nearby restaurant or gang apartment.

Although the associate leaders do not have much power in the administration of the gang, they control the ordinary members. It comes as no surprise, therefore, that street soldiers are more loyal to their immediate leaders than to the top leaders. Street leaders usually recruit the ordinary members. Street leaders are sometimes involved in carrying out assignments, but their usual role is that of "steerer"—that is, they bring the street soldiers to their target and identify it for them. Street leaders do not initiate plans to attack specific people.

Among ordinary members, a few tough ones are known as shooters; they carry out most of the gang's assaults. The bulk of the soldiers watch the streets, guard the gambling places, and collect protection fees.

One of the leaders acts as the treasurer and maintains the gang's bank account. The money is used for rent, food, guns, bail, lawyers' fees, and other expenses.

In New York City, most gangs have their own apartments in Chinatown, Queens, and Brooklyn. The apartments are used as headquarters and for ammunition storage, and are occupied mainly by street soldiers. The leaders do not live in them, although they drop by occasionally to talk to the members.

Except for the Ghost Shadows and the Flying Dragons, no other gang in New York's Chinatown has splinter groups in other cities. The Ghost

Shadows have chapters in Boston, Chicago, Baltimore, Houston, and Toronto, and police in New York City believe that the groups are nationally, or even internationally, linked. When a Shadows leader was at war with another of the gang's leaders in 1977 and 1978, support groups from Boston and Chicago came to New York to lend assistance.

Recruitment and Membership

Some youths join the gangs voluntarily, while others are coerced. Before the mid-1970s, most youths were volunteers. Members treated one another as brothers, and it appeared that there was much camaraderie among them. However, from the mid-1970s through the early 1980s, many youths joined the gangs out of fear (for example, *Sing Tao Jih Pao*, June 28, 1977, 1).

Since the early 1980s, gangs have employed both subtle and crude methods to recruit new members. Gang members may treat potential members to a good meal, show them their expensive cars, and provide them with the companionship of teenage girls. Easily impressed adolescents may decide to join the gang, so that they can enjoy the putative benefits of membership. If potential recruits are unimpressed by what the gang members offer, gang members send street soldiers to beat them up, a cruel way of convincing them that their lives are more secure if they are gang members than if they are alone.

Normally gang members recruit youths who are not doing well in school or who have already dropped out. They look for youngsters who are "vulnerable." Those most likely to find gang life attractive and exciting are the young newcomers who have little or no command of English, poor academic records, and few job prospects. Gang youths also approach adolescents who hang around video arcades, basketball courts, bars, and street corners, and those who talk and act arrogantly. Both seasoned members and those who have been in the gang for only a short time carry out recruitment activities. Some members who have been affiliated with the gang for as little as six months can begin recruiting their own members.

Once a youth decides to join the gang, he goes through an initiation ceremony that is a simplified version of the Chinese secret societies' recruiting rituals. The youth takes his oaths, burns yellow paper, and drinks wine mixed with blood in front of the gang leaders and the altar of General Kwan, a heroic figure of the Triad subculture. The oaths taken by new recruits (Appendix 3) are, in essence, similar to the thirty-six oaths of the Hung societies.

DYNAMIC CHARACTERISTICS

Conformity to peer pressure is a strong characteristic of Chinese gang members. For instance, after six Ghost Shadows abducted and raped a white woman, two of the offenders initially opposed killing the victim. However, when the other four argued that she had to be killed, the two immediately consented.

Nevertheless, group cohesion, as this term is generally understood, appears to be weak. Intragang conflicts erupt frequently, and members sometimes transfer from one gang to another. Within a Chinese gang, there are usually two or more cliques, each consisting of a leader, one or more associate leaders, and several soldiers. These cliques usually distrust and dislike one another, and the tensions among them are easily exacerbated whenever illegal gains are not distributed properly. A review of the history of Chinese gangs indicates that leaders are constantly plotting to have one another killed.

Some intragang conflicts are instigated by tong elders who are associated with a particular clique. These mentors prefer to have a divided rather than a united gang; therefore, they intervene to ensure that no particular clique gains enough power to challenge the supremacy of the tong.

Attachment to the gang is not absolute. Some members, especially those who are strong enough, can drop out of the gang at will. A typical reason for leaving the group is marriage. If a member marries, other members respect the importance of family life and leave the married member alone if he so desires, especially if he becomes a father. A member might also leave if he becomes a victim of violence. A final reason for withdrawing from gang life is imprisonment. The experience of incarceration causes some members not to return to their gangs after they get out of jail.

To date, no gang member has been killed or injured by his peers simply because he decided to leave the gang. However, if a member joins a rival gang, he can provoke retaliation from his former associates. For example, a former Flying Dragons member who joined and became a senior member of the Freemasons was shot to death by members of his former gang (*World Journal*, March 15, 1983, 24). Likewise, a former Shadows member who joined the White Tigers was seriously wounded by three Shadows. On the other hand, if the leaders of the two gangs involved can reach agreement about the transferral of members, changing membership and allegiance can be arranged satisfactorily.

Although it is not uncommon for gang members to move from one gang to another, the average time a Chinese youth stays with a gang is unknown. Law enforcement authorities have observed that gang members who are in their late twenties or early thirties still maintain close associations with street members even after they are married and have their own legitimate businesses.

Another indicator of group cohesiveness or the lack of it is gang members' behavior toward their fellow members when they are arrested and prosecuted. Normally, convicted members are not very supportive of one another, especially when they find themselves abandoned by their gang or tong. They become furious when their legal fees are not paid or when their families are neglected financially. When abandoned, indicted members may turn in other members to the prosecutor.

NORMS AND VALUES

The norms and values of the Chinese street gangs are transmitted to them by tong members, who acts as mentors and may belong to a Hung society. Gang members are inspired by the Triad societies' role in patriotic uprisings and their ideas of loyalty and righteousness. Gang members see themselves as nationalistic, loyal, and righteous. Some of the major norms and values of the gang are:

1. Do not commit burglary: Gang members view burglars as low-life criminals who lack character. They prefer to extort or rob a person for money.
2. Do not victimize the poor: The gangs usually victimize only merchants and rich people. Since the mid-1980s, Chinese residents are being increasingly robbed by young gang members in the streets of Chinatown. These young and probably peripheral members are being stigmatized as *lan jia* ("rotten kid") by the core seasoned members.
3. Do not use drugs or become involved in drug trafficking: Drug use and drug trafficking are viewed as immoral and risky.
4. Do not harm rivals' families or relatives: Revenge is not only acceptable but expected. A revengeful person is viewed as a good member. However, vengeful acts should be directed only at the enemy himself or his gang. The enemy's families or relatives should not be harmed under any circumstances.
5. Ganging is a way to earn a living: Ganging should not be for fun or to increase one's reputation. It is purely an alternative way to make a living.

6. Never harm cops or cooperate with them: Although gang members do not trust law enforcement authorities, they still see them as people doing their jobs.

Although most gang members still follow these rules, a few are increasingly neglecting these norms and values, especially gang kids who belong to the newly emerging gangs active in the outskirts of Chinatown, Queens, and Brooklyn. Leaders of the traditional gangs, as mentioned in Chapter 7, are also ignoring the rules by becoming involved in drug trafficking.

COMPARISON OF CHINESE GANGS AND OTHER ETHNIC GANGS

How different are Chinese gangs from other ethnic gangs? Some researchers report that Chinese gangs are similar to other ethnic gangs in several ways. For instance, Robinson and Joe (1980) found that the functions and characteristics of the Chinese gangs in Vancouver, Canada, were identical to those of American gangs. However, the gangs Robinson and Joe studied were atypical Chinese street gangs. Young teenagers with no connection to adult organizations formed these gangs. They resembled American street-corner gangs or athletic clubs, and were similar to the Bugs in San Francisco and the Continentals in New York, which were started by native-born Chinese-Americans. These non-Triad-affiliated gangs followed the patterns of other ethnic gangs, but they were very different from the powerful, criminally oriented gang of foreign-born Chinese that were associated with tongs and Triad subculture.

Like Robinson and Joe, Takagi and Platt (1978) suggest that Chinese gangs, like other ethnic gangs, are involved only in petty crimes. In their view, the tongs and other adult associations, rather than the gangs, are responsible for the organized racketeering activities and violence within the Chinese communities. Takagi and Platt's findings are not supported by other data. Violence in Chinatown is caused by street gangs.

In contrast to scholars of gang delinquency, law enforcement authorities argue that Chinese gangs are unlike other ethnic street gangs. A former captain in the Fifth Precinct suggests that Chinese gangs should not even be considered as "youth" gangs because of the way they are controlled and the age of the leaders:

> [Chinese gangs] are well-controlled and held accountable to the various associations in the Chinatown area. They are the soldiers of Oriental organized crime, with strong ties to cities throughout the

> United States. The associations have international ties in banking, real estate, and import/export businesses and are suspected of being involved in narcotics and alien smuggling. Members of the street gangs range in age from the mid-teens to early twenties. The street leaders are in their early twenties and thirties, with the highest leader being a mature middle-age or senior adult generally in charge of one of the associations. (New York City Police Department, 1983, 3)

Likewise, Spataro found a network of Chinese organized crime that is not duplicated by other ethnic groups. His conclusion was based on the following observations: (1) The street gangs dispatch manpower or hit men or both to support related gangs in other cities (for example, Toronto, Boston, New York); (2) weapons are supplied to out-of-town gang members; (3) gangs provide information to each other on potential extortion victims moving into their cities; and (4) the gangs provide sanctuary to out-of-town fugitives (1978, 14-15).

Furthermore, an Intelligence Division officer in New York City proposes that Chinese criminal groups are not typical street gangs both because they are well structured and because there is so much money at stake.

> First, I will say they are very mobile. They have connections with Chinese criminal groups in other cities, and they can obtain support from those groups when they are on the run. Second, there are more means available to the Chinese gangs. They make a lot of money by becoming a gang member and if they are in trouble with the law, legal services are offered to them by the tongs. Third, they are more violent because there is so much money at stake. (From an interview conducted for this study)

From the perspective of law enforcement authorities, Chinese gangs have these unique characteristics: (1) They are closely associated with and controlled by respected adult organizations within the community; (2) Gang leaders invest their money in legitimate businesses. They are mature and spend a large amount of time doing business, even though they still maintain close relationships with street members; (3) Chinese gangs form national or international networks; (4) The gangs are influenced to a great extent by the Triad societies; (5) Chinese gang members normally do not go through various stages in which they graduate from delinquent behavior to serious crime. New members are often assigned to carry out the most serious assaults; (6) Chinese gangs control large amounts of money and making money is their main motive; and (7) Chinese gangs systematically victimize the community in ways no ordinary street gangs possibly could. In sum, their strong affiliation with powerful adult organizations, their high level of mobility, and their businesslike methods of wiping out rivals suggest that they more closely resemble adult criminal organizations than typical youth gangs.

From our study of Chinatown gangs, we can see that they resemble Cloward and Ohlin's (1960) concept of criminal gangs. Chinese gangs develop in ethnic communities in which adult criminal groups exist and in which the adult criminals serve as mentors and role models for the gang members. They not only provide the youths with jobs but also offer them an illegitimate opportunity structure. The youths can start working as street soldiers and then go on to become lieutenants, gang leaders, and eventually core members of the tong. Thus, a street youth can work his way up to become a respected, wealthy community leader through the illegitimate structure provided by adult organizations if he can survive his years as a gang member. For instance, Johnny Eng, the leader of the Flying Dragons who was arrested in Hong Kong for heroin trafficking, was elected the national chief of staff of the Hip Sing prior to his downfall (*Centre Daily News*, September 16, 1985, 20).

Nevertheless, gangs such as the Ghost Shadows and the Flying Dragons do not strictly follow the subculture pattern in Cloward and Ohlin's classification. Their long history of street violence shows that, besides securing income, the gangs fought constantly with rival gangs to establish their power to shake down the community. This use of violence to win status is consistent with Cloward and Ohlin's definition of conflict subculture. It is hard to imagine in any case how criminal gangs can protect their illegal sources of income without violently subduing rival gangs to prevent them from encroaching on their territory. Even though gang involvement in street violence is not condoned by the adult organizations and is not in the best interests of the gangs themselves, the gangs presumably think that they must instill fear in rival groups as well as in the community as a whole.

What is the evidence for Cloward and Ohlin's third delinquent subculture, the retreatist? In a study of gangs in three cities, Fagan (1989) found drug use widespread among black, Hispanic, and white gangs, regardless of the city. Moore's Los Angeles gangs (1978) and Hagedorn's Milwaukee gangs (1988) were heavily involved in drug use and dealing. However, drug use among Chinese gang members is rare. Although gang leaders are involved in drug trafficking, they themselves are not drug users. Tong members do not tolerate drug use in the gangs, and the gangs themselves are reluctant to recruit anyone who uses drugs. If a member begins using drugs, he is expelled from the gang. For Chinese gang members, gambling is the most prevalent activity in "getting high."

Thus, Chinatown gangs have the characteristics of two of the subcultures described by Cloward and Ohlin: the criminal and the conflict subcultures. Because gang leaders are concerned mainly with the lucrative heroin trade and investment in legitimate businesses, and they are closely associated with certain tong leaders, they adhere more to norms and values of the criminal subcultures as depicted by Cloward and Ohlin. Young members are mostly concerned with their macho image and therefore are more prone to commit violent acts and predatory crimes. These young members seem to be most congruent with Cloward and Ohlin's conflict subculture. Consequently, instead of labeling Chinese gangs as either criminal or conflict gangs, it is perhaps more important to consider the age and rank of the gang members and their criminal propensity.

Unlike Chinese gangs that are closely associated with the well-established adult groups, gangs formed by young Vietnamese and Korean immigrants have no adult group to emulate. As a result, Vietnamese and Korean gangs are not as well organized as the Chinese gangs. Without the stable income from protection and extortion operations that Chinese gangs enjoy, and without a lucrative commercial district to claim as a territory, Vietnamese and Korean gangs are forced to become involved primarily in extortion, robbery, and burglary. These gangs resemble Cloward and Ohlin's conflict gangs because they are prone to excessive use of violence, they lack supervision by adult criminal elements, and they are inaccessible to an illegitimate opportunity structure.

CHARACTERISTICS THAT FACILITATE THE PERSISTENCE OF GANGS

From the information in this chapter, we can isolate three unique characteristics that cause Chinese gangs to persist. First, unlike black and Hispanic gangs (Moore et al. 1978; Hagedorn 1988), Chinese street gangs are not based on youth fads or illicit drug use. Instead, they are closely related to their communities' social and economic life. This relationship enables Chinese gangs to become deeply enmeshed in the legitimate and illegitimate enterprises in their communities. Opportunities for money, power, and prestige through various ventures are bestowed on Chinese gang members. No such distinctive opportunity exists for other minority gangs.

Second, unlike other ethnic gangs, which operate primarily in deteriorated poor neighborhoods, Chinese gangs flourish in rapidly developing and economically robust Chinese communities that are closely tied to Chinese societies in Southeast Asia. Chinese gangs can thus become engaged in financially rewarding domestic and international ventures. Other ethnic gangs are hampered by both the lack of lucrative criminal opportunities in their own neighborhoods and the absence of contacts outside those neighborhoods.

Third, Chinese gang members are embedded in the legendary Triad subculture. By emulating Triad initiation rites and internalizing Triad norms and values, they can claim a certain legitimacy within their communities. This legitimacy enables them to instill a level of fear that no other ethnic gang can match because the community does not view them merely as street thugs.

Nevertheless, the nature, values, and norms of Chinese gangs could change in the future. Chinese gangs with no ties to the tongs and Triad subculture are emerging in newly established Chinese communities. These gangs not only are unfamiliar with Triad norms and values, but their criminal patterns such as street mugging and household robbery are also markedly different from the traditional Triad-inspired gangs.

REACTIONS TO GANGS AS A REASON FOR THEIR PERSISTENCE

The continued existence of Chinese street gangs depends not only on their distinctive characteristics but also on the reactions of law enforcement authorities and the Chinese communities to them and to the problem they present. In New York City, the number of street gang members has never exceeded four hundred at any one time. However, their impact on the community is profound and far-reaching. Because of the gangs' systematic extortion and reckless shootings, the once festive community is gradually turning into a ghost town in the late evening.

Due to the enormous media publicity bestowed on violence involving Chinese gangs, the American public is now aware of the gang problem in Chinatown and they are becoming increasingly reluctant to go there. As a result, businesses in Chinatown are losing American as well as Chinese customers. A police officer of the Fifth Precinct notes:

> The gang problem is serious because it affects so many innocent people. Whenever there is a shootout, bystanders are hurt. The gang problem has damaged the image of Chinatown. Although statistically

> it is still a low crime area, people do not believe Chinatown is a safe place. Just like Central Park. The park is a low crime area and yet people are afraid to go there. It is the same with Chinatown. You will be surprised how many people call me on the phone and ask, "I am coming down to Chinatown tomorrow evening with my wife and children. Is it safe?" The perception of Chinatown as an unsafe place is enormous. They do not want to come to Chinatown for sightseeing or shopping. At one time, business was down about 40 percent. (From an interview conducted for this study)

Some people worry that Chinatown may become another deserted ethnic community. This result seems unlikely, however, because of the continuous influx of new immigrants and the increase in investment money from Hong Kong and Taiwan. Many large businesses from overseas are opening branches in the community, and new immigrants are moving into the area by the thousands each year. Although people are afraid to live in the community, they do not want to give up the many conveniences they enjoy in Chinatown. For the present, they just change their life-style, not their residence.

Social Control in Chinatown

Informal social control within New York's Chinatown is provided primarily by the Chinese Consolidated Benevolent Association and its major association members. When disputes arise, residents seek the aid and assistance of their association and conflicts are settled with the help of one or more respected community leaders. When peaceful informal negotiating channels fail, individuals or groups who are involved in the personal or business conflicts may turn to some of the shady figures that have gang connections for help. As a result, conflicts among residents may evolve into a gang conflict when two rival gangs represent two hostile parties.

The local police precinct, however, is at the forefront of the battle against Chinese gangs. Within the precinct, the Gang Task Force gathers information about the gangs and maintains a file containing members' names, nicknames, photographs, dates of birth, car license numbers and models, affiliated gangs, and other related data.

There is also a special unit known as the Robbery Identification Program (RIP) that deals mainly with predatory crimes such as extortion and robbery. When a victim reports a crime, the RIP Unit will take the complaint by filling out a UF61 or UF49 form. The form is then sent to the Precinct Detective Squad (PDU). Officers from the RIP Unit will interview the victim, get descriptions of the perpetrators, show the victim the photos of registered gang members, or prepare sketches of offenders. The officers may drive the victim around the area for possible identification of the offenders. If the suspects are arrested, the victim will have to identify the perpetrators in the line-up. If the victim positively identifies the suspects, the case is turned over to an assistant district attorney for consideration of prosecution.

Besides the Fifth Precinct, a unit within the Manhattan District Court has as its major responsibility the investigation of Chinese gangs' activities. This unit is known as the Oriental Gang Unit or Jade Squad. Its small staff of eight officers (recently trimmed to three) works closely with the assistant district attorneys who prosecute gang-related cases. The Federal Bureau of Investigation has also become involved in some of the more serious cases (*New York Times*, January 13, 1985, A1).

For these law enforcement authorities, the task of controlling Chinese criminals can be frustrating and futile. First, there is the language barrier. Chinese people not only speak the major dialect of Chinatown, which is Cantonese, but also communicate with one another in Mandarin, Toisanese, Taiwanese, and other dialects of the Fujianese, Hakka, and Chiu Chao. Besides, Chinese gang members have many Triad slang words to use when they talk among themselves. Most American police officers have difficulty identifying the dialect spoken by suspects, to say nothing of the content of the communication. In addition, in order to identify a gang member accurately, law enforcement agents have to know his English name, Chinese name, and nickname. Most gang members have one or more nicknames by which they are known among their peers. And a suspect's Chinese name is pronounced differently in different dialects. For example, the English words Chin (Toisanese), Chen (Mandarin), Chan (Cantonese), and Tang (Taiwanese) all denote the same Chinese surname.

Second, most crime goes unreported in Chinatown. Although businesses are constantly victimized by gang members, they are not willing to seek help from the police; without complaints, the police can do nothing. Law enforcement authorities are amazed at the reluctance of Chinese victims to report a crime. Even though the local precinct now has bilingual officers to handle a special Chinese-language hot line, reaction from the community has not been as enthusiastic as expected.

Not only do victims remain silent, but the community in general does not cooperate with police investigations. Whenever there is a shootout, the police have difficulty obtaining information. The scene of the crime may be filled with Chinese people, but these potential witnesses say they did not see the offenders or pretend that they do not speak English. After the East Broadway shootout in which a four-year-old boy was shot, the police were so frustrated and angered by the way the community responded to their investigation that the Fifth Precinct's chief of police made this statement at a news conference:

> Chinese people are the most uncooperative ethnic group pertaining to police investigations. I believe if the incident had occurred in other ethnic communities, there would be at least one person willing to provide information to the police. Here, there is no witness at all. All our information comes from our own investigation, the victims, and the informants. Our biggest obstacle in fighting the gangs is the community's uncooperative attitude. Our task is to help and protect the community, but if they do not support us, we do not know where to start our job! (*Centre Daily News*, June 7, 1985, 20; my translation)

Likewise, at the aftermath of the Golden Dragon Massacre in San Francisco, Police Chief Charles Gain accused Chinatown residents of "an absolute abdication of responsibility." He also charged that Chinese were living on a "subculture of fear," and they were too intimidated to report any crime to the police (Wu, 1977, 6).

Police attribute the unwillingness of Chinatown residents to come forward and cooperate with authorities to the residents' unwarranted fear of reprisals by gang members. The police constantly remind the community that no witness was ever hurt by gangsters, but so far Chinatown residents seem unconvinced. Thus, the police blame the docile Chinese victims and residents for tolerating the proliferation of vicious gangs within the community.

Community Response to the Gang Problem

While the police blame the community for the problem, Chinatown residents charge the police with not effectively combating the youths who terrorize their streets. A Chinese businessman who was extorted explained his refusal to the police this way:

> What good is it for me to report to the police? First, I do not believe the police can protect me. Second, I still want to do business here. I don't want them [the gang members] to come back and break my store or scare away my customers. Third, I do not want to lose face. If I make the incident public, how am I supposed to respond to my

> friends and colleagues? Finally, I do not believe the police are either effective or reliable. They don't care what has happened to me anyway. (From an interview conducted for this study, my translation)

Another victim rationalized his compliance with the extortionists' demand as follows:

> Three kids came to sell me a box of firecrackers for $300. After bargaining with them, I gave them $200. They did give me a huge box of firecrackers after I gave them the money. Why haven't I reported this to the police? Because, it cost me more than a thousand dollars to install the glass windows. If I do not comply, and they decide to come by at midnight and break the glass windows, who will pay for it? Obviously, the 109th precinct is not going to pay for it, and then I'll be the one who is doomed! (*World Journal*, March 2, 1988, 24; my translation)

Attitudes such as this often arise from the residents' belief that law enforcement authorities are too lenient with the gang members. Most Chinese immigrants do not know how the legal system works, and when they see someone who was arrested back on the streets several days later, their confidence in the system diminishes. Many residents want the police to be proactive rather than reactive. Said one angry restaurant owner, "We want the police to investigate any suspicious-looking people, question them on where they live, who their parents are, where their money comes from." A storekeeper took an even harder line. He insisted that "suspects should be arrested and punished. They should be beaten till they confess. And if they're underage, their parents have to be held responsible. Right now, the good people have no protection. Only the criminals have protection" (*New York Times*, January 19, 1974).

In addition to having little confidence in the police, Chinese victims are also reluctant to appear in court. As the Chinese saying goes, "When alive don't go to authority, when dead don't go to hell." People do not want to become involved with the courts because they are uncertain of the judges' impartiality. Besides, as the businessman quoted previously stated, for Chinatown residents to bring cases to American courts means humiliating themselves and the community at large. The complainant not only reveals the community's affairs to outsiders but also shows no respect for community leaders, who are traditionally accepted as mediators. A tong member explained the Chinese reluctance to go to court this way:

> Face is a very important factor. People here are very respectful to the elders. If there is a dispute, they prefer to have the matter settled by a mediator who is a community or association elder. In this way, all the parties involved are satisfied. (From an interview conducted for this study, my translation)

So many Chinese merchants in New York City were extorted that they threatened to close down all their business for a day to protest the inability of the criminal justice system to deal with the problem. On many other occasions, Asian business associations publicly appealed to their police precinct for protection from the extortionists (*Centre Daily News*, June 13, 1988, 22). Nevertheless, extortion remains to be the biggest problem facing the Asian store owners in the tri-state area of New York, New Jersey, and Connecticut.

Some businessmen did try to protect themselves from the gang by carrying guns (*World Journal*, April 20, 1989, 24). A businessman who owned a furniture store in Chinatown once shot and killed a gang member who demanded extortion money from him. In another incident, he shot at two gang members who attempted to ask for a "loan" from his friend. A few months after the last confrontation, however, he was shot execution-style in his office. Likewise, an employee of a restaurant in Queens killed a gang member who asked for extortion money. Within a year, the owner of the restaurant was shot to death. Although the cases are never solved, it is strongly suspected that the killings of the two businessmen were carried out by gang members as reprisals.

As an alternative, Chinese residents and businessmen attempt to cope with the gang problem through non-confrontative measures. In order to avoid being victimized, residents lock themselves in their apartments at nightfall. They try not to walk in the "gang zone" where street muggings often occur. If they have to, they will always have someone accompany them. Paranoid parents who find that their kids are being recruited by the gangs will send the kids back to their home countries or move out of New York City.

When darkness falls, Chinatown streets are quiet, and most places of business, except for restaurants, are closed. To protect themselves from extortion and victimization by street gangs, store owners have begun to hire only people with whom they are acquainted. They admit only recognized customers into their establishments after dark, close their businesses early, or, associate themselves with criminal elements for protection. Some of the retail stores in Chinatown display their tong membership certificates in their main entrances to show that they are under the protection of certain tongs. Recently, service-oriented businesses in Chinatown such as hair salons have been victimized so often by gang members who refuse to pay after haircuts that they plan to require payment before any service can be rendered (*World Journal*, August 14, 1989, 24).

As long as law enforcement authorities and community residents misunderstand each other and do not work together, however, no control mechanisms will be effective in the Chinese communities, and gangs will persist. As we have seen, various aspects of the Chinese communities create opportunities for criminal elements to exploit their own kind. Even if some of the overt crimes are brought under control, subtle victimization may become the norm.

9

TRIAD SUBCULTURE AND BEYOND

In this concluding chapter, we return to three general questions raised in Chapter 1. The first is the interrelationship of Triad societies, tongs, and street gangs. Are these organizations part of a structurally integrated, international criminal syndicate known as the Chinese Mafia? If so, how are these organizations related? If not, are there unique characteristics shared by all of them?

The second issue is the evolution of Chinese crime groups in the United States. What role will these organizations play in the future? Will they replace Italian American crime groups and become the major organized crime problem in this country? Is Ianni's theory (1974) of ethnic succession in organized crime adequate for predicting the future of Chinese crime groups?

The third topic is the association between the emergence of Triads, tongs, and gangs and the dramatic increase in Southeast Asian heroin in the United States. Are the two phenomena, as some law enforcement officials and the media propose, causally related?

JIANG HU: A SOCIETY APART

Law enforcement authorities in North America charge that Triad societies, tongs, and Chinese street gangs are structurally related. This criminal conglomerate, called the "Chinese Mafia," has its headquarters in Hong Kong and Taiwan. From there, the crime cartel monitors heroin trafficking and other racketeering activities in the Golden Triangle, Hong Kong, and other parts of the world (Robertson 1977; Bresler 1981; Posner 1988). Nonetheless, little evidence sustains this charge. As discussed in the previous chapters, these three types of organizations are neither vertically nor horizontally integrated, and therefore it is misleading to assume that the three groups are routinely involved in coordinated, worldwide criminal conspiracies.

Despite the lack of structural integration, however, members of these groups know, consult with, and even cooperate with one another sporadically in carrying out certain legal and illegal activities. They can easily communicate with one another because members all share Triad norms and values. These shared values and norms also lead members of the various groups to view one another as "insiders" or "brothers" and enable them to shift membership or maintain membership in more than one group. In order to understand better how the groups are interrelated, it is necessary to take a look at the nature of Triad subculture within the context of Chinese society and culture.

Social scientists such as Sellin (1938), Cohen (1955), Miller (1958), Cloward and Ohlin (1960), and Wolfgang and Ferracuti (1982) have theorized that certain subcultural norms and values are related to crime and delinquency. Within a heterogeneous society, certain groups of people may neither accept nor follow conventional values and norms because of the group's particular status. It is not uncommon, in fact, to find a wide variety of subcultural norms and values embedded in a dominant culture. In exploring the subculture of juvenile delinquency, Cohen notes:

> the notion of culture is not limited to the distinctive ways of life of [such] large-scale national and tribal societies. Every society is internally differentiated into numerous sub-groups, each with ways of thinking and doing that are in some respects peculiarly its own, that one can acquire only by participating in these sub-groups and that one can scarcely help acquiring if he is a full-fledged participant. These cultures within cultures are "subcultures." (1955, 12)

Wolfgang and Ferracuti further suggest how subcultures are related to the dominant culture in their study of the subculture of violence.

> A subculture implies that there are value judgments or a social value system which is apart from and a part of a larger or central value system. From the viewpoint of this larger dominant culture, the values of the subculture set the latter apart and prevent total integration, occasionally causing open or covert conflicts. The dominant culture may directly or indirectly promote this apartness, of course, and the degree of reciprocal integration may vary, but whatever the reason for the difference, normative isolation and solidarity of the subculture result. There are shared values that are learned, adopted, and even exhibited by participants in the subculture, and that differ in quantity

and quality from those of the dominant culture. Just as man is born into a culture, so he may be born into a subculture. (1982, 99–100)

While more than a billion Chinese around the world are committed to the Chinese mainstream cultures such as Confucianism, Taoism, and Buddhism, there are also hundreds of thousands of Chinese who belong to a subculture initiated by the *Xia*, crystallized by the vagabonds of Lian Shan, secularized by the Hung and Ching societies, and inherited by members of the Triad societies, tongs, and gangs.

As we saw in Chapter 2 and as we will briefly review here, Triad norms and values have thrived in social milieus where the dominant culture was perceived as alien and foreign. When Hung and Ching societies were formed during the Qing (Ch'ing) dynasty, Manchu foreigners controlled China, and living conditions among the poor were deplorable. Marginal and illiterate people such as laborers, peasants, vagabonds, priests, and sailors were all initiated into these secret societies. By joining the societies, the underclass had nothing to lose, and it was the only way for them to express their dissatisfaction with the establishment and the dominant cultures. In the secret societies, they found a Triad "family" and were surrounded by "brothers" with similar problems.

When the Qing dynasty was overthrown and the Republic of China was established, Triad subculture again blossomed in politically chaotic and economically deprived Shanghai and its French and British concessions. Hung and Ching leaders were able to recruit the marginals, the unemployed, and the laborers. With the sanctions of corrupted Kuomintang officials and the support of foreigners who needed secret society members to maintain law and order within their concessions, Hung and Ching members dominated the rampant drug importation and distribution, gambling, and prostitution operations in Shanghai.

After the Chinese Communists took over China, the Triad subculture flourished in the British colony of Hong Kong. Peddlers and workers who tried to survive in a disorderly environment ruled by foreign government formed many Triad societies. Since many Hong Kong residents were refugees who fled China during and after the civil war between the Kuomintang and the Communists, they needed a powerful organization to protect them while they were away from their homelands.

When Chinese immigrants traveled to Southeast Asia, Europe, and North America, they took Triad values with them. In the United States, tongs mainly comprised people who are discriminated against by both the host society and the Chinese elite groups. The gangs also are made up of young immigrants alienated from American society and ostracized by other ethnic groups and native-born Chinese. In the gang, inspired by Triad principles, these marginal newcomers can find their own identity and place in society.

In short, those who are unable or unwilling to become assimilated into either the dominant culture or the elite culture of overseas Chinese societies find Triad subcultural norms and values attractive. In all societies where Triad norms and values ascended, the dominant cultures were alien cultures from the Chinese point of view. The milieus where Triad subculture flourishes are strikingly similar to those where the mafia subculture emerged (Blok 1974; Nelli 1976; Arlacchi 1987; Duggan 1989).

Underclass Chinese are thereby most likely to become part of the Triad subculture, especially if they do not belong to a well-established family or district association. They are alienated from the dominant culture, and they are also not accepted by Chinese elite groups. In other words, working-class Chinese have no status in either the host society or their own community. For them, the only practical way to achieve status is to adopt Triad norms and values and to become part of an organization that can supply money, fame, and companionship.

According to Wolfgang and Ferracuti, there are two major subcultural values: (1) concordant values which are tolerated, and (2) discordant values which are not tolerated. The first type are "tolerated differences that are not disruptive, that do not cause injury or possess potential threat of social injury to the dominant culture," and the second type are "conflicting differences that are disruptive, that do cause injury or possess potential threat of social injury to the dominant culture" (1982, 40). In this regard, a host society's social control agencies would most likely classify Triad norms and values as discordant values not to be tolerated. The Chinese, however, have a different view, because Triad subculture is deeply rooted in a society in which most people are either peasants or laborers. For centuries, corrupt officials and landlords have repeatedly exploited underclass Chinese. Although most of the underclass prefer to remain law-abiding rather than to transform themselves into rebellious Triad members, they nevertheless view Triad societies as vanguards of the poor and the powerless. They may even prefer to be extorted occasionally by some of the Triad members than to be harassed constantly by government officials.

Among the Chinese, members of the Triad subculture are called Dark Society Elements, and the shady world in which they dwell is called the Dark Society or *Jiang Hu* (literally, "rivers and lakes." It denotes the members' rootlessness). Once a person is initiated into the world of Jiang Hu, he has to internalize, cherish, and observe Triad norms. In the romantic world of Jiang Hu, members view themselves as patriotic, heroic, righteous, and loyal. Chinese conventional norms and values such as filial piety, attachment to family and village, and nonradical philosophy are replaced by loyalty to the organization and its members, rootlessness, and radicalism. Within this world, a powerless and detached person can become connected to a legendary and honorable society.

A Jiang Hu person is not necessarily a criminal or a bad person. He is simply someone with a different way of life and a different set of values. Once initiated into the Triad subculture, a person can justify his infraction of the laws as inevitable because one of the most famous maxims of the subculture is "I am a Jiang Hu man, I am not in control of my fate." In other words, being a member of the subculture, he has a very different set of values and norms to be observed. He has to seek revenge if someone attacks him or his "brother"; he has to help his "brother" even if the "brother" commits a heinous crime; and he can never dissociate himself from his group's involvement in illegal activities. In sum, Triad subcultural norms and values are such that a "good" member of the subculture will break the laws of the conventional society even though he has no intention of committing a crime for personal gain. The more a person is committed to the norms and values of Jiang Hu, the less likely he is to be able to avoid defying the laws.

At any rate, Jiang Hu people are involved in the exploitation and intimidation of the rich and powerful, and in the provision of illegal services. Besides, they have always monopolized extortion and protection rackets, gambling, and prostitution. Members of the subculture believe they are simply making a living in an alternative way—a way that is justifiable because it redistributes wealth in an imperfect society.

Secret societies such as the Hung and the Ching, Triad societies in Hong Kong, and tongs and street gangs in the United States, are all members of the Triad subculture. These groups share the same norms and values, worship the same god (General Kwan as depicted in *The Three Kingdoms*), memorize the same Triad poems and slang, and adopt the same initiating ceremony, using similar Triad paraphernalia. Members of all these organizations view one another as "brothers" of the same "Triad Family."

If we examine the nature of the interrelationships among Chinese secret societies and criminal organizations from a subcultural perspective, we are better equipped to evaluate the phenomenon more realistically. It is important to bear in mind that cultural integration does not necessarily preclude structural integration. On the contrary, cultural integration among Chinese crime groups could only enhance their structural integration if they decide to integrate one another structurally, perhaps temporarily for certain occasions or situations.

The assumptions that Triads, tongs, and gangs are primarily culturally integrated, and that they have the potential to integrate structurally when the occasions arise, should guide law enforcement authorities in developing more flexible and effective strategies to cope with Chinese crime groups. In other words, law enforcement organizations and strategies should be structured to fight them both separately and collectively. Policies that stress one approach over the other would only be partially successful.

ETHNIC SUCCESSION IN ORGANIZED CRIME

Ianni (1974) proposed that different ethnic groups in the United States have used and continue to use organized criminal activity as a means of social mobility. Before the Italian Mafia, organized crime groups formed by the Irish and Jews preyed on their own communities through various protection and racketeering activities. When these early immigrants became part of the mainstream of American society, other ethnic groups lower on the social scale, such as the Hispanics and blacks, began to move into organized street crime and vice activities.

Now it seems to be the turn of the Chinese. As we saw in Chapter 1, social control agencies in the United States propose that the "Chinese Mafia" is already a formidable group. Triad societies, tongs, and Chinese street gangs have been labeled "emerging crime groups," "new crime cartels," and "nontraditional organized crime" by American law enforcement authorities. They tend to compare the Chinese gangs with Italian crime organizations, emphasizing that the Chinese gangs, as they follow the paths of the Italian gangs, will ultimately emerge as organized crime groups.

Before we see how Italian and Chinese groups compare, we should perhaps note that not all scholars are convinced there is a nationwide Italian crime syndicate called the Mafia or La Cosa Nostra (Smith 1975). According to Morris and Hawkins, there is no doubt that "small groups of criminals organized for carrying out particular kinds of crime" and well-organized crime groups involved in "the supply of consumer goods and services for which there's a widespread demand" do exist in our society. However, they question whether there is "a national syndicate which dominates organized crime throughout the country—one large nationwide criminal organization which controls the majority, if not all, of the local undertakings" (1970, 211). A study by Reuter (1983) of bookmaking, gambling, and loansharking revealed that these activities were not tightly controlled and monopolized by any well-organized Italian crime group.

Be that as it may, in comparing the Italian and Chinese crime groups, Goldstock (President's Commission on Organized Crime 1984b) proposed that La Cosa Nostra is the American version of the Sicilian Mafia, and the tongs are the American branches of the Triad societies. He suggested that Italian and Chinese crime groups are similar in several ways. First, both the Sicilian Mafia and the Triad societies were formed to save their countries from foreign influences. Both organizations have been instrumental in the success of various political movements in their countries. Members of both groups have immigrated to various parts of the world and both groups have long histories of criminal activity.

Second, members have to go through elaborate initiation ceremonies. Third, the rules of the Sicilian Mafia, such as reciprocal aid, absolute obedience, silence in the face of authority, and secrecy, are similar to the Triad's thirty-six oaths. Fourth, both La Cosa Nostra and the tongs established their strongholds within their respective communities—Little Italy and Chinatown.

Fifth, their illegal activities are similar: gambling, vice, and protection rackets. Both groups also invest their money in similar legal businesses, such as the garment industry, restaurants, and movie theaters. Sixth, La Cosa Nostra families have their own arbitration agents, known as the Commission, and the tongs have the Chinese Consolidated Benevolent Association (CCBA) to mediate disputes among themselves.

Goldstock found, however, that although the Triads and tongs are similar to the Sicilian Mafia and La Cosa Nostra in historical development, structure, norms, values, and criminal patterns, there are two major differences between them. First, while the Italian crime groups have penetrated the mainstream of American society, the Chinese groups are still confined to their ethnic community. Second, members of La Cosa Nostra and the Commission are all purely criminals, whereas the tongs and the CCBA consist of both criminals and law-abiding people.

When comparing Chinese groups with the Italian groups within the context of ethnic succession in organized crime, I believe that the dissimilarities between them are more crucial than their similarities. Tong members have been in the United States for over a century. Although they are responsible for various racketeering activity within the Chinese communities, they have neither infiltrated the American society nor victimized people who are not Chinese. In comparison with the Italian crime families, the tongs' role in American crime is minor. It is hard to imagine how the tongs will be able to surpass the Italian crime groups or how such a move by the tongs would provoke fierce competition from criminal organizations of other ethnic groups.

Language and cultural barriers, rather than competition, are the main factors that compel members of the Triad subculture in the United States to confine their activities to their own communities and to victimize only their own people. Because Chinese criminals here normally do not and could not relate to American society, they have little desire to expand their activities to a society that is so alien to them. Even if they were willing to do so, they would not be able to establish close relationships with public officials through corruption. Unlike Italian crime groups, other ethnic crime groups, such as the blacks and Hispanics, have not been successful in bribing the predominantly white officials for protection of their illegal activities. As Ianni pointed out:

> While it is a maxim in the underworld that graft and corruption are color-blind and that police and politicians will take graft regardless of the color of the hands that delivers it, it is difficult to imagine that blacks will be able to insinuate themselves into the kinds of social relationships with white politicians within which deals are made, bribes are offered or sought and protection developed. (1976, 147)

Because of their unique cultural background, Chinese criminals are in no better position than blacks or Hispanics to corrupt public officials. Without protection from police or politicians, the Chinese groups' ability to expand their criminal networks outside their communities is seriously hampered.

Another major dissimilarity between La Cosa Nostra and the tongs is that La Cosa Nostra consists mostly of criminals, while the tongs consist of mainly upright people. Most members of the tongs are law-abiding workers or business people who have nothing to do with the core members' criminal activities. Besides, tong activities are also checked closely by Taiwanese government officials here in the United States. Even though some core members are shady and corrupt, they cannot become overtly involved in illegal activities. After all, the tongs as organizations are not crime groups; they have many other civic and political responsibilities.

Finally, for the tongs to emerge as organized crime groups they must get control of the gangs, without whose full support they may never be able to impose their authority at the street level. Mistrust and misunderstanding between the tongs and the street gangs are mutual and rampant. Just as the tongs do not always feel obliged to provide the gangs with the support they want, the gangs do not feel compelled to follow the instructions of the tongs.

Goldstock suggested that the CCBA is equivalent to the Commission of La Cosa Nostra. He is correct only insofar as the CCBA mediates disputes among the tongs. However, the CCBA cannot settle gang conflicts, and it does not oversee and control the criminal activities of the tongs, as the Commission does with La Cosa Nostra.

In sum, one may conclude tentatively that, to the present, there has never been a Chinese Mafia on either the national or international level. Furthermore, the differences between the Chinese crime groups and the Italian crime groups are greater than their similarities. It is inappropriate to propose that the Chinese groups are now at the stage where the Italian groups were during the 1930s and that they will proceed to become the preeminent crime organization in the United States.

In fact, other than heroin trafficking, Chinese crime groups have not been able to expand their traditional criminal activities such as extortion, gambling, and prostitution from their own communities to non-Chinese communities. Furthermore, it is also very unlikely that these crime groups will be able to dominate other activities such as controlling labor unions, the waste industry, and other criminal activities that victimize non-Chinese people. Undeniably, what concerns law enforcement authorities the most and leads scholars of organized crime to propose that Chinese crime groups will become prominent is the fact that Chinese are importing the bulk of Southeast Asian heroin into the United States. Thus, a discussion of ethnic succession in organized crime would not be complete without mentioning Chinese involvement in heroin trafficking in the United States and other parts of the world.

NON-TRIAD CHINESE CRIMINALS AND THE HEROIN TRADE

Known as "China White" on the streets, as opposed to "Brown Heroin" from Mexico, heroin from the Golden Triangle in Southeast Asia has dramatically increased on the streets of New York City. According to law enforcement authorities, heroin from Southeast Asia constituted only 3 percent of the total available in New York City in 1982. The figure increased dramatically to 40 percent in 1986, and, by 1987, 70 percent of the city's supply came from Southeast Asia. Nationwide, China White represents 40 percent of the heroin smuggled into the United States. Between 1986 and 1987, the Drug Enforcement Administration (DEA) seized nine hundred pounds of Southeast Asian heroin. In the following two years, much more Southeast Asian heroin was found in Bangkok, Hong Kong, and Canada in cargoes that were destined for the United States. During the same years, DEA agents also seized many hundreds of pounds of heroin in various American cities, all bound for New York City, where more than half of the heroin addicts in the United States live.

Due to its purity (normally 90 percent or more on the wholesale level and about 40 percent on the retail level), China White has become a popular drug among the drug traffickers and addicts (*New York Times*, August 6, 1989, E5). Prior to the emergence of China White, heroin available to street addicts was normally 3 to 4 percent pure. As a result, treatment practitioners are observing a dramatic increase in heroin overdose and heroin-related illnesses.

The Changing Guard in Heroin Trafficking

Although Chinese have been involved in smuggling a few pounds of heroin into the United States for a long time, heroin importation and wholesale business before 1986 was generally dominated by Italian crime groups. The famous "French Connection" case in the 1960s shows that Italian criminals were actively involved in importing large amounts of heroin from Southwest Asia into the United States via Europe.

Starting in 1986, the heroin trade began to change hands. At the beginning, customs officials in Los Angeles, San Francisco, and New York international airports found that there was an enormous increase in heroin trafficking by Chinese passengers. Most of these cases involved passengers from Taiwan, Hong Kong, China, Thailand, or other Asian countries who attempted to smuggle ten to twenty pounds of heroin by hiding the drug in their bodies or luggage. Offenders were mostly drug couriers who are unemployed, gamblers, or restaurant and factory workers. They were paid about $10,000 for each trip. The men behind the crime were rarely implicated.

When law enforcement authorities began to scrutinize Asian passengers in major international airports, the traffickers changed their operations. Instead of having drug couriers hand-carry limited amounts of heroin into the United States, Chinese traffickers began to smuggle huge amounts in cargoes coming to the United States. For example, in September 1986, thirty-three pounds of China White were found inside furniture arriving in Newark, New Jersey, from Bangkok (*World Journal*, September 6, 1986, 3). Within the next six months, in at least three separate incidents, drug agents intercepted more than a hundred pounds of Southeast Asian heroin in cargoes arriving at New Jersey seaports (for example, *World Journal*, February 17, 1987, 24).

After these incidents, instead of decreasing their criminal propensity, Chinese traffickers simply got bolder. Within the next two and a half years, excluding the more than twenty cases that have implicated Chinese traffickers from around the world, law enforcement authorities confiscated many thousands of pounds of China White in Bangkok, Canada, Hong Kong, and the United States in several major cases. For example, in December 1987, four Chinese were arrested for importing 165 pounds of heroin into the United States by hiding the drug in nylon sport bags. Federal agents also confiscated more than $1 million cash stashed in safe boxes in Chinatown banks or briefcases (*Centre Daily News*, December 27, 1987, 24; *World Journal*, January 28, 1988, 24). Two months later, Thailand police seized 2,822 pounds of heroin concealed in bales of rubber sheets bound for a Chinese company in New York City (*New York Newsday*, February 14, 1988b, 5). Within the same month, federal drug agents found 165 pounds of heroin hidden inside the oriental statues arriving in Chicago from Bangkok. When Chinese traffickers from New York showed up in Chicago to pick up the statues, they were arrested (*New York Newsday*, February 22, 1988, 21). A month later, Johnny Kon, a major heroin trafficker from Hong Kong, was arrested in New York City for importing more than a thousand pounds of heroin into the United States (*New York Times*, March 15, 1988, B5). More than a dozen people, including a Caucasian former police officer, were taken into custody.

The arrests of major Chinese traffickers in the United States and Hong Kong kept on. DEA officers in Oakland, California, grabbed about seventy pounds of heroin when they searched boxes of tea leaves from Southeast Asia (*Centre Daily News*, March 19, 1988, 24); in a federal operation named "Operation Bamboo Dragon," forty Chinese traffickers in Hong Kong and the United States were arrested for operating a drug and gun smuggling ring (*Centre Daily News*, April 18, 1988, 1); two Taiwanese merchants in San Gabriel, California, were arrested for smuggling seventy-seven pounds of heroin by concealing the drug in can openers (*Centre Daily News*, June 30, 1988, 3); a prominent community leader and businessman in Boston's Chinatown was detained for sequestering 180 pounds of heroin in bean sprout washers imported from Hong Kong (*Centre Daily News*, September 10, 1988, 24); in February 1989, in an undercover operation initiated by the Organized Crime Drug Enforcement Task Force, American, Canadian, and Hong Kong drug agents arrested a major Chinese drug broker named Peter Woo and his associates in New York, Canada, Hong Kong, and Singapore and seized eight hundred pounds of heroin and $3 million in cash (*New York Times*, February 22, 1989, B5); in another international joint operation named "Operation Red Star," officials in China, Hong Kong, Canada, and the United States confiscated ninety pounds of heroin concealed in umbrellas arriving in

New York via China, Hong Kong, and Canada (*World Journal,* May 9, 1989, 6).

Besides cargo shipments, another major smuggling method employed by the Chinese traffickers is to hide the drug in boxes and mail them to the United States. The boxes are normally sent from Hong Kong via Oakland, California, and arrive in New York City. Drug traffickers hire Chinese residents in New York City who are eager to make $10,000 to $20,000 for simply agreeing to receive the boxes and turn them over to the importers.

Thus, over the past three years, we have observed that Chinese heroin traffickers around the world are adopting many innovative measures to smuggle heroin from the Golden Triangle to the heroin markets in Australia, Europe, and North America. Based on the number of arrests and the huge amount of heroin seized over the past three years, it is safe to conclude that Chinese traffickers are now one of the most active groups in international heroin trafficking. On many occasions, law enforcement officers have discovered that Chinese traffickers were aided by Americans who had previously served in social control agencies or the Chinese were working closely with drug dealers of other ethnic origins for distributing the drug. So far, Chinese are active only in the importation and wholesaling of heroin, leaving the marketing and retailing activities to non-Chinese dealers.

If the Chinese continue to dominate the heroin business, law enforcement officials predict that the Triads, tongs, and Chinese gangs will expand their illegal operations and penetrate American society through the heroin business. The enormous profits from heroin smuggling will lead them to money laundering, corruption, and the infiltration of legitimate businesses by investing drug money in real estate and restaurants.

The Rise of a New Class of Chinese Drug Traffickers

Before we conclude that Triads, tongs, and Chinese gangs are responsible for the dramatic increase in Southeast Asian heroin in the United States, it is important to study Chinese drug traffickers and their affiliation with the Triad subculture. Are they members of the Triads, tongs, and gangs, or are they mostly opportunistic businessmen or criminals with no connection to the Triad subculture?

Several facts are known about drug trafficking among the Chinese. Chinese heroin traffickers are not involved in retailing the drug. They normally bulk-sale it to Italian, black, or Hispanic dealers. They are also closely associated with Dominican crime groups. They are mostly independent entrepreneurs who own small businesses such as restaurants, trading companies, or retail stores. Their businesses are "fronts" for the heroin trade. Most of them start to trade with the intention of doing it only once, but the huge profits are appealing, and it is not easy for them to terminate their operations. Most low-level couriers are heavy gamblers or illegal aliens who are in debt. When arrested, Chinese traffickers are cooperative and do not resist. They take their arrest as their fate. Their normal reaction is *zhen dao mei* ("what bad luck!"). They do not see themselves as bad or as criminals; rather, they view themselves as entrepreneurs whose primary goal in drug dealing is to make money.

One type of evidence that could be used to show that Chinese drug traffickers are part of an organized syndicate is a predictable method of operation. However, the methods these drug traffickers use are diverse. Drugs are smuggled into the United States via air and sea, concealed in luggage, furniture, frozen food, statues, machines, and even goldfish. The drugs arrive in various American cities from all parts of the world.

The complex nature of the Chinese heroin trade thus makes it almost impossible to predict where the drug will originate, via what routes and methods it will be smuggled into the United States, and where will it arrive. Nor is it easy to pinpoint what type of individual or group is dominating the trade. Since 1986, Chinese with diverse backgrounds have been continuously involved in large-scale heroin and cocaine trafficking. Among those arrested for the crime are illegal aliens from China, Hong Kong, Taiwan, Thailand, and other Asian countries; U.S. permanent residents; and American citizens who are community leaders, business people, restaurant owners, workers, and the unemployed.

A senior drug enforcement official suggested the differences between drug traffickers of Italian and Chinese origin.

> Unlike the Mafia traffickers, who have more clearly defined organizations and chains of command, the Asian importers are working in looser fashion. When we talk about Asian organized crime, there is, I suppose, a question of definition. If you are talking about a crime cartel like the traditional Italians with dons and capos and territories, it doesn't exist within the Chinese. Instead, what agents see are loose confederations of traffickers gradually infiltrating themselves into extortion, massage parlors, and gambling rackets traditionally controlled by street gangs, who in turn are allegedly under the aegis of the ostensibly legitimate business associations, the tongs. (*New York Newsday*, February 14, 1988a, 5)

Not only are Chinese traffickers loosely knit, but they are also not necessarily related to Triads, tongs, or gangs. Drug Enforcement Administration agents in New York suggest that there is no evidence to prove that Triads, tongs, and gangs dominate the heroin trade. These agents describe the trafficking groups as ranging from loose confederations of businessmen and smugglers who collaborate on a single deal to complex organizations.

> The ones who are responsible for the importation and the financing are basically . . . the business people—generally, importers and exporters and financiers. Those are the ones who are responsible for either financing or smuggling. They are rarely responsible, however, for the distribution. Distribution is generally the responsibility of the gangs. So what you have is a working relationship between business and the gang people, and very often, not always the case, but very often, the business people don't even touch the heroin. They make the arrangements for the heroin to go directly from southeast Asia to the gang, where the gang is then responsible for distribution (United States Senate 1986, 70-71).

Johnny Kon, the person who was arrested for importing hundreds of pounds of heroin into the United States, is a typical non-Triad-affiliated drug smuggler. Kon emigrated from Shanghai to Hong Kong in 1965 to take a job with a fur company. Around 1968, he moved to Vietnam, where he sold furs to American soldiers and made his first contact with narcotics dealers. Although he became a major heroin trafficker, he remained in the fur business and was never a member of the Triad subculture (*New York Daily News*, March 27, 1988, 4). The same is true for other major Chinese traffickers such as Lai King Man of Hong Kong, Dennis Lai of San Francisco, Alice Lai and Chi Wai Wong of San Gabriel, California, Hu Kin Shiang of Boston, and Peter Woo of New York. Dennis Lai is an American-born wealthy businessman who also is vice-president of the Asian Pacific American Chamber of Commerce; Alice Lai and Chi Wai Wong are well-to-do entrepreneurs; Hu Ki Shiang is vice-president of an Indo-Chinese association, and Peter Woo is the former president of the Chinatown Democratic Club and owner of a few businesses. None of these major traffickers are associated with Triad, tong, or gang organizations.

In short, one can conclude that the heroin trade in the United States is an "equal opportunity employer" for Chinese from all walks of life who want to get rich quickly. Drug trafficking is also a desperate measure taken by some poor newcomers and gamblers to solve their financial problems.

Although Hong Kong Triad societies dominate the heroin business in Netherlands and Australia, no evidence sustains the allegation that they, along with the tongs and Chinese gangs, play a dominant role in heroin trafficking in the United States.

It is safe to say that a new generation of non-Triad Chinese criminals is emerging on the American crime scene. These non-Triad criminals are responsible for the bulk of the heroin imported into the United States, and they are more likely than people of the Triad subculture to infiltrate the larger society through drug trafficking, alien smuggling, money laundering, and other types of white-collar crimes. They are wealthier, more sophisticated, and better connected with their associates outside the United States. They are not committed to the rigid Triad subcultural norms and values, thus enabling them to assemble quickly when the criminal opportunity arises and to dissolve after the criminal conspiracy is carried out.

Thus, we are observing the development of a subculture of drug trafficking among the Chinese in the United States, Hong Kong, Canada, Australia, Europe, and other parts of the world. Members of this subculture include import-export businessmen, community leaders, restaurant owners, workers, gamblers, housewives, and the unemployed. It is extremely difficult to penetrate this subculture because members have no prior criminal records, no identifiable organization, and no rigid structure and norms and values. They can conceal their criminal activities through their involvement in lawful business activities. Their involvement in criminal activities is sporadic rather than continuous. In other words, they may participate or invest in one heroin deal, collect the illegal gains, and put the money in real estate or other legal businesses such as restaurants. They may not be involved in any illegal activities for a prolonged period of time until another opportunity arises. Since their illegal activities are not predatory crimes, they can thrive with or without the assistance of members of the Triad subculture.

Thus, it will have far-reaching, unfortunate consequences if law enforcement authorities focus only on the Triads, tongs, and Chinese gangs, and view them as the only crime groups responsible for the heroin trade and other racketeering activities in the Chinese communities or mistakenly label those non-Triad criminals as part of the Triad subculture and attempt to fight them as such. What we need to do is to focus our attention on the development of both the Triad subculture and the Chinese drug trafficking subculture simultaneously and to prevent the coalition of these two equally destructive forces.

APPENDIX 1

THIRTY-SIX OATHS OF THE HUNG SOCIETIES

(EXTRACTED FROM BRESLER 1981, 32-36)

1. After having entered Hung Mon, I ought to treat the parents, brothers, sisters, and wives of my brethren as my own home folks. I shall be killed by five thunderbolts if I do not keep this oath.
2. I shall help my brethren to bury their parents and brothers by offering or giving financial or physical assistance. I shall be killed by five thunderbolts if I pretend to have no knowledge of their trouble.
3. When Hung brethren come to my home, I shall provide them with board and lodging. I shall be killed by myriads of swords if I treat them as outsiders.
4. I shall accord recognition to all Hung brethren when they produce their signals, otherwise I shall be killed by myriads of swords.
5. I shall not disclose the secrets of the Hung family even to my natural parents or brothers or my spouse. I shall never disclose secrets for money. Otherwise, I shall be killed by myriads of swords.
6. I shall not betray my own brethren. If I happen to have arrested one of my brethren owing to a misunderstanding, I must release him at once. I shall be killed by five thunderbolts if I do not keep this oath.
7. I shall offer financial assistance to my brethren when they are in trouble, in order that they may pay their passage fee, etc. I shall be killed by five thunderbolts if I do not keep this oath.
8. I shall be killed by myriads of swords if I have done any harm to my brethren or incense master.

9. I shall be killed by five thunderbolts if I commit indecent assaults on my brethren's wives, sisters, or daughters.
10. I shall be killed by myriads of swords if I embezzle cash or property from my brethren.
11. I shall be killed by five thunderbolts if I do not take good care of my brethren's wives or children or other things when they are entrusted to my care.
12. I shall be killed by five thunderbolts if I have reported false particulars about myself for the purpose of joining Hung Mon tonight.
13. I shall be killed by myriads of swords if I change my mind about my Hung Mon membership after this night.
14. I shall be killed by five thunderbolts if I secretly assist an outsider or rob my own brethren.
15. I shall be killed by myriads of swords if I take advantage of my brethren's weaknesses and make unfair deals with them by force.
16. I shall be killed by five thunderbolts if, acting contrary to my own conscience, I convert my brethren's cash and property to my own use.
17. If I have wrongly taken my brethren's cash or property during a robbery, I must return them to my brethren. I shall be killed by five thunderbolts if I do not keep this oath.
18. If I am arrested for having committed an offense, I deserve punishment and should not pass the blame to my brethren. I shall be killed by five thunderbolts if I do not keep this oath.
19. If any of my brethren has been killed or arrested, or has gone some place else for a long time, I shall arrange to help his wife and children who appear to be helpless. I shall be killed by five thunderbolts if I pretend to have no knowledge of them.
20. When any of my brethren has been assaulted or scolded by others, I must come forward to help him if he is right, or advise him to stop if he is wrong. If he has been repeatedly insulted by others, I shall inform other brethren and arrange to help him financially or physically. I shall be killed by five thunderbolts if I pretend to have no knowledge of the matter.
21. If it comes to my knowledge that the government is seeking any of my brethren who have come from other provinces or overseas, I must immediately inform him so that he may make good his escape. I shall be killed by five thunderbolts if I do not keep this oath.

22. I must not conspire with outsiders to cheat my brethren by gambling. I shall be killed by myriads of swords if I do so.
23. I shall not sow discord among my brethren by making false reports about any of them. I shall be killed by myriads of swords if I do so.
24. I shall not appoint myself as incense master without authority. After having entered Hung Mon for three years, the loyal and faithful ones may be promoted by the incense master or by the support of the brethren. I shall be killed by five thunderbolts if I do any unauthorized act of promoting myself.
25. If my natural brothers are involved in a dispute or lawsuit with my Hung brethren, I must not help any party against the other, but have to advise them against it. I shall be killed by five thunderbolts if I do not keep this oath.
26. After having joined Hung Mon, I must forget all previous grudges against any of my brethren. I shall be killed by five thunderbolts if I do not keep this oath.
27. I must not trespass upon the land occupied by my brethren. I shall be killed by five thunderbolts if I pretend to have no knowledge of my brethren's rights and consequently injure their rights.
28. I must not convert, or intend to share, any cash or property obtained by my brethren. I shall be killed if I have malicious ideas about it.
29. I must not disclose any address where my brethren store their wealth and have any malicious ideas about the address. I shall be killed by myriads of swords if I do not keep this oath.
30. I must not protect outsiders and oppress my Hung brethren. I shall be killed by myriads of swords if I do not keep this oath.
31. I shall not oppose others or act unreasonably or violently by taking advantage of the influence of our Hung brethren. I must be contented and honest. I shall be killed by five thunderbolts if I do not keep this oath.
32. I shall be killed by five thunderbolts if I commit indecent assault on the small boys and girls who are my brethren's family folk.
33. I must not inform the government, for the purpose of getting a reward, when my brethren have committed a big offense. I shall be killed by five thunderbolts if I do not keep this oath.
34. I must not take the wives and concubines of my brethren, and must not commit adultery with them. I shall be killed by myriads of swords if I do this purposely.

35. When speaking to outsiders, I must be careful never to use Hung phrases or disclose Hung secrets, which could cause trouble. I shall be killed by myriads of swords if I do not keep this oath.
36. After having entered Hung Mon, I shall be loyal and faithful, and shall endeavor to overthrow Ch'ing (Qing) and restore Ming by co-ordinating my efforts with those of my brethren, although my brethren and I may not be in the same profession. Our main aim is to avenge our Five Ancestors.

APPENDIX 2

THIRTY-SIX STRATEGIES OF THE HUNG SOCIETIES

(EXTRACTED AND TRANSLATED FROM SHU N.D., 119)

1. To cross the ocean without letting the sky know. To cheat all the people around.
2. To surround Wei country in order to rescue Chao country. If an ally is surrounded by enemy, attack the enemy's country to save the ally.
3. To kill a person with someone else's knife. To eliminate a victim without being personally involved.
4. To stay home and let the enemy come to attack you. To eliminate the tired enemy with your refreshed army.
5. To rob while there is a fire. To commit a crime amidst social unrest.
6. To pretend to hit the east and actually attack the west. To pretend to attack one place and strike the unguarded primary target.
7. To create something out of nothing. To confuse the enemy with false information.
8. To attack the enemy through the least suspected routes while launching an explicit yet fake attack plan.
9. To stay at a distance while two conflicting parties are attacking each other.
10. To pretend to be innocent when caught.

11. To put Chang's hat on Lee's head. To confuse the enemy by identifying Lee as Chang and vice versa.
12. To steal if the situation allows.
13. To beat the grass and scare the snake. To hit two enemies with one attack.
14. To utilize the identity of a deceased man.
15. To persuade the tiger to leave its mountain. To persuade the army or householder to leave the city or house so that one can attack the place off-guard.
16. To pretend to set loose a person right before arresting him.
17. To throw a stone to call forth the jade. Limited self-revelation or exposure to bring forth the hidden enemy.
18. To magnify one's own strength.
19. To solve a problem by treating the causes rather than the consequences.
20. To steal after creating chaos.
21. To transform oneself into a totally new person in a crisis situation.
22. To occupy a country while passing through it.
23. To make friends with groups from far away while conquering the surrounding groups.
24. To blame someone you do not want to have open conflict, point the finger at someone else while you are making the verbal assault.
25. To steal the dragon and replace it with a phoenix. That means to steal a real thing and replace it with a fraudulent one, or to send an innocent marginal member to the authorities to bear the burden of the heinous crime of an important offender.
26. To kill a person and scare the rest.
27. To pretend to be an insane person when caught.
28. To destroy the bridge after crossing it, that is, to prevent the enemy from following.
29. To commit a crime in such a way that the incident seems to be caused by natural forces.
30. To overpower the host and take over his place.
31. To use women as bait.
32. To attack or rob a place while it is unguarded.

33. To obtain information about the enemy by counter-intelligence activities.
34. To lure the enemy's pity by intentionally hurting oneself.
35. To apply the domino principle.
36. To walk away from the scene if there is no better option.

APPENDIX 3

OATHS OF A CHINESE STREET GANG

(SOURCE: NEW YORK CITY POLICE DEPARTMENT)

I, Surname ______________, First Name ______________, Born 19___ Month ______________ Date ______________ Time ______________ State ______________ County ______________, now voluntarily and wholeheartedly join into the xxxxxxxxxxxxxx Association (Tong). After being admitted into the Tong (said of rulers), those who obey the mandate of heaven will live, while those who defy it will perish. As long as I live, I am a member of the xxxxxxxxxxxx Tong. We are all each other's brothers; even if I die, I am still a member. No remorse as long as I live. If I do, the heaven and earth will destroy me.

1. After I join, I am going to follow, to obey all of the rules and regulations of the Tong. If I do not, I will die under the condition of being shot.
2. Today I join the xxxxxxxxxxxxxxx Tong. My date of birth must be true; if not, I will be destroyed by electric shock.
3. The secret of the association must be kept. If not, I will die under the condition of being stabbed a thousand times.
4. If the tong runs into difficulty or is in danger, anyone who knows about it and does not provide assistance will be destroyed by electrical shock and/or burned by fire.

5. The Tong officer is the advisor of all events. If anyone tries to get rid of or kill him, the punishment is death.
6. All brothers must unite as real brothers. If anyone is found to be a traitor, he will be punished by death.
7. If anyone overextends his authority and sends out an order to benefit himself or to try to gain more power, he will be punished publicly.
8. When our brothers run into trouble or danger, we must respond and provide assistance. Anyone who has money must give money; anyone who has strength must give strength. Give what you can; do your best. Anyone who ignores will be stabbed to death a thousand times.
9. We are all each other's brothers; we must never spy or sell out our brothers. If there is hatred and hostility between us, public judgment should rule. Never dwell on it. (Following the public judgment between the hateful brothers, put the feelings in the past.)
10. If one of our brothers is captured or goes on a long journey, leaving his wife and children behind and defenseless, we must try our best to help them. If anyone appears to do good but really means to deceive others, he will be punished. If anyone tries to take advantage of a member's wife, the punishment is death.
11. Never be disrespectful to your parents or abuse your brother, sister, or sister-in-law. Anyone who commits any of the above shall be punished.
12. If one is not authorized by the Tong's officer to know the Tong's secret, he shall not try to peep or spy on it. If he does so, he will be treated as a traitor and will be punished publicly.

Every member must follow the above rules and regulations. Now your name is displayed in heaven; you shall not try to ruin it on earth. Once you join the Tong, you should have confidence in it. You must be loyal to the Tong until you die. If anyone tries to betray the Tong, the punishment is death. If one acts positively externally and negatively internally, heaven is his justice; his death will be close. The sword and knife should cut him to pieces; lightning should destroy his identity (trace); therefore he will be in hell eternally with no hope for reincarnation. Since the sole judgment is heaven and God, one who is loyal to the Tong will be blessed by God. The heaven and earth are my parents; the sun and moon shine upon us. Following the brotherhood ceremony, we use the incense to pray to God to protect and look over us.

Display all of the names in heaven; if the incense breaks, the heads fall.

I, Surname ________________ First Name ________________ Born 19____ Month ________________ Day________________ Time ________ State ________________ County ________________. Now we join our blood-brother ceremony before God-General Kwan. All of us hereby pledge to be loyal and to protect the xxxxxxxxxxxx Tong.

Tonight we pray to heaven as our father, earth as our mother, the sun as our brother, the moon as our sister, we all should enjoy everything together, resolve all of our anxieties together. Even though we are not born on the same day, we will die together on the same day.

APPENDIX 4

MEMBERSHIP IDENTIFICATION OF A CHING MEMBER

(AUTHOR'S TRANSLATION)

Membership Identification of a Ching Member

-1-

MAY OUR RIGHTEOUS SPIRIT LAST FOREVER

-2-

BLANK

-3-

SPREAD THE SPIRIT OF NATIONALISM

PHOTO

____________________ Rank

Branch

____________________ Recipient

PROMOTE ETHICS AND MORALITY

-4-

PRINCIPAL GOALS OF MEMBERS

1. Unified struggle to rejuvenate our nation
2. Re-unification of China under the guidance of the Three Principles
3. Sacrifice ourselves and devotion to our country's leader
4. Elimination of the violent and protection of the innocent
5. Recover our lost land by means of our everlasting righteous spirit

---

-5-

THE THREE GENERATIONS OF RECRUITING MASTERS

Third Generation Master's Rank ________________ Branch __________
Last Name ________ SEAL First Name ________ Second Name ________
Residence: Province ________ County ________
Occupation: ____

Second Generation Master's Rank ________________ Branch __________
Last Name ________ SEAL First Name ________ Second Name ________
Residence: Province ________ County ________
Occupation: ____

First Generation Master's Rank ________________ Branch __________
Last Name ________ SEAL First Name ________ Second Name ________
Residence: Province ________ County ________
Occupation: ____

-6-

BRIEF INTRODUCTION TO THE RECRUITING MEMBER'S BRANCH

This branch is ________________________, full fleet of 83 boats, 2 boats retired, 4 boats in renovation, 1 boat is the flag boat, the color of the flag is orange, with a golden top.
Sail the dragon flag when harbored; sail the phoenix flag when at sea; drink the water from Chang Liu; burn the wood from Kuen mountain.

-7-

THE THREE GENERATIONS OF RULE MASTERS

(This form is similar to page 5.)

-8-

BRIEF INTRODUCTION TO THE RULE MASTER'S BRANCH

(This form is similar to page 6.)

-9-

THE THREE GENERATIONS OF PRINCIPAL MASTERS

(This form is similar to page 5.)

-10-

BRIEF INTRODUCTION TO THE PRINCIPAL MASTERS' BRANCH

(This form is similar to page 6.)

-11-

TEN RESOLUTIONS

1. Do not cheat the master or damage the ancestors' reputation.
2. Do not look down upon the pioneers of the Pang.
3. Do not reveal the gang's secrets to outsiders.
4. Do no commit robbery or illegal sex.
5. Do not create chaos by irresponsible speech.
6. Do not attempt to promote one's rank.
7. Do not disrupt the Pang's regulations.
8. Do not exaggerate one's position.
9. Do not promote one's benefits at the expense of the public.
10. Do not exploit the powerless people.

-12-

TEN MUSTS

1. Must obey parent.
2. Must work hard.
3. Must respect seniors.
4. Must be lenient as elder brother and tolerant as younger brother.
5. Must maintain harmony as husband and wife.
6. Must maintain good relationships with neighbors.
7. Must have faith in friendship.
8. Must chastise the mind and discipline the body.
9. Must constantly yield the right of way to other people.
10. Must help the elderly and sympathize with the poor.

-13-

TEN MUST NOTS

1. Students must not follow two principal masters.
2. Father and son must not belong to the same principal master.
3. Students must not look for another principal master after their initial principal master's death.
4. Principal masters must not initiate students after retirement.
5. Principal masters must not initiate someone who is not accepted by their students
6. Students of a principal master must not have different ranks.
7. Members of a group must not act as recruiting masters for their own group.
8. Students must not act as principal masters right after their principal master's death.
9. Students must not defame one another.
10. Members must not upgrade their ranks.

-14-

TEN ABSTENTIONS

1. Promiscuity
2. Murder
3. Robbery
4. Obscene language
5. Testifying at a trial
6. Illegal drugs
7. Exploiting the people
8. Exploiting minorities
9. Exploiting the powerless
10. Smoking and drinking

-15-

THE TWENTY-FOUR SENIOR RANKS

THE TWENTY-FOUR JUNIOR RANKS

BIBLIOGRAPHY

BOOKS, JOURNAL ARTICLES, AND MONOGRAPHS IN ENGLISH

Allen, Glen, and Lynne Thomas. "Orphans of War." *The Toronto Globe and Mail* 1, no. 12 (1987): 34-57.

Arlacchi, Pino. *Mafia Business: The Mafia Ethic and the Spirit of Capitalism.* New York: Verso, 1987.

Attorney General of California. California Organized Crime and Criminal Intelligence Branch. *Proceedings of the Conference on Chinese Gang Problems.* Sacramento, California, 1972.

Badey, James R. "Federal Coordination Is Needed to Head Off Growing Threat from Vietnamese Criminals." *Organized Crime Digest* March 11, 1987, 1-6.

———. *Dragons and Tigers.* Loomis, Calif.: Palmer Enterprises, 1988.

Bax, Arie. "Chinese Organized Crime in Amsterdam." Paper prepared for the Public Hearings on Asian Organized Crime, New York City, October 23-25, 1984.

Beach, Walter G. *Oriental Crime in California.* Stanford, Calif.: Stanford University Press, 1932.

Blok, Anton. *The Mafia of a Sicilian Village 1860-1960.* New York: Harper & Row, 1974.

Bresler, Fenton. *The Chinese Mafia.* New York: Stein and Day, 1981.

Chang, Henri. "Die Today, Die Tomorrow: The Rise and Fall of Chinatown Gangs." *Bridge Magazine* 2 (1972): 10-15.

Chernow, Ron. "Chinatown, Their Chinatown: The Truth Behind the Facade." *New York Magazine* June 11, 1973, 39-45.

Chesneaux, Jean. *Popular Movements and Secret Societies in China, 1840-1950.* Stanford, Calif.: Stanford University Press, 1972.

Chevigny, Bell Gale. "I Wor Kuen: The Harmonious Fist of Radical Chinatown." *Village Voice*, September 10, 1970.

Chin, Ko-lin. *Chinese Triad Societies, Tongs, Organized Crime, and Street Gangs in Asia and the United States.* Unpublished Dissertation, Department of Sociology, University of Pennsylvania, 1986.

Chin, Ko-lin, Ting-fung May Lai, and Martin Rouse. "Social Adjustment and Alcoholism Among Chinese Immigrants in New York City." *International Journal of the Addictions* 25 (1990): forthcoming

Chin, Rocky. "New York Chinatown Today: Community in Crisis." *Amerasia Journal* 1, no. 1 (1971): 1-32.

Chinese-American Planning Council. *Outlook: The Growing Asian Presence in the Tri-State Region*. New York: Chinese-American Planning Council, 1989.

Chinese Business Guide and Directory: 1989-1990. New York: Key Publications, Inc., 1989.

CLEU LINE. Co-ordinated Law Enforcement Unit. *Asian Crime*. Victoria: Province of British Columbia, Ministry of the Attorney General, 1985.

Cloward, Richard A., and Lloyd E. Ohlin. *Delinquency and Opportunity: A Theory of Delinquent Gangs*. New York: Free Press, 1960.

Cohen, Albert K. *Delinquent Boys: The Culture of the Gang*. New York: Free Press, 1955.

Cressey, Donald R. *Theft of the Nation*. New York: Harper & Row, 1967.

Daly, Michael. "The War for Chinatown." *New York Magazine*, February 14, 1983, 31-38.

Dillon, Richard H. *The Hatchet Men: The Story of the Tong Wars in San Francisco's Chinatown*. New York: Coward-McCann, Inc., 1962.

Duggan, Christopher. *Fascism and the Mafia*. New Haven, Conn.: Yale University Press, 1989.

Emch, Tom. "The Chinatown Murders." *San Francisco Sunday Examiner and Chronicle*, September 9, 1973, 6-14.

Fagan, Jeffrey. "The Social Organization of Drug Use and Drug Dealing Among Urban Gangs." *Criminology* 27, no. 4 (1989): 633-67.

Fairbank, John King. *The Great Chinese Revolution 1800-1985*. New York: Harper & Row, 1987.

Fessler, Loren W. (ed.). *Chinese in America: Stereotyped Past, Changing Present*. New York: Vantage Press, 1983.

Fight Crime Committee. *A Discussion Document on Options for Changes in the Law and in the Administration of the Law to Counter the Triad Problem*. Hong Kong: Fight Crime Committee, Security Branch, 1986.

Grace, Michael, and John Guido. "Hong Kong 1997: Its Impact on Chinese Organized Crime in the United States." Washington, D.C.: United States Department of State, Foreign Service Institute, May 1988.

Gong, Ying Eng, and Bruce Grant. *Tong War!* New York: N.L. Brown, 1930.

Hagedorn, John M. *People and Folks: Gangs, Crime, and the Underclass in a Rustbelt City*. Chicago: Lakeview Press, 1988.

Hirschi, Travis. *Causes of Delinquency*. Berkeley: University of California Press, 1969.

Horowitz, Ruth. *Honor and the American Dream*. New Brunswick, N.J.: Rutgers University Press, 1983.

Huang, Ken, and Marc Pilisuk. "At the Threshold of the Golden Gate: Special Problems of a Neglected Minority." *American Journal of Orthopsychiatry* 47 (1977): 701-13.

Ianni, Francis A.J. *A Family Business*. New York: Russell Sage Foundation, 1972.

———. *Black Mafia: Ethnic Succession in Organized Crime*. New York: Simon & Schuster, 1974.

———. "New Mafia: Black, Hispanic and Italian Styles." In Francis A. Ianni and Elizabeth Reuss-Ianni. (eds.), *The Crime Society*. New York: New American Library, 1976.

Joe, Karen. "Kai-Dois (Bad Boys): Gang Violence in Chinatown." Paper submitted for presentation at Sixth Annual Undergraduate Research Conference sponsored by Rho Chapter of California Alpha Kappa Delta, University of California, Los Angeles, May 9, 1981.

Jue, Linda. "Fear: Taiwan's Deadly Export." *San Francisco Focus*, April 1985, 72-79.

Kaplan, David E., Donald Goldberg, and Linda Jue. "Enter the Dragon: How Hong Kong Notorious Underworld Syndicates Are Becoming the Number One Organized Crime Problem in California." *San Francisco Focus*, December 1986, 68-84.

Klein, Malcolm. *Street Gangs and Street Workers*. Englewood Cliffs, N.J.: Prentice-Hall, 1971.

Klein, Malcolm W., and Cheryl L. Maxson. "Street Gang Violence." In Marvin Wolfgang and Neil Weiner (eds.), *Violent Crime, Violent Criminals*. Beverly Hills, Calif.: Sage Publications, 1987.

Kornhauser, Ruth Rosner. *Social Sources of Delinquency*. Chicago: University of Chicago Press, 1978.

Kuo, Chia-Ling. *Social and Political Change in New York's Chinatown: The Role of Voluntary Associations*. New York: Praeger, 1977.

Kwong, Peter. *The New Chinatown*. New York: Hill and Wang, 1987.

Landesco, John. *Organized Crime in Chicago: Part III of the Illinois Crime Survey, 1929*. Chicago: University of Chicago Press, 1968.

Lee, Henry. "Blood of the Flower." *New York Daily News Magazine*, February 5, 1989, 8-9.

Leng, Veronica W. F. "The Oriental Gang Unit in New York City's Chinatown." N.p., 1984.

Lethbridge, H. J. *Hard Graft in Hong Kong*. Hong Kong: Oxford University Press, 1985.

Light, Ivan. "From Vice District to Tourist Attraction: The Moral Career of American Chinatowns, 1880-1940." *Pacific Historical Review* 43 (1974): 367-94.

Loo, Christopher K. *The Emergence of San Francisco Chinese Juvenile Gangs from the 1950s to the Present*. M.A. thesis, San Jose State University, 1976.

Los Angeles County Sheriff's Department. "Asian Criminal Activities Survey." N.p., 1984.

Lyman, Stanford M. *The Asian in North America*. Santa Barbara, Calif.: ABC-Clio, Inc., 1977.

McCoy, Alfred W. *The Politics of Heroin in South-East Asia*. New York: Harper & Row, 1973.

MacGill, Helen Gregory. "The Oriental Delinquent in the Vancouver Juvenile Court." *Sociology and Social Research* 12 (1938): 428-38.

Mak, Lau-Fong. *The Emergence and Persistence of Chinese Secret Societies in Singapore and Peninsula Malaysia*. Ph.D. dissertation, University of Waterloo, Ontario, 1977.

Matza, David. *Delinquency and Drift*. New York: John Wiley, 1964.

Meskil, Paul. "In the Eye of the Storm." *New York Daily News Magazine*, February 5, 1989, 10-16.

Miller, Walter B. "Lower Class Culture as a Generating Milieu of Gang Delinquency." *Journal of Social Issues* 14, no. 3 (1958): 5-19.

———. *Violence by Youth Gangs and Youth Groups as a Crime Problem in Major American Cities*. Washington, D.C.: U.S. Department of Justice, 1975.

Moore, Joan W., Robert Garcia, Carlos Garcia, Luis Cerda, and Frank Valencia. *Homeboys*. Philadelphia: Temple University Press, 1978.

Morgan, W. P. *Triad Societies in Hong Kong*. Hong Kong: Government Press, 1960.
Morris, Norval, and Gordon Hawkins. *The Honest Politician's Guide to Crime Control*. Chicago: University of Chicago Press. 1970.
Nee, Victor G., and Brett de Barry Nee. *Longtime Californ'*. Stanford, Calif.: Stanford University Press, 1986.
Nelli, Humbert S. *The Business of Crime*. Chicago: University of Chicago Press, 1976.
New York City Police Department, Fifth Precinct. *Gang Intelligence Information*. New York, 1983.
Posner, Gerard. *Warlords of Crimes*. New York: McGraw-Hill, 1988.
Poston, Richard W. *The Gang and the Establishment*. New York: Harper & Row, 1971.
President's Commission on Organized Crime. *The Cash Connection: Organized Crime, Financial Institutions, and Money Laundering*. Washington, D.C.: U.S. Government Printing Office, 1984a.
———. *Organized Crime of Asian Origin: Record of Hearing III—October 23-25, 1984, New York, New York*. Washington, D.C.: U.S. Government Printing Office, 1984b.
Reuter, Peter. *Disorganized Crime*. Cambridge, Mass.: MIT Press, 1983.
Rice, Berkeley. "The New Gangs of Chinatown." *Psychology Today* 10 (1977): 60-69.
Robertson, Frank. *Triangle of Death: The Inside Story of the Triads—the Chinese Mafia*. London: Routledge and Kegan Paul, 1977.
Robinson, Norman, and Delbert Joe. "Gangs in Chinatown: The New Young Warrior Class." *McGill Journal of Education* 15 (1980): 149-62.
Schwendinger, Herman, and Julia S. Schwendinger. *Adolescent Subcultures and Delinquency*. New York: Praeger, 1985.
Seagrave, Sterling. *The Soong Dynasty*. New York: Harper & Row, 1985.
Sellin, Thorsten. *Culture Conflict and Crime*. New York: Social Science Research Council, 1938.
Shaw, Clifford R., and Henry D. McKay. *Juvenile Delinquency in Urban Areas*. Chicago: University of Chicago Press, 1942.
Short, James F., and Fred L. Strodtbeck. *Group Process and Gang Delinquency*. Chicago: University of Chicago Press, 1965.
Smith, Dwight C. *The Mafia Mystique*. New York: Basic Books, 1975.
Spataro, Michael F. "Report on International Chinese Street Gangs and Triad Organized Criminal Activities." Paper presented at the First Annual Meeting on Chinese Triad Societies, New York Police Academy, 1978.
Spergel, Irving A. "Youth Gangs: Continuity and Change." In Norval Morris and Michael Tonry (eds.), *Crime and Justice: An Annual Review of Research* 12. Chicago: University of Chicago Press, 1989.
Sung, Betty Lee. *Gangs in New York's Chinatown*. New York: Department of Asian Studies, City College of New York, Monograph no. 6, 1977.
———. *Transplanted Chinese Children*. New York: Department of Asian Studies, City University of New York, 1979.
———. *The Adjustment Experience of Chinese Immigrant Children in New York City*. New York: Center for Migration Studies, 1987.
Surovell, Hariette. "Chinatown Cosa Nostra." *Penthouse*, June 1988, 40-46.
Sutherland, Edwin H. *Principles of Criminology*, 4th ed. Philadelphia: J.B. Lippincott Company, 1947.
Takagi, Paul, and Tony Platt. "Behind the Gilded Ghetto: An Analysis of Race, Class and Crime in Chinatown." *Crime and Social Justice* 9 (1978): 2-25.

Teng, Ssu-yu. *Protest and Crime in China: A Bibliography of Secret Associations, Popular Uprisings, Peasant Rebellions.* New York: Garland Publishing, Inc., 1981.

Thompson, Jennifer. "Are Chinatown Gang Wars a Cover-Up?" *San Francisco Magazine*, February 1976.

Thrasher, Frederic M. *The Gang: A Study of 1,313 Gangs in Chicago.* Chicago: University of Chicago Press, 1927.

Tracy, Charles A. "Race, Crime, and Social Policy: The Chinese in Oregon, 1871-1885." *Crime and Social Justice*, Winter 1980, 11-25.

U.S. Attorneys and the Attorney General of the United States. *Drug Trafficking: A Report to the President of the United States*, August 3, 1989.

U.S. Department of Justice. *Oriental Organized Crime: A Report of a Research Project Conducted by the Organized Crime Section.* Federal Bureau of Investigation, Criminal Investigative Division. Washington, D.C.: U.S. Government Printing Office, 1985.

———. *Report on Asian Organized Crime.* Criminal Division. Washington, D.C.: 1988.

———. *NIJ Reports.* No. 214. May/June 1989.

U.S. District Court. "Government Version of the Offense of Ghost Shadows Members." New York, 1985a.

———. "Indictment of Bamboo United Members." New York, 1985b.

———. Sentencing Memorandum: Ghost Shadows Members, 1986.

U.S. House of Representatives. Public Hearings on Emerging Ethnic Crime Group Involvement in Heroin Trafficking. Select Committee on Narcotics Abuse and Control. JFK International Arrivals Terminal, 1987.

United States Senate. *Emerging Criminal Groups.* Hearings before the Permanent Subcommittee on Investigations of the Committee on Governmental Affairs. Washington, D.C.: U.S. Government Printing Office, 1986.

Ward, J.S.M., and W.G. Stirling. *The Hung Society.* London: The Baskerville Press, 1925.

Weijenburg, Richard. "Chinese Organized Crime in the Netherlands." Paper prepared for the Public Hearings on Asian Organized Crime, New York City, October 23-25, 1984.

Whyte, William Foote. *Street Corner Society.* Chicago: University of Chicago Press, 1943.

Winterton, Michael J. "The Collation of Crime Intelligence with Regard to Chinese Triads in Holland." *The Police Journal*, January 1981, 34-57.

Wolfgang, Marvin E., and Franco Ferracuti. *The Subculture of Violence.* Reprint of 1967 edition. Beverly Hills, Calif.: Sage Publications, 1982.

Wu, Robin. "What the ***** Is Goin On?" *Bridge Magazine*, Fall 1977, 5-11.

Yablonsky, Lewis. *The Violent Gang*, Rev. Ed. Baltimore: Penguin Books, 1970.

BOOKS, JOURNAL ARTICLES, AND MONOGRAPHS IN CHINESE

Chen, Kuo-ping. *Chao Pu (Ching Societies).* Taipei: Chang Yan Books, 1946.

Chi Zong-xian. *Pang Wei, Xuan Ju, yu Bao Li (Gangs, Election, and Violence).* Taipei: Jiao Dian Publishing Co., 1985.

Chu Shin-liu. *Mei Kuo Wah Fu (Chinatowns in America).* New York: Chinese-American Research Institute, 1985.

Committee to Obtain Justice for Henry Liu. *Ji Nian Jiang Nan (In Memorial of Henry Liu)*. San Francisco: Athens Printing Co., 1985.

Fu Shiang-yuan. *Ching Pang Ta Hen (Bosses of the Ching Pang)*. Hong Kong: Chung Yuan Publication, 1987.

Fung Tze-yu. *Wah Chao Ge Ming Shi (History of Overseas Chinese Revolution)*. Shanghai: Commercial Publication, 1947.

Huang Dao. "Kua Kuo Shi Dai de Xiang Gang Hei Sher Wei" (The Internationalization of Hong Kong Organized Crime). *The Nineties*, December 1984, 68-72.

Jian Yi Jia Li Xu Zhi (Courtesy Rules of the Green Pang). N.p.: N.d.

Jin Shi. "Xi Shuo Tai Wan Ba Ta Bang Pai" (The Largest Taiwanese Gangs). *World Journal Weekly*. December 8-14, 1984, 30-35.

Lau Bing-bing. *Chen Chi-li Zhen Han (The Impact of Chen Chi-li)*. Taipei: Lian Hong Publisher, 1984.

Li Chen-dong. *San Guo, Shui Hu, yu Xi You (The Values of Three Classical Novels)*. Taipei: The Buffalo Book Co., 1981.

Liu Pei-chi. *Mei Kuo Wah Chao Shi Xu Bian (A History of the Chinese in the United States of America II)*. Taipei: Li Min Publications, 1981.

Ong, Benny. Keynote Speech at the Chih Kung Annual Meeting. New York, 1988.

Peoples University and First National Archive. *Tien Ti Wei (Heaven and Earth Society)*. Three Volumes. Peking: Peoples University Press, 1980.

Ping Shan-cho. *Chung Kuo Pi Mi Sher Wei Shi (The History of Chinese Secret Societies)*. Taipei: Commercial Publications, 1935.

Pung Sung-pu. *Pang Wei Shi Li Zhen Wen (The Power of the Pangs)*. Hong Kong: Chung Yuan Publisher, 1987.

Shaw I-sun. *Pi Mi Sher Wei Shi Liao (Historical Materials of the Secret Societies)*. Peking: Peking University Press, 1935.

Shu Wen-li. *Hung Mun de Pi Mi (The Secret of Hung Society)*. Hong Kong: Contemporary Publisher, N.d.

Shuai Xue-fu. *Chung Kuo Pang Wei Shi (History of Chinese Pangs)*. Hong Kong: Contemporary Publisher, 1961.

Sun Cheng-tao. *Mei Kuo Wah Ren Zhen Shi (A Brief History of Chinese in America)*. Taipei: Overseas Chinese Society, 1962.

Sun Yat-sen. *San Ming Zhu Yi (The Three Principles of the People)*. Taipei: Li Ming Publication, 1977.

Tang Jun-yi. *Chung Kuo Wen Hua de Jing Shen Jia Zhi (The Spiritual Values of Chinese Culture)*. Taipei: Cheng Chung Publisher, 1974.

Wei Da Fa Shi. *Chung Kuo Pang Wei (Chinese Gangs)*. Chungking: Shuo Wen Publications, 1949.

Zhang Sheng. *Xiang Gang Hei She Hui Huo Dong Zhen Xiang (The Activity of Hong Kong Organized Crime)*. Hong Kong: Tien Ti Books Co., 1984.

NEWSPAPER, NEWSLETTER, AND MAGAZINE ARTICLES IN ENGLISH

Asiaweek

November 11, 1988: "Unmasking the Triads," 52-57.

Business Week

March 5, 1984: "The Future of Hong Kong," 50-64.

Canal Magazine
December 8, 1978: "Interview with Nickey Louie," 1.

Dallas Morning News
September 14, 1986: "Asian Organized Crime Growing in Dallas," 1A.

Far Eastern Economic Review
May 15, 1986: "Headlines Bolster Plan to Get Tough with Triads," 50-51.

Los Angeles Times
July 19, 1987: "Crime Gangs Known as Triads Are a Fact of Life in Hong Kong," 6.

New York Daily News
September 14, 1970: "Chinatown's Youth Picket Honorable Elders: Seek Benevolent Association Gym," 4.
October 17, 1976: "Shooting Kills Boy, Hurts 2 in Chinatown."
November 21, 1982: "Police Quiz Gangs in NYU Party," 6.
February 20, 1983: "13 Slain in Seattle," 3.
March 15, 1983a: "Flying Dragons Leader Slain," 5.
March 15, 1983b: "The Toughest Gangster on Pell Street," 4.
February 19, 1985: "A Fed Indictment Hits 25 Members of Chinatown Mob," 3.
May 22, 1985: "Boy, 4, Shot in Chinatown, Fights for Life," 3.
February 19, 1986: "Girl Is Found Strangled," 5.
April 10, 1987: "Crossfire Hits Girl, 6; Chinatown Thug Wounded," 5.
March 27, 1988: "The Making of King Kon," 4.
July 24, 1989: "New 'Chinatown' Turf," 15.

New York Newsday
February 20, 1985: "Cops Still Seek Worst Chinese Gang."
September 29, 1987: "Asian Gangs Move into Drugs," 7.
February 14, 1988a: "The Asian Connection: A New Main Line to U.S.," 5.
February 14, 1988b: "Record Heroin Bust Sends Agents Searching in NY," 5.
February 22, 1988: "Feds Nab 6 Men on Heroin Charges," 21.
February 22, 1989: "$1 Billion in Heroin Seized in Queens," 5.
June 2, 1989: "Chinatown Struggle Predicted," 6.

New York Post
August 6, 1970: "Chinatown's Eagle Held in Slaying."
February 24, 1971: "Seven Wounded, One Held in Chinatown Clash," 11.
September 17, 1986: "Chinatown Casino Busted—14 Nabbed," 13.
October 20, 1988: "Hong Kong Help$ Chinatown Grow," 58.

New York Times
January 15, 1964: "Chinatown Extends Its Borders as 7,000 Refugees Settle in City," 33.
November 16, 1969: "Influx of Chinese Spurs Educators."
February 22, 1971: "Peking Gains Favor with Chinese in U.S.," B2.
January 19, 1974: "Street Crime Casts a Pall of Fear over Chinatown."
December 1, 1976: "Festive Chinatown Is a Place of Terror to the Merchants Who Offend Gangs," B1.
December 29, 1981: "Asian Investors Battle for Footholds in Chinatown," A1.
December 24, 1982: "Gunmen Firing Wildly Kill 3 in Chinatown Bar," A1.
October 24, 1984: "Asian Crime Groups Held Active in U.S.," A1.
January 13, 1985: "Chinese Organized Crime Said to Rise in U.S.," A1.

April 21, 1985: "Murder Trial Illuminates Taiwan's Dark Thoughts," E2.
September 17, 1985: "Asian Crime Group Hit by U.S. Arrests," A1.
November 25, 1985: "Vietnamese Gangs Active in Florida," 14.
January 30, 1986: "Why Asians Succeed Here," *Magazine*, 75.
June 1, 1986: "Mining Chinatown's 'Mountain Gold'," C1.
July 20, 1986: "Chinatown Plan is Key to Dispute," 12.
August 3, 1986: "Tape Depicts Asian Gang with U.S. Branches," 26.
September 14, 1986: "Satellite Chinatowns Burgeon Throughout New York," *Magazine*, 7.
December 25, 1986: "Commercial Rents in Chinatown Soar as Hong Kong Exodus Grows," A1.
June 28, 1987: "Police Say Teen-Agers Were Slain After Trying to Break Up a Fight," 30.
July 9, 1987: "Californian Sees Rise in Asian Gangs," A20.
August 11, 1987: "Group 41 Undercover: Chasing the Heroin from Plush Hotel to Mean Streets," B1.
September 13, 1987: "City's Third Chinatown is Emerging in Brooklyn," 74.
November 5, 1987: "2 Are Slain as a Gang Opens Fire in a Chinatown Gambling Parlor."
January 29, 1988: "Why Do Asian Pupils Win Those Prizes?" A35.
February 10, 1988: "Chinatowns Find New Venues," C1.
February 20, 1988: "New York's Chinese: Living in 2 Worlds," L29.
March 15, 1988: "Top U.S. Target in Heroin Trade Seized at Hotel," B5.
May 8, 1988: "Hong Kong Sees Rising Emigration as Peril," 15.
June 12, 1988: "A Chinatown Businessman Is Charged in a Slaying," 34.
June 21, 1988: "Hispanic Dropout Rate is Highest in Study of New York City Schools," A1.
December 12, 1988: "Chinese Gangs Exercise Vast Power in Hong Kong."
February 22, 1989: "Heroin Seizure at 3 Queens Sites Is Called Biggest U.S. Drug Raid," B5.
August 6, 1989: "Intelligence-Gathering Among the Addicts of New York City," E5.

Newsweek
June 19, 1989: "A Bad Omen for Hong Kong," 27.

Newsweek on Campus
April 1984: "The Drive to Excel," 4-14.

Organized Crime Digest
August 9, 1989: "Chinese Triads Pushing the Mafia Aside; Focusing on Heroin Smuggling, Extortion," 3-4.

San Francisco Chronicle
November 18, 1986: "California's Solid Ties to Hong Kong," 1.
March 26, 1988: "Police Say Asian Youth Gangs Growing," A2.

San Francisco Examiner
May 10, 1987: "Golden Dragon Massacre: Pain Still Felt a Decade Later," B1.

South China Morning Post
April 8, 1987: "Police to Help in US Murders," 3.
June 8, 1987: "Mass Exodus of Triads Denied," 1.
July 28, 1987: "Deadly Code of Secrecy," 13.

July 24, 1988: "UK Triad Crime 'to Increase'," 7.

Wall Street Journal

March 30, 1988: "Hong Kong's Exodus Starts as 1997 Nears," 14.

Washington Times

January 28, 1986: "Chinese Gangs and Heroin Cast Lawless Shadow," A1.

NEWSPAPER, NEWSLETTER, AND MAGAZINE ARTICLES IN CHINESE

Centre Daily News

June 7, 1985: "Precinct Chief Complains about the Lack of Cooperation," 20.

June 18, 1985: "A Gambling Club on Bayard Street Got Robbed," 20.

August 16, 1985: "Fook Ching Members Extorted a New Jersey Restaurant Owner," 20.

September 16, 1985: "Annual Meeting of the Hip Sing Association Adjourned, Key Officials Elected," 20.

September 18, 1985: "Chung Shing Jewelry Got Robbed Again," 5.

October 12, 1985: "Youth Gang Member Killed and Burned by Rival Gang Members," 20.

October 29, 1985: "Clash between Chinese and Hispanic Students," 11.

November 21, 1985: "Shadows Leader Arrested in Taiwan," 20.

January 8, 1986: "Jade Squad Member Analyzes Youth Gang Situation in Chinatown," 20.

March 10, 1986: "Chinatown Girl Murderer Nabbed, No Link to Gangs," 1.

March 21, 1986: "Mainland China Immigrants Have Problems Coping in a New Environment," 19.

March 31, 1986: "High Incidence of Depression among Chinatown Residents Due to Poor Living Conditions," 20.

February 21, 1987: "One Killed, One Wounded in Brooklyn Gang Fight," 20.

April 11, 1987: "Andy Liang Shot on East Broadway," 20.

May 27, 1987: "ABC will Air a 4-part Series on 'The Chinatown Wars'," 24.

September 21, 1987: "Midnight Murder in Chatham Square," 24.

November 9, 1987: "A Dragon Busted for Shooting Tung On Members," 24.

December 1, 1987a: "Sun Yee On Member Testified That 80% of the Restaurants Pay Protection Money," 4.

December 1, 1987b: "Hong Kong Triads Establishing Branch in Taiwan," 5.

December 27, 1987: "More Arrests in Multimillions Heroin Case," 24.

January 29, 1988: "Chinese Gangs Follow Chinese Businessmen to Long Island," 24.

February 8, 1988: "Estimated 160,000 Triad Members in Hong Kong," 4.

March 5, 1988: "The First Time A Chinese Gang Leader Was Arrested for Heroin Trafficking," 24.

March 19, 1988: "DEA Confiscated $70 Million Worth of Heroin," 24.

April 18, 1988: "Operation Bamboo Dragon Crushed a Major Chinese Heroin Ring," 1.

May 4, 1988: "Is Paul Ma a Drug Kingpin?" 24.

June 13, 1988: "Flushing Merchants Appeal to the Local Police Precinct for Protection from Gangs," 22.

June 30, 1988: "$50 Million Heroin Nabbed in San Gabriel, California," 3.

July 14, 1988: "Hong Kong Triads Control Heroin Smuggling in Australia," 3.
September 10, 1988: "Undercover Drug Agents Busted Chinese Heroin Traffickers in Boston and New York," 24.
December 22, 1988: "Undercover Cops Arrested 19 Orientals for Operating Prostitution Houses," 18.
January 28, 1989: "Police Raids Wo Sheng Wo's Base in West Berlin," 5.
April 13, 1989: "Fook Chow Youths Ranging from 20 to 30 Years Old Were Arrested for Heroin Smuggling," 24.
May 5, 1989: "Restaurant in Elmhurst Slained," 21.
July 7, 1989: "Two Chinese Drug Traffickers Slain by Manila Police," 13.

China Daily News
March 7, 1985: "Two White Tigers Arrested for Extortion in Flushing," 20.
October 13, 1987: "Chinese Youth Slain in Woodside's Golden Q Billiard Hall," 16.
June 23, 1989: "Police Raid Massage Parlors, Arrest 81 Korean Women," 10.
July 18, 1989: "Shootout in a Chinese Restaurant in Queens," 3.

China Post
September 10, 1976: "Shootout on Bayard Street."

China Times
February 22, 1984: "Gang Fight on East Broadway," 1.
October 24, 1984: "Tong Overshadows Chinese Image in the U.S.," 3.
October 29, 1984: "The Impact of the Hearings on Asian Organized Crime," 3.

China Times Weekly
May 12, 1985: "A Special Report on Oriental Massage Parlors in the United States," 65-67.
May 19, 1985: "Big Circle Rumble in Hong Kong," 72.
November 10, 1985: "Triad Members As Peddlers," 71-72.
January 26, 1989: "The Crisis of Modern Hung Societies," 52-55.

China Tribune
January 18, 1976: "A Revival of Chinese Gangs?"
June 18, 1976: "Black Eagles Member Attempts Suicide in Jail."
December 1, 1976: "Internal Conflict in the Flying Dragons," 1.
December 11, 1976: "Restaurant Owners Slain by Chinese Youth Gang Members," 1.
February 2, 1977: "President of Flying Dragons Arrested," 1.
May 19, 1977: "Shadows Leaders Ask for Community's Understanding," 1.

Chinese Journal
June 5, 1976: "The Clash between West Coast Gangsters and New York Chinatown Gangsters," 24.

Mei Tung News
May 23, 1988: "Taiwanese Gangs in the United States," 5.

Mei Wah Report
October 6, 1985: "The History of Chinese Street Gangs in the United States," 16-21.
June 14, 1988: "The Bloody Tongs," Part I, 162-68.
June 28, 1988: "The Bloody Tongs," Part II, 60-63.
January 25, 1989: "Hong Kong 14K Dominates Taiwan Gambling Industry," 63-65.

Sing Tao Jih Pao

March 21, 1977: "More than 50% of Chinatown Residents Earned Less than $6000 Annually."

June 28, 1977: "Ghost Shadows' President Nickey Louie Arrested for Beating Youths Who Refused to Join the Gang," 1.

January 29, 1988: "Several Sun Yee On Leaders Received Prison Terms," 28.

August 21, 1989: "Six Vietnamese Youths with Uzi Machine Guns Robbed a Night-club Near Chinatown," 24.

August 22, 1989: "Prison Sentence for A Hong Kong Crime Figure in California," 22.

August 23, 1989: "Ching Pang in Taiwan Recruiting Members," 40.

August 30, 1989: "Chinese Organized Crime Dominates Gambling and Extortion Rackets in New Zealand Chinatowns," 34.

Ting Ting Daily News

October 14, 1987: "Two Mainland Criminals Arrested with Guns," 1.

World Journal

March 28, 1977: "800 Days in Jiang Hu."

October 22, 1982: "Six Shadows Are Accused in the Rape and Murder of a Caucasian Woman," 24.

February 25, 1983: "Mr. Chan's Description of the Killings in Seattle's Chinatown," 3.

March 15, 1983: "Slain Chinese Youth's Body Found on Long Island," 24.

October 26, 1984: "Chinatown Leader Denied Charges by the President's Commission," 1.

December 1, 1984: "Taiwanese Gang Members Active in Los Angeles Area," 24.

December 8, 1984: "4 Chinese Youths Robbed in Chinese Restaurant," 20.

January 25, 1985: "14K Members Arrested for Drug Trafficking in Taiwan," 4.

February 17, 1985: "Shootout in Los Angeles' Chinatown," 3.

March 25, 1985: "Kowloon Police Arrest Bamboo United New Recruits," 5.

May 3, 1985: "Cops and Robbers Shoot Out in Hong Kong," 1.

May 13, 1985: "Organized Crime Groups Control Commercial Sex," 5.

May 19, 1985: "Police Arrest Members of Two Triad Groups," 7.

June 4, 1985: "Taiwan Supreme Court Indictment in Henry Liu Case," 4.

June 15, 1985: "14K Factions Ready for a Showdown," 6.

July 29, 1985: "Four Hooded Robbers Slay Massage Parlor Operator," 1.

September 9, 1985: "Ghost Shadows Leader Shot to Death at the Entrance of a Mott Street Gambling Den," 20.

October 23, 1985: "Chinatown Store Owners Extorted by Many Gangs," 16.

October 25, 1985: "Survey Shows Most Peddlers Are Triad Members," 15.

September 6, 1986: "Taiwanese Drug Traffickers Arrested," 3.

September 23, 1986: "Four Asians Arrested for Heroin Trafficking," 20.

December 27, 1986: "Ghost Shadows and Flying Dragons Clash on Mott Street," 24.

January 14, 1987: "Three Vietnamese Gang Members Arrested in Boston, Wanted in San Francisco for a Murder Case," 3.

February 17, 1987: "DEA Nabbed Chinese Heroin Traffickers," 24.

April 22, 1987: "Hong Kong 14K Active in Smuggling Heroin into the U.S.," 20.

June 30, 1987: "A 14-Year-Old Killer," 22.

August 16, 1987: "Chinese Youth Shot to Death Execution-Style Inside his Luxury Car," 24.

September 6, 1987: "Police Raided Sun Yee On Holdouts," 22.
November 4, 1987: "Chinese Gangs Extended Their Activities out of Chinatown," 3.
November 13, 1987: "Dice Was Arrested for Selling Drugs to Undercover Drug Agents," 24.
January 5, 1988: "Shootouts in Elmhurst Street," 20.
January 6, 1988: "Chinese Drug Trafficking Increased Dramatically in '87," 36.
January 14, 1988: "Fook Ching and Ghost Shadows Involved in Gun Battle after Negotiation Failed," 24.
January 17, 1988: "Golden Star Member Found Dead in a Car," 25.
January 28, 1988: "Lai Kim Mun Arrested with $400,000 Cash," 24.
March 2, 1988: "Flushing Merchants Endured Financial Loss Without Solving the Problem," 24.
April 7, 1988: "A Hispanic Man Was Shot to death by Asian Gunmen in Jackson Heights, Queens," 24.
April 23, 1988: "On Leong Delegates Meeting in Chicago," 19.
April 24, 1988: "Many Gamblers Arrested in Chicago Chinatown," 3.
May 19, 1988: "Chinese Students Dominate Presidential Scholars Awards," 3.
October 24, 1988: "43 Kilograms of Heroin Seized in Australia," 20.
November 13, 1988: "Hung Mun may Register as Civil Association," 6.
November 22, 1988: "Hong Kong China White All Over the World," 3.
December 11, 1988: "Chih Kung Tang Dissociates Itself from Communist Party," 3.
March 20, 1989: "Sex Salons Invade Queens," 24.
April 20, 1989: "Chinese Businessmen Carry Guns for Self-Protection?" 24.
May 9, 1989: "Operation Red Star Nabbed Heroin Traffickers," 6.
May 25, 1989: "Hong Kong Drug Traffickers Active in Australia," 7.
July 25, 1989: "Andy Liang's Suspected Killer Acquitted," 24.
August 14, 1989: "Hair Salon Owners Plan to Change Practice as a Result of Gang Members' Refusal to Pay for Service," 24.
August 24, 1989: "Hip Sing Annual Meeting Will Be Held in New York Next Month," 24.
August 26, 1989: "Johnny Eng Indicted for Two Heroin Cases," 28.

INDEX

ABOUT THE AUTHOR

Ko-lin Chin is a senior research analyst for the New York City Criminal Justice Agency. He has published several articles on drug use and criminality, including *Violence as Regulation and Social Control in the Distribution of Crack* and *Initiation into Crack and Cocaine: A Tale of Two Epidemics*.